ANCIENT ICE
MUMMIES

JAMES H. DICKSON

To P.F. from C.E.

First published 2011

The History Press
The Mill, Brimscombe Port
Stroud, Gloucestershire, GL5 2QG
www.thehistorypress.co.uk

British Library Cataloguing in Publication Data.
A catalogue record for this book is available from the British Library.

ISBN 978 0 7524 5935 6

Typesetting and origination by The History Press
Printed in Great Britain
Manufacturing managed by Jellyfish Print Solutions Ltd

Contents

Preface

At the invitation of the Innsbruck University botanists Sigmar Bortenschlager and Klaus Oeggl, I have been involved in the scientific investigations of the 5200-year-old Tyrolean iceman, otherwise known as Ötzi, since the spring of 1994. This was less than three years after the discovery of this astonishing survival from such a very long time ago. To be so involved was, and still is, a wonderfully satisfying, undreamt of combination of my two major interests – bryology, which is the study of bryophytes (mosses and liverworts), and archaeology. To my great pleasure mosses have proved more relevant in the Ötzi investigations than I could have guessed when I first began to identify them 17 years ago.

Rightly, Ötzi was a sensation and has remained so over the 20 years since the finding because more and more fascinating discoveries have been made by scientists of various disciplines concerning his life and death. However, some aspects of Ötzi's fame have given me much concern. In dealing with the ancient frozen corpses that are the subject of this book and making deductions about them from scientific studies, it is best to try to behave like an expert witness at a murder trial in a court of law while facing a clever advocate for the defence. Everything must be taken into account, presented concisely and what is well-established fact and what is speculation must be clearly distinguished. If speculation there has to be, then it must be absolutely obvious that that is just what it is. All too often in watching the numerous television programmes about Ötzi and reading books, newspaper and web articles that deal with glacier bodies and other mummies, I have been all too conscious of untrammelled speculation and a far from complete knowledge of the broad scope of the particular topic by the speaker or writer.

Though by far the most investigated and publicised, Ötzi is not the only ancient human body from a glacier to have been studied. There are also the Porchabella Shepherdess and the Theodulpass Mercenary, both from Switzerland, and Norbert Mattersberger, poacher, from Austria, as well as Kwäday Dän Ts'ìnchí Man (Long Ago Person Found) from British Columbia. All four have special features of interest, scientific and otherwise.

Though there are now various well-produced books by the Iceman Museum in Bozen (Bolzano), for the general English-speaking public, by far the best-known book is Konrad Spindler's bestselling *The Man in the Ice*. There were reviews by Paul Bahn in the *Times Literary Supplement* and by Lawrence Barfield in the well-known archaeological journal *Antiquity*. Both were very well qualified for the task. Paul Bahn is very heavily critical and deservedly so in my view. Lawrence Barfield's review is long in description but short on praise. Then came the book *Iceman* by American journalist Brenda Fowler; it also provided strong criticism of Konrad Spindler.

So, in this book I have tried to assess the scientific discoveries concerning the five ancient glacier bodies and what can reasonably deduced from them, without either undue sensationalism or excessive speculation. That has involved evaluating and marrying together many different lines of science – anthropology, medicine, chemistry, isotopes, DNA, ecology, zoology and botany, not to mention traditional archaeology. This was not any easy task. I offer my gratitude to those specialists who have read drafts that I sent them. However, I must take full responsibility for the assessments presented here.

Jim Dickson

Acknowledgements

My continuing work on ancient glacier mummies has been supported financially by the Royal Society of Edinburgh, the Royal Society of London, the Austrian Academy of Sciences, the Botanical Institute of the University of Innsbruck, the Sealaska Heritage Institute (Juneau Tlingits), the Carnegie Trust for the Universities of Scotland, the Leverhulme Trust, the author Jean Auel, the Royal British Columbia Museum, the British Council (Toronto), the Yakutat Tlingits, the Bryological Fund of the University of British Columbia and the Lloyd-Binns Fund of the Glasgow Natural History Society.

With regard to individuals concerning Ötzi, my thanks go first and foremost to Klaus Oeggl who, in sending me the mosses, made the years of my research career after 1994 very congenial ones. My first *Scientific American* article led to my meeting Geneviève Lécrivain who has been a great help to me in many ways, not least in searching the literature which led consequently to very useful discussions of the literature in French among others. Jenny and I have carried out very fruitful fieldwork high in the mountains of Austria, Italy and Switzerland and in low-lying parts of Germany and France. During my numerous sojourns in Innsbruck I have had stimulating discussions with Klaus Oeggl and enjoyed his company on fieldtrips. Another Austrian to whom I am very grateful is Andreas Heiss who has been very helpful in translating some of the Ötzi literature published in German.

During a long career, some of my happiest days in the field anywhere have been spent hunting Ötzi mosses, mostly with Wolfgang Hofbauer, yet another Austrian to whom I am most grateful. There have also been Ronald Porley, Gordon Rothero and Andrew McMullen. In the Innsbruck Botany Institute the following deserve my thanks: Sigmar Bortenschlager, Jean-Nicolas Haas, Peter Acs, Andreas Gruber, Sylvia Klein, Werner Kofler and Alexandra Schmidl.

At various other places, with regard to both Ötzi and mummies in general, in alphabetical order by surname, there are: Horst Aspöck, Paul Bahn, Ronald Beckett, Martina Bertini, Aimé Bocquet, Roberta Bottarin, William Chaloner, Daniel Cherix, Finbarr Conolly, David Crompton, Peter Dickson, Andrea Dolfini, Desmond Duthie, Eduard Egarter Vigl, Markus Egg, Jörg Feldman, Angelika Fleckinger, Andrea Fuganti, David Getz, Lydia Giuntini, Walter Gössler, Geoffrey Grime, Linda Handley, Mogens Hansen, Stefan Hochuli, Andrea Hofbauer, Grant Hughes, Stefanie Jacomet, Bruno Kaufmann, Lutz Klassen, Eva Krupp, Walter Kutschera, Andreas Lippert, Elizabeth and James MacDonald, Michel Magny, Karl-Joseph Müller, Valentin Müller, Wolfgang Müller, William Murphy, Tamsin O'Connell, Maria-Anna Pabst, Annaluisa Pedrotti, Patrizia Pertner, Pierre Petrequin, Christine and

Albert Piguet, Johanna Platzgummer, John Raven, Ann Reichert, Thomas Reitmeimer, Michael Shand, Alison Sheridan, Ghisan Sherl, Torstein Sjøvold, the late Gyula Skultéty, Harald Stadler, Nigel Thorp, Peter Vanesis, Alastair Wardlaw, Roderick Watt, Walter Wenzel, Caroline Wilkinson, Claude Wyss, Astrid Sapelza, Albert Zink, Elizabeth Rastbichler Zissernig.

With regard to Kwäday Dän Ts'ìnchí Man (Long Ago Person Found), my thanks are due, in alphabetical order by surname, to: Elaine Abraham, Bert Adams, John Baldwin, Owen Beattie, Bruce Bennett, Judy Brakel, Adolf Ceska, Geno Cisternos, Brian Coppins, Julie Cruikshank, Greg Eikland, Catherine English, Tangres Gallicano, the late Sarah Gaunt, Myra Gilliam, Daniel Gilliken, Sheila Greer, Greg Hare, Susan and Bill Hanlon, Carla and Al Harvey, Roxanne Hastings, Elaine and Richard Hebda, Florence Joe, Joe Homer, Wayne Howell, Gayle and Guy Immega, Robert Johnson, Rose and Brian Klinkenberg, Nicole Lantz, Olivia Lee, Bruce Leighton, Bill Lucey, Al Mackie, Kjerstin Mackie, Lee Mennell, Lance Miller, Mat Moran, Petra Mudie, Liz and John Nylen, Frances Oles, Dorothy Paul, Catherine Powell, Pauline Rafferty, Judy Ramos, Michael Richards, Irma and John Schnabel, the late Peggy and Wilfred Schofield, William Schroeder, Joyce Skaflestad, Suzanne and Norman Smith, Mary Stensvold, Daniel Straathof, Greg Streveler, Carol and John Thilenius, Nancy and Robert Turner, Delmar Washington, Rosita Worl, Sandie and Vic Wratten. The Champagne and Aishikik First Nations granted permission for my work.

1

Well-preserved Bodies: Mummies

Norbert Mattersberger. That is a name with a ring to it, even if it is known to few, certainly few in the English-speaking world. Nonetheless, it has a claim to fame. It was the name of a man who melted headless and partly legless out of a glacier high in the mountains of East Tyrol, Austria, in 1929. He had lived from the last decade of the eighteenth century until he disappeared out hunting chamois in 1839. His body, buried very quickly after discovery, was the only ancient glacier mummy with an authentic real name.[1] What is a mummy? This term applies to much more than the very famous bodies of the ancient Egyptians. What exactly is a glacier mummy as distinct from a permafrost mummy and what is an ancient glacier mummy as distinct from a modern one? These are all questions needing answers which this chapter tries to provide.

Fig. 1.1 The only photograph of the remains of Norbert Mattersberger and his rifle as found in 1929. (*Harald Stadler, University of Innsbruck*)

ANCIENT HUMAN REMAINS

Some skeletal remains of our very remote ancestors are millions of years old. One of the best known of these discoveries has been called Lucy and she had lived in Ethiopia. Many parts of her skeleton were found. According to the Americans Donald Johanson and Maitland Edey, Lucy is approximately 3.5 million years old and her skeleton is the oldest, best preserved one of any erect-walking human ancestor. Later, we have another good skeleton of a 3-year-old of the same hominin from the same region. Now we have parts of the skeleton of an even more exciting human ancestor from the Ethiopia of no less than 4.4 million years ago. She is nicknamed Ardi, after the formal name *Ardipithecus ramidus*.[2] Ardi walked on her two feet on the ground but used all four limbs when in the trees.

Sometimes merely very small parts of skeletons are found but nonetheless they can be very important. Such an example in Britain is Boxgrove Man. He lived about half a million years ago in Sussex, but only one incomplete shin bone and two teeth (from a second person) were found in the sediments that also enclosed worked flint tools and the butchered bones of large mammals.[3] There are now two very recent examples of exceedingly important discoveries from very small remains of humans. The place is a Siberian cave called Denisova and the period about 30,000 to 50,000 years ago. No less than 28 authors were involved in the DNA analysis of a finger bone of a juvenile. The result indicates a previously unknown type of human.[4] Also published in late 2010, the microscopic examination of the debris between the teeth of Neanderthals from Iraq (about 44,000 years ago) and Belgium (about 36,000 years ago) yielded striking results. From starch grains and other microscopic plant structures called phytoliths the four authors made tentative identifications of the plants and claim that they had been eaten after being cooked.[5]

In North America, Kennewick Man lived some 9500 years ago along the Columbia River, which flows between the states of Washington and Oregon. His almost complete skeleton was discovered and the study of the skull caused great, unfortunate controversy.[6] Such an old and almost complete skeleton is a very rare discovery in North America and is of great scientific interest. Whole or partial skeletons of people who died during the last few to several thousand years are very numerous discoveries from many parts of the world. Much can be deduced from such skeletal remains, very old and not so old, and more will be revealed as science advances. However, researchers are limited in what they can achieve with only bones to investigate. How much better it is to have not just bones but all the soft tissues as well.

Executed men who lived around 2000 or so years ago at Tollund and Grauballe in Jutland, Denmark, and at Lindow, northern England, became bog bodies, that is to say they were found when peat digging exposed them.[7] As revealed to the public on television in early 2006, the partial but very dramatic bog bodies of two murdered men were found in bogs about 40km apart in central Ireland. They had lived about 2300 years ago and perhaps will become very famous, as the scientific results are fully published (see Figs 1.2 and 1.3). All these five bodies from peat bogs are mummies – not just skeletons, but retaining to a greater or lesser degree flesh, innards, eyes and hair. When all or part of the soft organs have

Fig. 1.2 Head of the mummified body of Cloneycavan man, Ireland. (*Finbarr Conolly, Dublin, National Museum of Ireland*)

Fig. 1.3 Mummified hand of Old Crogan man, Ireland. (*Finbarr Conolly, Dublin, National Museum of Ireland*)

been preserved many more scientific techniques come into play and the lifestyles of the deceased can potentially be revealed in great detail.

The term 'mummy' is used by archaeologists and anthropologists to mean any well-preserved human body. It does not just apply to elaborately treated corpses such as those of the Egyptian pharaohs whom people, stimulated by some none too rigorous or scholarly television broadcasts and books, find so endlessly fascinating. The American Arthur Aufderheide, in his 2003 book *The Scientific Study of Mummies*, gives the definition of mummy as '... for most people "mummy" induces a mental image of a corpse with soft tissues sufficiently preserved to resemble a once-living person'. This scientist gives further precision as 'a physically preserved corpse or tissue that resembles its living morphology but resists further decay for a prolonged post-mortem interval'. His book deals with mummies from all over the world and from all aspects.[8] A book which deals comprehensively with Egyptian mummies is that by Salima Ikran and Aidan Dodson.[9] All but a very small minority of mummies worldwide have resulted from five different but interacting causes: embalming, desiccation, saltiness, waterlogging and freezing. The first three causes interconnect, as do the second two. Desiccation is part of embalming and many frozen bodies have come into contact with liquid water, as was the case with both Ötzi and Kwäday Dän Ts'inchí Man.

EMBALMING

Over a period of some 3000 years until about 2000 years ago, numerous mummies were skilfully prepared in ancient Egypt.[10] The corpses were carefully treated by evisceration, removal of the brain and the application of a great range of substances including natron, or divine salt, which was a naturally occurring combination of compounds of sodium. Natron was mainly sodium chloride, which is halide or common salt, but also contains bicarbonate, which is baking powder, and carbonate and sulphate. The embalmers also used incense, frankincense, myrrh, resin, various oils, cassia, cinnamon, beeswax and onions. In the body and cranial cavities the embalmers placed fillings such as lichen, sawdust, chopped straw or other materials. Finally, the mummies were wrapped in linen bandages. The Egyptians mummified not only humans but also other creatures such as shrews, baboons, dogs, crocodiles, hippopotamuses and birds like ducks, falcons and ibises. Cats were mummified in large numbers. 'Cats became the official deity of Egypt in the form of the goddess Bastet; the huge numbers of cats sacrificed and mummified indicates that Egyptians were breeding domestic cats', says Carlos Driscoll and three others in the *Scientific American*.[11]

For soft organic tissues to survive indefinitely decay must be prevented and that means no water at temperatures above freezing, or else bacteria, fungi and other decomposers, microscopic and otherwise, will thrive. The reason for the use of natron is to induce this dryness; afterwards, the near rainless, warm climate of the Egyptian desert allowed preservation through the ages in shallow graves or in deep tombs.

No other culture has had such a detailed, highly complex procedure as the ancient Egyptians. The aboriginal Canary Islanders, the Guanches, mummified their dead and placed them in dry caves, natural tunnels in the thick lava flows of these almost entirely volcanic subtropical islands. The preparation of the bodies consisted only of evisceration and the cavity was filled with plant material which could be canary pine, dragon's blood tree, tree heather, grass or moss, as well as mineral particles. Whether any chemical treatment by application of liquids was ever used is unclear and, if there was, it may only have been applied to corpses of the upper classes.[12]

Long ago as the beginnings of Egyptian mummification were, this famous process was not the earliest artificial preparation of the dead. The people of the Chinchorro culture of Chile started elaborate mummification even earlier. In 1995 Bernardo Arriaza of the University of Tarapacá, Chile, stated:

> Black mummies were externally painted with a black manganese coating, hence their name. They were the most complex of all [the varied Chinchorro mummies]. To make these black mummies, the body was altered to such an extent that they were converted into sophisticated statues or death images because of the reinforcement of their inner skeletal structure and removal of most of the soft tissue. They were literally disassembled and reconstructed bodies.[13]

These mummies just discussed in this section are artificial mummies – specially prepared to be mummies. Those mummies now to be discussed are mostly natural ones, with no deliberate human intervention such as embalming involved.

SALTINESS

The importance of the preservative qualities of salt is very clearly shown by the discoveries of the well-preserved human remains in the old salt mines in Austria. In 1734, workers in the salt mine at Hallstatt, Upper Austria, found an ancient corpse entombed by a collapse of the ceiling of a salty tunnel. The body was buried in the local church. Recently called the 'Man in the Salt', the miner had lived about 2000 years ago, as we now know. Sadly, no such discoveries have been made recently during the period of productive scientific investigations of mummies.[14] At Hallein and Dürrnberg, south of Salzburg, the pine torches and other equipment of the Iron Age salt miners have been found and, more productive scientifically, their preserved faeces (coprolites) as well. In the Innsbruck Botanical Institute, pollen analyses of these human coprolites by Klaus Oeggl and colleagues of Innsbruck University are producing interesting results. In these ancient human stools, Horst Aspöck of Vienna University found eggs of several different internal parasites including roundworm, liverfluke and whipworm, all three together in four separate samples. More recent work by Klaus Oeggl and his colleague Werner Kofler on the pollen from coprolites from Dürrnberg produced a variety of results: the miners had eaten four types of cereals including broomcorn millet, they may have used *Nigella sativa* (black seed) medicinally, may have drunk mead (deduced from the high amounts of meadowsweet pollen) and may have used mugwort to control the intestinal parasites.[15]

DESICCATION

The arid climates in parts of Peru and Chile have led to the preservation of many mummies of which the recently discovered tattooed woman of the Moche people from some 1600 years ago is a very noteworthy example.[16] In the province of Xinjiang, north-westernmost China, neither evisceration nor embalming was used. Nonetheless, the exceedingly dry climate producing salty soils, formed under the blistering summers, as well as the cold winters, ensured preservation of an astonishing variety of mummies. There are children and adults of different racial origins, some with all their grave goods and beautiful clothes including tartan worn by one group from about 3000 to 3500 years ago at Hami. The Chinese professor Wang Binghua has stressed that the excellent preservation of the best of the mummies relates to burial in well-ventilated shallow graves during the sub-zero winter, cold arresting the initial autogenic decomposition, and then immediately followed by the great summer warmth[17] (see Plate 1).

The oldest known mummy from North America is that of Spirit Cave Man from about 9500 years ago in Nevada. Only 160cm tall (5ft 2in) and aged about the mid-forties, he was poorly mummified by desiccation alone because little of the soft tissues are preserved: some skin, ligaments, eye tissue and musculature, and remnants of the large intestine and colon. The head hair of a dark colour had been at least shoulder length. Helen Edgar of Ohio State University wrote that:

> He lived to around the age of 45, and was not very robust or muscular. He had many genetic abnormalities of the spine that lead to some to some pathological changes and probably caused him quite a bit of lower back pain. However, he had little or no osteoarthritis in his arms or legs. Sometime before his death the front of his head was fractured, possibly by the action of another person. He survived this injury, but may have died because of three severely abscessed teeth.[18]

WATERLOGGING

The very opposite preserving medium of desiccation is waterlogging. Here the crucial factor is the oxygenless conditions that pertain under the water table of peat bogs; the actions of decomposers such as many bacteria that need oxygen are inhibited or totally prevented. Already mentioned, the best known bog bodies are those of the Tollund and Grauballe men who lived between about 2000 and 2400 years ago. Both these men had infestations of pinworm, an intestinal parasite.[19] They had been killed and buried in the peat, as had Lindow Man from Cheshire, England, who also lived about 2000 years ago. Another well-known Danish mummy is that of a woman of about 20 years who lived in the Bronze Age at Egtved in southern Jutland.[20] She had been interred in an oaken coffin which must quickly have become waterlogged. This allowed preservation of her brain, face and hair as well as her clothing. There were a variety of artefacts including a little birch bark container with a dried crust inside, the remains of an alcoholic drink which has been discussed in detail by my late wife, Camilla, and I in relation to similar discoveries in Scotland.[21]

FREEZING

The very long-term preservative action of sub-zero temperatures is best shown by the Siberian woolly mammoths intact after tens of thousands of years with, when melted out, flesh palatable to the local carnivorous fauna. From central Alaska, near Fairbanks, some 36,000 years ago came Blue Babe, the well-preserved frozen body of an extinct Bison.[22] In the regions where the ground stays frozen (continuous permafrost), such as northernmost North America, there have been accidental burials of indigenous people, some found very well preserved when excavated after hundreds of years in the frozen state.[23]

A particularly noteworthy case, unique in one respect as far as I know in the studies of frozen bodies, is that of the corpse of an old woman who lived 1600 years ago on St Lawrence Island, in the Bering Sea, between Alaska and Siberia. She had died traumatically having been accidentally trapped in her house by a landslide or earthquake. What makes the case unique is the asphyxiation by the inhalation of fragments of a moss (three-ranked hump moss). She had suffered from coronary arteriosclerosis, emphysema, a curved spine and marked anthracosis (lungs blackened by smoke inhalation). She had simple tattoos on her hands.[24] At Barrow on the north coast of Alaska at about the year 1500, five people were killed when drifting sea ice crushed their house; three of the corpses (two women and a man) became little more than skeletons, but two women, both naked, were so well

preserved as to allow thorough medical examination of the soft tissues. Both were in good health but suffered from arteriosclerosis from eating too much fat and meat. One had had pneumonia and anthracosis.

In western Greenland freeze-dried bodies including not just adults but also babies and children have been found at three places, Pisissarfik, Qilakitsoq and Unartog.[25] Qilakitsoq serves as a good example. There, around 1475, eight people had been buried in shallow, plant-lined hollows on rocky ground: six adult women, a boy of about 4 years and a 6-month-old baby (see Figs 1.4 and 1.5). All were fully clothed in skins of harp and ringed seals and caribou. The inner parka (tight-fitting anorak) of one of the women had been made

Fig. 1.4 Mummified baby, Greenland. (*Hansen and Gulløv, 1989*)

Fig. 1.5 Facial tattoos of the mummified women, Greenland. (*Hansen and Gulløv, 1989*)

of the skins of no less than five different birds, including two types of duck. The boy had insoles made of a locally growing grass. Five of the women had facial tattoos. Only the young- est woman lacked them. Their teeth were in good state in that there were no caries (decay), as is so typical of modern people with their excessively sugary food. However, there were clear signs of wear pro- duced by use of the teeth as tools for preparing animal sinews. There were no artefacts whatever with the bodies.

From stable isotope analyses (about which technique much more later), the diet of the boy was estimated as 75 per cent from marine sources and the rest from the land. This is very likely to have been much the same for the other people too. Microscopic examination of the faeces of one of the women revealed pinworm. However, little in the way of what was obviously food was found but the authors thought that several mosses, including a bog moss had been deliberately eaten. This I doubt unless the people had been in dire straits, that is to say starving to death. There is much more about the importance of mosses in the studies of ice mummies later in this book. The only other parasite recognised was the head louse found on five of the mummies. The cause or causes of death were not firmly established though one of the women had probably died of cancer. On p. 91 it is stated that disease transmitted by the lice 'cannot be entirely excluded' as having contributed in some way to the deaths of the women.

An example of fine preservation by freezing has been investigated in detail by the Canadian anthropologist Owen Beattie of the University of Alberta. This concerns interred sailors who died during the ill-fated exploration of the Canadian Arctic archipelago by Sir John Franklin, commanding two Royal Navy ships in the mid-nineteenth century. The point of the expedition was to find the Northwest Passage, a sailing route westwards through archipelago. Everybody, in all 129 officers and men, on the two ships HMS *Terror* and HMS *Erebus*, perished and their sad fate for long remained a mystery. They had eaten food from tins. However, the tins had been poorly made and inadequately sealed with lead. It now seems possible that everyone's health was affected by the lead they inadvertently ingested. The ships became beset in the ice with the subsequent protracted loss of all hands and their southwards struggle to survive included cannibalism. Before that, however, in 1846 three crewmen, two from HMS *Erebus* and one from HMS *Terror*, had died and had been buried on land and the burials became frozen. The exhumations which took place in the mid-1980s revealed the state of preservation of the mummies to be outstandingly good.

All three had very high levels of lead in their soft tissues. This may have weakened them and two showed signs of tuberculosis and one of pneumonia. However, the lead poisoning as a cause of the whole tragedy has recently been doubted.[26]

Two more examples of superb preservation by freezing can be given. In some cases, there is beautiful preservation of the frozen bodies of children, both boys and maiden girls, sacrificed then buried on the summits of the Andean mountains. According to the Spanish chroniclers, children were selected for sacrifice because their purity made them more acceptable to live with the gods. There was much beautiful clothing and grave goods such as pottery and objects of precious metals, gold and silver. Some of the peaks are well over 6000m (more than 20,000ft). The summit of Amapato reaches 6310m and that of Llullaillaco 6739m. On both these mountains sacrifices were carried out by the Incas several hundred years ago. The Ice Maiden, also called 'Juanita', was found on Amapato. Living in the second half of the fifteenth century, she was in her early teens and had been killed by a blow to the right side of her head which fractured her skull. The ceremonial complex on Llullaillaco, where there were at least three burials, is the highest archaeological site in the world. There were a young woman, a girl and a boy of about 7. He was wearing a red tunic, leather moccasins, fur anklets, a silver bracelet and a sling wrapped around his head; he also had a bag containing coca leaves, a little bag containing hair and two figurines, one representing a man and the other a llama. The girl had a sleeveless dress and a shawl with pins and a metal plaque on her forehead. There were several pottery items, figurines of precious metal and bags of food. The young woman was about 15 years old and had a feathered headdress[27] (see Plates 2 and 3).

The second example of superb preservation concerns the burials in areas of discontinuous permafrost in Central Asia. The corpses, as in the cases of the Pazyryk people of the Altai, such as the Ukok Princess or the Ice Maiden and the Warrior or the Horse Man of about 2500 years ago, show elaborate decorative tattoos. The corpses were first eviscerated and the cavities filled with vegetable matter. Interred deeply and then covered with substantial mounds of boulders, the splendidly attired deceased and magnificent grave goods, including gold objects, became frozen in the great winter cold. The mounds of boulders allowed flow

Fig. 1.6 Retrieval of mummified First World War soldiers from the Alpine front. (*Pejo Museum, Italy*)

Fig. 1.7 The mummified soldiers melting upside down from the glacier. (*Pejo Museum, Italy*)

of frigid air right into the burial chamber.[28] Beautifully decorated horses were sacrificed and buried alongside skilled horse riders, often referred to as Scythians. Their habits had been described by Greek Herodotus (484–*c*.425 BC). The archaeological discoveries tally well with that historian's account[29] (see Plates 4 and 5).

A frozen body that gained much publicity some 10 years ago is that of the mountaineer George Mallory who, along with Andrew Irvine, may or may not have climbed Mount Everest in 1924; the corpse lay prone on a steep, gravelly slope at 8300m (27,000ft) when found in 1999, 75 years after the fatal fall.[30] During recreational mountaineering, many unfortunate people die each year in the Alps, some by falling into crevasses. According to Lawrence Barfield in his *Antiquity* review, hundreds of people die in the Alps annually and Ötzi was the sixth body recovered in 1991. Konrad Spindler specifies 200 fatalities (Spindler 1, p. 131). If a fall into a crevasse does not lead instantly to death, hypothermia will usually be fatal very quickly. Such bodies normally get carried along by the moving ice and, in so doing, may become fragmented. Finally the corpse may be found lower down the glacier or pieces come out the melting snout. In his well-known book, *The Man in the Ice*, the late Konrad Spindler has related some recent examples from Tyrol, such as the bodies of two young men who took 38 years to travel 300m down the glacier. An even more recent example (from 2004), but not because of recreation, is the discovery of the frozen bodies of three Austro-Hungarian soldiers of the First World War who died in 1918 fighting to retake the peak of San Matteo on the border of Austria and Italy (see Figs 1.6 and 1.7).

UNUSUAL CASES

The majority of mummies fall into the principal categories just discussed. However, for the sake of completeness, mention is necessary of the following few cases as examples of rare types of mummification: Copper Man, the St Bees Man, the self-mummified Buddhists of Japan and smoked mummies in Papua New Guinea.

That heavy metals such as copper in contact with organic materials can have a preservative effect has been discussed by Arthur Aufderheide. He cites the case of the 1500-year-old
mummy of a miner known as Copper Man from the copper ore rich Chuquicamata in
northern Chile, but the hyper arid climate of the Atacama Desert could have been crucial in
the mummification. As related on the web pages of Dr John Todd, excavation of the ancient
St Bees priory in Cumbria, England, revealed the very well-preserved body of a man of
some 40 years who had lived during high medieval times. The corpse had been enveloped
in a double linen shroud coated with 'probably beeswax' and all inside a hard shell of lead
– 'not so much a coffin as a wrapper'. The fine preservation is attributed to 'the combined
effects of the lead sheath, which excluded moisture and the beeswax coating of the shroud
which excluded all air' and resulting biochemical changes which 'acidified and dehydrated
the tissues, so killing off the bacteria which normally cause decay, and producing glycerol
which acted as a preservative'. This example appears to be unique.

Professor Iwataro of the St Marianna University School of Medicine in Japan has
investigated an extraordinary kind of mummification, referred to as self-mummification,
undergone by Buddhist monks in Japan during the seventeenth to twentieth centuries.[31]
The claim is that by greatly restricting their diet for prolonged periods to 'bark of pine trees
and meat of Torreya nuts' and by drinking lacquer from the urushi tree before entomb-
ment they enhanced their chance of becoming mummies. Referring to China, Arthur
Aufderheide in his large text on mummies states that conscious efforts aimed at self-mummification are very ancient in Asia, certainly much older than Buddhism. In the case of the
Japanese, he considers that slow starvation and terminal water restriction were major factors
in soft tissue preservation, but makes no mention of either the eating of conifers or of the
drinking of lacquer.[32]

According to Ronald Beckett of Quinnipiac University, Connecticut, the Anga tribe of
the Central Highlands of New Guinea until recently made mummies by treating the corpses
with smoke. Stopped by missionaries for some decades, the process with some unique features has now begun again. The use of smoke for mummification has been practised by the
Maori of New Zealand and Ibaloi of the Philippines, but the Anga use of a hut is peculiar to
them. Coated with red ochre clay, specially chosen important people were mummified in a
sitting position. The mummies then attended ceremonies and meetings.[33]

PERMAFROST AND GLACIER MUMMIES

With the principal exceptions of Ötzi and Norbert Mattersberger, most of the frozen bodies
mentioned above are best not referred to as ancient icemen or icewomen. Though frozen,
they had died for some reason such as disease or from violent causes, like sacrifice, and then
many of them had been deliberately interred in frozen ground. Their preservation had to do
with freezing in or on the ground, not within or under glacier ice. They have sensibly been
called permafrost mummies by Konrad Spindler.

In German, there is a well-established word, *gletschermumie* (glacier mummy), for bodies
melted from glaciers. A particularly good example of the use of this term is in the book by
Markus Egg and colleagues of the Roman Germanic Museum in Mainz *Die Gletschermumie*

vom Ende der Steinzeit aus den Ötztaler Alpen (The Glacier Mummy of the End of the Stone Age from the Ötztal Alps); this has magnificent photographs of Ötzi and his clothing and equipment, as does the much more recent *Kleidung und Ausrüstung der Kupferzeitlichen Gletschermumie aus den Ötzaler Alpen* (Clothing and Equipment of the Copper Age Glacier Mummy from the Ötzal Alps) by Markus Egg and Konrad Spindler.

Have there been any discoveries of ancient human remains from European glaciers prior to the finding of Ötzi? The answer is yes. There are not just Norbert Mattersberger, already mentioned, but also the Theodulpass Mercenary and the Porchabella Shepherdess, the latter two from Switzerland. All have their own especially interesting features and they are discussed later in this book. Ancient corpses melted out of glaciers present intriguing questions, several of them different from those that arise from permafrost mummies or from other kinds of mummies. What had they been doing where they were found; where had they come from (A going to B or B going to A or A back to A) and by which routes; who were their kin and did they die as a result of an unfortunate accident or not?

Ötzi, who is the main concern of this book, had well-preserved gear and clothing that he had carried and worn on his fatal last journey. Crucially, because he retained his shrivelled but intact alimentary tract holding food residues, we can answer some or all of these special questions. Because of this, ancient glacier mummies have great scientific importance and should be recognised as a distinct subset of frozen corpses. Ötzi, the Theodulpass Mercenary, the Porchabella Shepherdess and Norbert Mattersberger all had a good reason for being high in the mountains but it seems unlikely that any of them had been there purely for fun. However, climbing high mountains out of curiosity was not unknown long ago, though perhaps it was rare, as this example, kindly drawn to my intention by Harold Stadler, shows.[34] In 1387 six priests from Luzern in Switzerland climbed the nearby mountain called Pilatus (2130m high) to fathom the myth of the spirit of the Roman governor Pontius Pilate haunting a small lake near the peak. Unfortunately they could not find anything proving or disproving the matter. Even more unfortunately for the curious clerics, their adventure was regarded as sacrilegious by their superiors and led to a long imprisonment.

Fig. 1.8 Ötzi shortly after being ripped from the ice in 1991. (*Elisabeth Zissernig, University of Innsbruck*)

Most glacier bodies derive from mountaineering mishaps and fighting on the alpine front during the First World War. These sad accidents are not the particular concern of this book. The Italians Dr Michel-Gabriel Paccard and Jacques Balmat reached the summit of the highest peak in Western Europe, Mont Blanc (4807m or about 15,800ft), as early as 1786. However, alpinism as a popular organised sport can be thought of as an activity beginning to be very serious in the second half of the nineteenth century. The Alpine Club was set up in 1857 in London and soon after other nations followed suit by founding such clubs. For Europe I use the term 'ancient glacier mummy' to mean a well-preserved corpse from earlier than 1850.[35] So, dying in 1839, Norbert Mattersberger qualifies, though not by very much, to be called an ancient glacier mummy. In great contrast is Ötzi who, alive well over 5000 years ago, is by far the most ancient of the glacier mummies and, certainly too, by far the most famous and liable to remain so for all time. I doubt that there will ever be another Ötzi – no ancient glacier mummy so very ancient and so full of fascinating information will ever be found[36] (see Fig. 1.8).

THE TYROLEAN ICEMAN – ÖTZI

It was extremely fortunate that a corpse happened to be noticed very high in the Alps on 19 September 1991 by man and wife, Hugo and Erica Simons. This is because, since then, there has been almost no such great melting of the snow and ice to reveal the spot. The late summer of 2007 is an example, as I know from personal experience. Out hiking in the Ötztal (Venoste) Alps at about 3200m (about 10,500ft), right on the border of Austria and Italy, the German couple were only very slightly off the usual track when they saw the head and upper back of the man protruding through the ice. Hugo took a photograph with the second last shot on his film. The photograph and the discoverers instantly became very well known. The body lay only a mere 92m south of the frontier which follows the main watershed of the Ötztal Alps. These mountains form beautiful and dramatic terrain with towering peaks reaching altitudes well above 3000m.[37]

The finding of the frozen, complete body of a man who had lived well over 5000 years ago was not just unprecedented but totally unexpected. The iceman, often called Ötzi, is the oldest, best preserved human ever found and is deservedly spoken and written of in superlatives. With the body were a set of clothes and much gear including items never before seen in the archaeology of such a remote period or, indeed, any period other than very recent times. The English archaeologist Lawrence Barfield's splendid way of putting it in a review article in *Antiquity* is:

> With some justification he has been claimed as the most exciting find since Tutankhamun. Both were mummies; the similarity ends there. Tutankhamun was a find which was expected, an intact royal tomb sought for over several campaigns of excavation; the Iceman was an accidental find and a unique case of conservation which had figured in no archaeologist's wildest dreams.

I would add another important difference, indeed a difference significant in the eyes of the scientist, which is that the body of the Egyptian had been grossly altered by the mummifiers, rendering some types of scientific investigation difficult or impossible. In contrast is the iceman's body which was intact, including all the innards, allowing a greater diversity of studies to take place. So, I would immediately go much further than Lawrence Barfield and claim that Ötzi is greater by far than Tutankhamun, the boy pharaoh who lived long after the iceman.

The name Ötzi – rhymes with tootsie – is a pleasing, humanising one. The *Innsbruck* 1 volume of Ötzi studies uses no less than six names for him: *Homo tirolensis*, Similaum or Hauslabjoch or Tisenjoch man or mummy, ice man or iceman. In *Innsbruck* 2 Lorelies Ortner states: 'There are more than 500 different appellations for this unique find … the readers of the texts no longer have a dead body but a fascinating relative called *Ötzi* (inhabitant of the Tyrolean valley Ötztal).' *Ötz* is Tyrolean German word meaning pasture, a vegetation type which some would link to Ötzi's way of life. Another name I like is Hibernatus, which the French use, and which, again, is humanising.[38]

The discovery of Ötzi immediately raised many questions and various claims were made, some plausible and some absolutely not so. There was even a book quickly published claiming preposterously that the whole thing was a hoax. Konrad Spindler and the first investigators of Ötzi's DNA with total justification quickly and disparagingly dismissed this cynical nonsense. What had Ötzi been doing so high in the mountains; where was his home; how did the corpse come to be so well preserved and intact; how did he come to die? Questions such as these and many others were addressed in books such as *Der Jeuge aus dem Gletscher* (The Witness from the Glacier) which, unfortunately, was never published in English. This had been written by Lawrence Barfield and his Austrian co-authors, Ebba Koller and Andreas Lippert. Soon afterwards there was the much more famous *Der Mann im Eis* (The Man in the Ice), written by the late Konrad Spindler in 1993, one of the professors of archaeology in Innsbruck University. In the light of much new scientific work, many of the ideas in these very quickly written books are now discarded or in need of substantial reinterpretation.

Like many millions of people around the world, I heard very soon of the discovery of Ötzi from the media. It was truly a sensation and, immediately, I wished that I was involved in the investigations and, indeed, I was so to be, but not until some two and a half years later. The moment, on 18 April 1994, that I opened a parcel from Klaus Oeggl, a professor of botany in Innsbruck University was a great one. Seeing 47 small glass vials more or less full of scraps of mosses was exciting. There was one especially full one containing a low-altitude, woodland moss, called in botanical Latin *Neckera complanata* and, in English, flat neckera. In the region where Ötzi was found, it does not grow above 1750m and yet the corpse had been found at almost twice that height above sea level. I realised at once that some at least, possibly many, of the mosses, not just the flat neckera, could be significant discoveries. They were potentially clues for understanding the lifestyle of Ötzi, for reconstructing the events of his last days and for deducing the ancient environment.

In 2001, when Werner Kofler in the Innsbruck Botanical Institute showed me a plant fragment on a microscope slide made from Ötzi's colon contents, I was totally taken aback but very pleasantly so. It was a tiny fragment of a leaf of a bog moss and that in itself was unexpected. People do not normally eat mosses of any kind. But, more than that, it was a particular species unknown in the territory we think Ötzi had occupied. So, how come?

It was another potentially big clue, but to what exactly? Foodstuff? Some distant geographical connection? A remnant of a wound dressing that had been sticking to his blood-stained fingers? Or just a chance accidental ingestion with no particular significance?

The Royal Society of London was founded in 1663 and so is one of the oldest learned societies in the world, and not just old but prestigious. So when in 1999 I read in a multi-author paper in the *Philosophical Transactions* of that society a claim that Ötzi had had an 'essentially vegan' diet I was astonished, but that time unpleasantly. It did not make sense. I wondered why such an improbable statement had been published and not merely because Klaus Oeggl and I had seen meat fibres in the tiny sample of food residue we had already examined by that time. Now we know from the DNA work of Franco Rollo of Camerino University in Italy that Ötzi had eaten both alpine ibex and red deer meat as part of his last meals. Of course, Ötzi was omnivorous, just as one would expect, or, if he had been vegan, then he gave up his principles in the last few hours of his life.

Konrad Spindler became famous worldwide with the publication of his book *The Man in the Ice*. He was the first person to realise fully that Ötzi had lived thousands of years ago, although Reinhold Messner, the famous alpinist, who saw the body before it was taken from the ice, thought that it was centuries old – not the result of a modern accident. Konrad Spindler's first and, surprisingly, only visit to the discovery site was by helicopter and he then gave the direction of the excavations in October 1991 and August 1992 to his colleague Andreas Lippert, who left Innsbruck soon after to become an archaeology professor in Vienna University.

In order to understand to the fullest extent the importance of scores of different mosses found inside, on and around the ancient corpse, I have climbed always accompanied to the site or its near vicinity several times from both the Italian and Austrian sides. These have been instructive visits from more than the point of studying moss ecology. The weather in the zone of perennial snow and ice, and even at much lower altitudes, can be treacherous even during the summer months in Tyrol. This I know from personal experience. On 17 August 2006 I roped up to Geneviève Lécrivain, Wolfgang Hofbauer, Klaus Oeggl and Andreas Gruber, the latter two being expert alpinists. We then tried to climb Similaun, which is the highest peak, reaching 3600m, within a few km of the Ötzi site. At first it was easy, even crossing the crevasses. But the day was a mixture of mist and sun and strong wind, and we stopped at about 3,400m where the final climb is up a much steeper slope which was covered in snow and the mist had become thick. We turned back down to the Similaun Hut and took note of a few mosses on the way. So I still do not know if any mosses grow on the very top. However, it will be few, perhaps just a couple or so.

Notes

1 Stadler, H. 2005. '"Untertan kontra Obrigkeit". Die Gletscherleiche des Wilderers Norbert Mattersberger vom Gradetzkees in Ostirol'. In J. Holzner and E. Walde (eds), *Brüche und Brücken*. Bozen, Folio, pp. 236–49.

2 Johanson, D.C. and Edey, M.A. 1990. *Lucy The Beginnings of Humankind*. Harmondsworth, Penguin, p. 28. The term hominid is now superseded by hominin, which includes Lucy (*Australopithecus afarensis*), *Ardipethicus*, *Kenyanthropus* and us (*Homo*). Berger, L.R. 2001. 'Viewpoint: Is it Time to Revise the System of Scientific Naming?' *National Geographic News*. Hecht, J. 2006. 'Amazing skeleton of a young ancestor'. *New Scientist*, 23 September. Shreeve, J. 2010. 'The Evolutionary Road'. *National Geographic*,

July, pp. 35–67. Braun, D.R. 2010. 'Australopithecine butchers'. *Nature* 466, p. 828. For a stimulating account of the early evolution of humans and biological nomenclature see Dawkins, R. 2010. *The Greatest Show on Earth*. London, Transworld.

3   Pitts, M. and Roberts, M. 1997. *Fair-weather Eden*. London, Century. Barton, N. 2005. *Ice Age Britain*. London, Batsford. There are clear signs of even earlier humans in Britain at Happisburgh, Norfolk. See Parfitt, S.A. *et al.* 2010. 'Early Pleistocene human occupation at the edge of the boreal zone in north-west Europe'. *Nature* 466, pp. 229–33. They found pollen of the tree hop hornbeam, a very important plant in the story of Ötzi. Today it is found almost nowhere north of the Alps and there very sparsely.

4   Reich, D. *et al.* 2010. 'Genetic history of an archaic hominin group from Denisova Cave in Siberia'. *Nature* 468, pp. 1053–60. Henry, A.G., Bropoks, A.S. and Piperno, D.R. 2010. 'Microfossils in calculus demonstrate consumption of plants and cooked foods in Neanderthal diets (Shanidar III, Iraq; Spy I and II, Belgium)'. *Proceedings of the National Academy of Sciences Early Edition*.

5   Ibid.

6   Chatters, J.C. 2001. *Ancient Encounters Kennewick Man and the First Americans*. New York, Simon & Schuster. Thomas, D.H. 2000. *Skull Wars*. New York, Basic Books. Dalton, R. 2005. 'Scientists finally get their hands on Kennewick Man'. *Nature* 436, p. 10. Anonymous. 2006. 'Too old to be buried'. *New Scientist*, 19 August, p. 7. Burke, H. *et al.* 2008. *Kennewick Man Perspectives on the Ancient One*. Walnut Creek, Left Coast Press. Dalton, R. 2010. 'Audit picks a bone with US relics office'. *Nature*, 464, p. 422.

7   Stead, I.M., Bourke, J.B. and Brothwell, D. 1986. *Lindow Man: the Body in the Bog*. British Museum, London. Turner, R.C. and Scaife, R.G. 1995. *Bog Bodies: New Discoveries and Perspectives*. London, British Museum Press. *Innsbruck* 3 contains the following two articles: Brothwell, D. 'European bog bodies: current state of research and preservation', pp. 161–72; Daniels, C.V. 'Selection of a conservation process for Lindow Man', pp. 173–81. Lynnerup, N., Andreasen, C. and Berglund, J. 2003. *Mummies in a New Millenium*. Copenhagen, Danish Polar Centre. This book contains the following three articles: Asing, P. 'The Grauballe Man. A Well-preserved Iron Age Bog Body. Old and New Examinations', pp. 50–6. Fischer, C. 'The Tollund Man', pp. 59–62. Asingh, P. and Lynnerup, N. 2007. *Grauballe Man: An Iron Age Bog Body Revisited*. Mosegaard, Jutland Archaeological Society. Kelly, E.P. No date. 'Kinship and sacrifice: Iron Age bog bodies and boundaries'. *Archaeology Ireland Heritage Guide* 35. Mannering, U. *et al.* 2010. 'Dating Danish textiles and skins from bog finds by means of 14C AMS'. *Journal of Archaeological Science* 37, pp. 261–8.

8   Aufderheide, A.C. 2003. *The Scientific Study of Mummies*. Cambridge University Press. See p. 1 for the tortuous history of the use of the word 'mummy'.

9   Ikram, S. and Dodson, A. 1998. *The Mummy in Ancient Egypt: Equipping the Dead for Eternity*. London, Thames and Hudson. Zivie, A. 2007. *The Lost Tombs of Saqqara*. Ankhtawy, Cara. Driscoll, C.A. *et al.* 2009. 'The Taming of the Cat'. *Scientific American* 300, pp. 56–63.

10 Ibid.

11 Ibid.

12 Anonymous. 1992. *Proceedings of the First Congress on Mummy Studies*. Two volumes. Archaeological and Ethnographical Museum of Tenerife. Rodríguez-Martin, C. 1996. 'Guanche mummies of Tenerife, Canary Islands'. *Innsbruck* 3.

13 Arriaza, B. 1995. *Beyond Death: The Chinchorro Mummies of Ancient Chile*. Washington, Smithsonian Institution Press. Arriaza, B. 1996. 'Preparation of the dead in coastal Andean preceramic populations'. *Innsbruck* 3, pp. 131–40. In his textbook Arthur Aufderheide states that the oldest Chinchorro mummy is from about 9000 years ago but the oldest artificially mummified body is from 7000 years ago, no less than 2000 years before the first mummified pharaoh.

14 Klein, H. 1961. 'Der Fundort des "Mannes in Salz"'. *Mitteilungen der Gesellschaft für Landkunde* 101, pp. 139–41. In his books Konrad Spindler discusses an even earlier man from 1573 preserved in the salt mine at Hallein, Austria.

15 Aspöck, H. 2000. 'Paläoparasitologie: Zeugen der Vergangenheit'. *Nova Acta Leopoldina* 83, pp. 159–81. Aspöck, H. *et al.* 2002. 'Parasitologische Untersuchungen von im Salz konservierten Exkrementen: Zur Gesundheit der Dürrnberger Bergleute'. In Dobiat, C. *et al.* (eds), *Kolloquien zur Vor- und Frühgeschichte* 7. Dürrnberg und Manching Wirtschaftarchäologie im ostkeltischen Raum, pp. 123–32. Bonn, Dr Rudolf Habelt. Aspöck, H. *et al.* 2007. 'The Dürrenberg miners during the Iron Age New

Results by Interdisciplinary Research'. *Beiträge zur Ur- und Frühgesichichte Mitteleuropas* 47, pp. 109–26. Oeggl, K. and Kofler, W. 2007. 'Pollen analysis of Human palaeofaeces from an Iron Age Salt Mine'. *Beiträge zur Ur- und Frühgesichichte Mitteleuropas* 47, pp. 115–26.

16   Williams, R.A. 2006. 'Mystery of the Tattooed Mummy'. *National Geographic*, June 2006, pp. 71–83.

17   Barber, E.J.W. 1991. *Prehistoric Textiles the Development of Cloth in the Neolithic and Bronze Ages.* Princeton University Press. Barber, E.W. 1999. *The Mummies of Ürümchi.* London, Macmillan. Mallory, J.P. and Mair, V.H. 2000. *The Tarim Mummies.* London, Thames & Hudson. Wang Binghua. 1999. *The Ancient Corpses of Xinjiang the Peoples of Ancient Xinjiang and Their Culture.* Peking.

18   The *Nevada Historical Society Quarterly* 40, no 1, 1997, has several articles on Spirit Cave Man. There is a very satisfactory suite of radiocarbon dates and assessments of palaeopathology. Like Kennewick Man, Spirit Cave Man is very controversial for socio-political reasons.

19   Stead, I.M., Bourke, J.B. and Brothwell, D. 1986. *Lindow Man: the Body in the Bog.* British Museum, London. Turner, R.C. and Scaife, R.G. 1995. *Bog Bodies: New Discoveries and Perspectives.* London, British Museum Press. *Innsbruck* 3 contains the following two articles: Brothwell, D. 'European bog bodies: current state of research and preservation', pp. 161–72; Daniels, C.V. 'Selection of a conservation process for Lindow Man', pp. 173–81. Lynnerup, N., Andreasen, C. and Berglund, J. 2003. *Mummies in a New Millenium.* Copenhagen, Danish Polar Centre. This book contains the following three articles: Asing, P. 'The Grauballe Man. A Well-preserved Iron Age Bog Body. Old and New Examinations', pp. 50–6. Fischer, C. 'The Tollund Man', pp. 59–62. Asingh, P. and Lynnerup, N. 2007. *Grauballe Man An Iron Age Bog Body Revisited.* Mosegaard, Jutland Archaeological Society. Kelly, E.P. No date. 'Kinship and sacrifice: Iron Age bog bodies and boundaries'. *Archaeology Ireland Heritage Guide* 35. Mannering, U. *et al.* 2010. 'Dating Danish textiles and skins from bog finds by means of 14C AMS'. *Journal of Archaeological Science* 37, pp. 261–8.

20   Glob, P.V. 1973. *The Mound People. Danish Bronze-Age Man Preserved.* London, Paladin. Dickson, C. and Dickson, J.H. 2000. *Plants and People in Ancient Scotland.* Stroud, Tempus.

21   Ibid.

22   Lister, A. and Bahn, J.M. 1995. *Mammoths.* London, Boxtree. Guthrie, R.D. 1990. *Frozen Fauna of the Mammoth Steppe.* Chicago University Press.

23   Ibid.

24   Duke, P. 1996. 'Mummies of the far north'. In Bahn, P.G. (ed.) *Tombs, Graves & Mummies.* London, Wiedenfield & Nicholson, pp. 174–9. Zimmerman, M.R. and Smith, G.S. 1975. 'A probable case of accidental inhumation of 1,600 years ago'. *Bulletin of the New York Academy of Medicine* 51, pp. 828–37. Zimmerman, M.R. 1996. 'Mummies of the Arctic regions'. *Innsbruck* 3, pp. 84–92. Figure 3 in Zimmerman's paper is a photomicrograph of the moss that caused asphyxiation. It is totally inadequate for the certain recognition of three-ranked hump-moss, a species which, on grounds of ecology, seems an unlikely one to have been inhaled. Hart Hansen, J.P. and Gulløv, H.C. 1989. 'The mummies from Qilakitsoq – Eskimos in the 15th century'. *Meddelelser om Grønland, Man and Society* 12, pp. 1–199. Lynnerup, N. 2003. 'The Greenland Mummies'. In Andreasen, C. and Berglund, J. (eds). *Mummies in a New Millenium.* Copenhagen, Danish Polar Centre, pp. 17–9.

25   Ibid.

26   Beattie, O. and Geiger, J. 1993. *Frozen in Time.* London, Bloomsbury. Notman, D. and Beattie, O. 1996. 'The paleoimaging and forensic anthropology of frozen sailors from the Franklin Arctic expedition mass disaster (1845-1848): a detailed presentation of two radiological surveys'. *Innsbruck* 3, pp. 93–106. Williams, G. 2010. *Arctic Labyrinth the Quest for the Northwest Passage.* Penguin Books, London.

27   Reinhard, J. 1996. 'Peru's Ice Maidens'. *National Geographic* 189, pp. 62–81. Reinhard, J. 2005. *The Ice Maiden Inca Mummies, Mountain Gods and Sacred Sites in the Andes.* Washington, National Geographic. Horne, P.D. 1996. 'The Prince of El Plomo: a frozen treasure'. *Innsbruck* 3, pp. 153–7. See also papers on the frozen mummies from Mount Llullaillaco, north-western Argentina, in Niels, N., Andreasen, C. and Berglund, J. (eds). *Mummies in a New Millenium.* Copenhagen, Danish Polar Centre. Ceruti, C. 2004. 'Human bodies as objects of dedication at Inca mountain shrines (north-western Argentina)'. *World Archaeology* 36, pp. 103–22. Reinhard, J. and Ceruti, M.C. 2010. *Inca Rituals and Sacred Mountains.* California, Corten Institute for Archaeology.

28   Ibid.

29 Bogucki, P. 1996. 'Pazyryk and the Ukok Princess'. In Bahn, P.G. (ed.). *Tombs, Graves & Mummies.* London, Wiedenfield & Nicholson, pp. 146–51. Millson, P. *et al.* 1997. *Horizon Ice Mummies.* BBC, London. Rolle, R. *Innsbruck* 1, p. 334. Bourgeois, J. and Gheyle, W. 2006. *Frozen Tombs of the Altai Mountains.* UNESCO, Ghent.

30 Hanneleb, J., Johnson, L.A. and Simonson, E.R. 1999. *Ghosts of Everest.* London, Macmillan.

31 Morimoto, I. 1993. 'Buddhist Mummies in Japan'. *Acta Anatomica Nipponica* 68, pp. 381–98.

32 Aufderheide, A.C. 2003. *The Scientific Study of Mummies.* Cambridge University Press.

33 Beckett, R., Berstein, J. and Lohmann, U. 2011. 'A Unique Field Mummy Conservation Project in Papua New Guinea'. *Yearbook of Mummy Studies* 1, pp. 11-17. Beckett, R., Berstein, J. and Lohmann, U. 2011. 'A Field Report on the Mummification Practices of the Anga of Koke Village, Central Highlands, Papua New Guinea'. *Yearbook of Mummy Studies* 1, pp. 19-27.

34 2002. *Maos Atem Rossinis Tränen und 999 andere unwichtige Tatsachen und Ereignisse der Welt- und Kulturgeschichte 42*, p. 153.

35 Dickson, J.H. 2011. 'Why Ancient Glacier Mummies are so special: The Ingesta are encoded Maps and Diaries'. *Yearbook of Mummy Studies* 1, pp. 45-50.

36 I make this prediction expecting to be proved wrong quickly. See the booklet *Bluff Your Way in Science* by Brian Malpass. That witty author gives examples of old scientists who, predicting that something cannot ever happen, are then proved wrong very soon afterwards. See also *Bluff Your Way in Archaeology* by Paul Bahn for another amusing read.

37 There is, however, precisely at the area of the site, a small deviation north-eastwards of the watershed which means that, despite being within the northwards drainage, the iceman lay in Italy and not in Austria.

38 Cadinot, V. 2005. 'Hibernatus Enquête sur un crime préhistorique'. *Science et Vie*, June, pp. 152–66. R'bibo, Y.S. 2011. 'Préhistoire Ouvert, tatoué, marquee … Le corps investi. Naissance de la Médicine'. *Science & Vie* 121, pp. 6–12.

2

Ötzi, the Tyrolean Iceman from 5200 Years Ago

ÖTZILAND

Lie of the Land

The region in which Ötzi was found is still referred to as Tyrol or Tirol. Since 1919, the southern part (Südtirol) has been part of Italy and the northern part (Nordtirol) remained Austrian. Various publications, including some of mine, call Ötzi the Tyrolean iceman. For the purposes of this book I have coined the term *Ötziland*. This area covers southernmost Ötztal (Nordtirol), southwards from about Sölden, and north-westernmost Südtirol, westwards to about Mals (Malles), eastwards to about Brixen (Bressanone) and southwards to about Bozen (Bolzano).

The very place where the body was found lies at 3210m above sea level, near Hauslabjoch and Tisenjoch (latitude 46° 50' N longitude 10° 50' E). The site is a long, narrow, shallow,

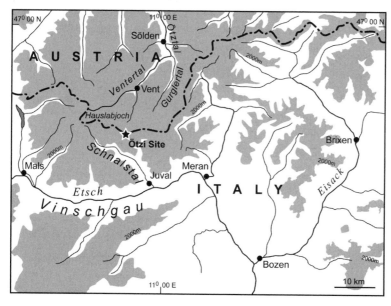

Fig. 2.1 *Ötziland* A.

Fig. 2.2 *Ötziland B.*

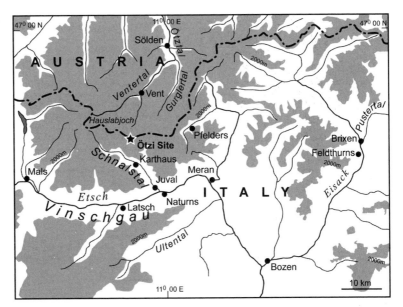

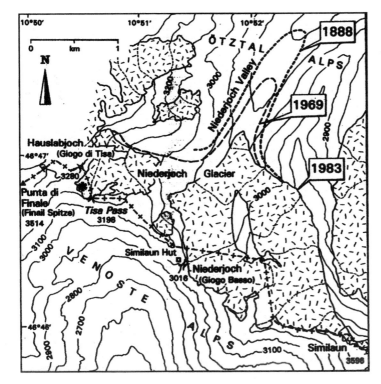

Fig. 2.3 Map with Ötzi site (star middle left) and glaciers. (*Baroni and Orombelli, 1996*)

rocky hollow. When free of snow and ice it can be seen to be strewn with boulders. There was coarse mineral sediment that was largely removed during the second excavation. Though it may have been part of the nearby Niederjoch glacier for some, perhaps even much or all, of the last 5000 years, there is no old ice in the hollow now, nor may there have been any at Ötzi's precise time.[1]

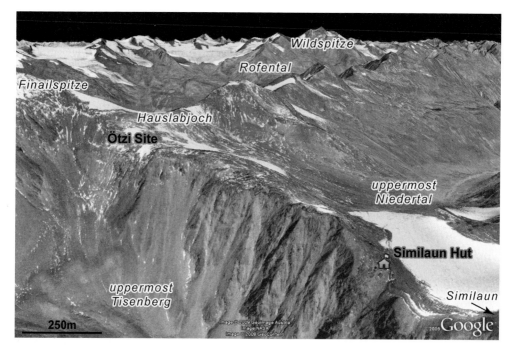

Fig. 2.4 Aerial shot by Google Earth. (*Google Earth*)

There are two long valleys which come up to the site and these are the very valleys which Ötzi may have traversed on his last journey or on earlier journeys too, if there were any, as is probable. From the north southwards there is Ötztal, which in its upper reaches splits into two; to the east is Gurglertal and to the west is Ventertal. The upper part of Ventertal also splits in two and it is its eastern branch, called Niedertal, which reaches nearest the iceman site. More than 15km to the south of the site is a broad valley through which the River Etsch (Adige) flows eastwards, the region being called Vinschgau (Val Venosta). From Vinschgau up towards the site comes the southeast–northwest-lying Schnalstal (Val Senales) and its side valley, Tisental (Val Tisa), which goes nearest the site (see Fig. 2.4).

Less than 1km to the west of the site is Finailspitze, which reaches 3514m, and less than 3km to the southeast is Similaun, reaching just less than 3600m. Reaching 3736m, 10km to the northwest, is Weisskugel and 12km to the north is Wildspitze, which reaches 3774m. These are the third and second highest peaks in all Austria. Well to the east in the Hohe Tauern of Osttirol (East Tirol), Grossglockner reaches 3798m and so is only a little higher than Wildspitze. Within *Ötziland*, as defined here, there is the considerable altitudinal range of well over 3000m, from 240m at Bozen, 500m at Meran (Merano) and 1360m at Sölden to 3774m at Wildspitze.

Rocks

The bedrock geology is varied in detail from very hard rocks like granites to much softer rocks such as limestone, which, being calcium carbonate, is soluble in water. There are outcrops of dolomite and marble which are greatly altered limestones. Also in *Ötziland* are gneisses and phyllites, as well as volcanic rocks such as basalts. Plate 6 is taken from the paper by Wolfgang Müller, of Royal Holloway College, London, with four others.[2] These rocks just listed were formed hundreds of millions of years ago but within the last few million years the recent numerous ice ages have dramatically altered the landscape. Glaciers have great erosive powers in grinding down bedrock and have dumped along their sides and at their ends as they melted moraines, as can be seen very clearly in Ventertal. In low-lying Vinschgau, where, as discussed in later chapters, we think Ötzi may have spent part or all of his adult life, there are very striking fan-shaped areas of debris brought down the steep slopes during and after the retreat of the glaciers.

Climate, Present and Past

Ötziland has a temperate climate, which varies not just from lowland to highland, but from north to south. The northern part is higher (1368m at Sölden) and wetter (851mm precipitation) and colder (mean annual temperature 2.8°C). The southern part descends to much lower altitudes (262m at Bozen), is drier (661mm annual precipitation) and much warmer (mean annual temperature 12.6°C). Not too far to the south, at the north end of Lake Garda, the climate is akin to the Mediterranean. In middle Vinschgau (Naturns to Mals) the climate is the most Continental of Ötziland. There the lowermost, south-facing slopes are warm and dry. The temperature and snow cover varies greatly with altitude and aspect, with permanent snow and glaciers above 2500m and especially above 3000m.

During the last few million years there have been very many marked changes in the Earth's climate which resulted from variations in the orbit of our planet.[3] In 2010, in the prominent scientific journal Nature, Daniel Sigman of Princeton University with two others published a figure showing 11 glacial periods in the last 800,000 years.[4] Having lasted some 100,000 years, the last ice age ended abruptly about 11,500 years ago. It has long been thought that after the last ice age until about 5000 or so years ago the climate was warmer than now, perhaps by a degree or so, which does not sound very much but that is more than enough to have made quite a difference to people's lives. This is the so-called Climatic Optimum when there was less ice in the Alps than now. Swiss scientists have even claimed that, there having been so little ice remaining, the Alps looked green with vegetation.[5] Thereafter, there was a decline but not necessarily a slow, steady one, but with changes, perhaps abrupt ones, to colder and warmer and back again. This cooling with advancing glaciers is known as the Neoglaciation.

There are now many new powerful scientific disciplines used to investigate the complex climatic changes over hundreds, thousands and millions of years. Before these new investigations it was realised that the climate of very recent times is not stable but subject to changes which can greatly affect our lives. Within the last 600 years or so in Europe there was a cooler period known as the Little Ice Age, which produced advancing glaciers. In the Alps the glaciers even overcame some villages and there were miserable wet, cold summers that greatly curtailed harvests so the people sometimes faced starvation, as in Scotland and elsewhere. There are paintings which show the alpine glaciers bigger than now and there are documents detailing the sufferings of ordinary people.[6] The few hundred years prior to the Little Ice Age were more favourable climatically – the Medieval Warm Period when crops could be grown at higher altitudes than afterwards.

Until quite recently most scientists would have argued that the fluctuations of climate before and since the last ice age could have had nothing to do with human activities. Now everyone knows about greenhouse gases such as carbon dioxide and methane thought to cause global warming, a very serious reality but unfortunately also a contentious topic.[7] So great has been the impact of humankind on the planet that some scientists, in order to stress the point, wish to designate the last 250 years as the Anthropocene (man/new). William Ruddiman of the University of Virginia argues that global warming began not just in the last few centuries but started when humankind began to chop down the woodlands 8000 years ago. Very recently, there is an idea that in the Americas the swift slaughter of many millions of plant-eating large mammals like mammoths and mastodons had dramatic consequences. There was no more intestinal methane being expelled into the atmosphere and so the climate suddenly cooled. This is the contention of Felisa Smith of the University of New Mexico and her co-authors. However, now other scientists believe that a cosmic impact caused the cooling and death of the large mammals.[8] So, the matter is controversial. Perhaps we should be cautious of these ideas but at least we can consider that the more we know about climate change the more complex the story seems to get.

Concerning the cold/warm fluctuations, producing glacier advances and retreats, since the last ice age, just how many there have been is not too clear. Certainly there have been more than a few. Raffaele De Marinis of Milan University and the journalist Giuseppe Brillante show not less than 16 in their book on Ötzi. Some of these fluctuations have been deduced from pollen analysis, discussed later in this chapter, such as those known as Rotmoos 1 and 2. Rotmoos is a peat bog high in the Ötztal Alps.[9]

Two more Italians, Carlo Baroni and Giuseppe Orombelli, studied the glaciers and the shape of the ground around the Ötzi site.[10] At the height of the last glaciation (c.20,000–25,000 years ago) the entire area had been completely snow- and ice-covered, apart from minor rocky outcrops sticking above the ice. The site was again completely covered certainly during the Little Ice Age. Fig. 2.3 shows that the Niederjoch Glacier between 1910 and 1982 receded about 900m and became fragmented. Close to the site, these two investigators recognised buried soils which had formed about 6400 and then 4400 years ago. This indicates quite prolonged mild conditions around the site at least twice between the end of the last glaciation and the early part of the Neoglaciation.

However, what was the climate precisely at Ötzi's time? Climate varies not just by the millennium and century, but by the decade, and so we cannot be very sure exactly what the conditions were that Ötzi had to endure during his short span of less than 50 years about 5200 years ago. The Italians wrote:

> As widely recognised, the exceptional preservation of the Iceman and of his artefacts requires that he was rapidly entombed at the time of death and remained so till he was discovered. We therefore deduce that during the last 5000 yrs. in this area conditions of greater glacier thickness and extent have prevailed ... Thus the Iceman reveals that about 5300–5050 cal yr B.P., a rapid climatic change took place, producing a persistent snow cover on previously deglaciated areas ... marks the beginning of the Neoglaciation in the Alps.

This claim was strengthened in 2004 and further in 2006 by global surveys of advancing glaciers, rising lake levels and descending timber lines. The investigations were by Frenchman Michel Magny, based in Besancon, Franche-Comté, and others, including Sigmar Bortenschlager and the Swiss Jean-Nicolas Haas, both of Innsbruck University. Their earlier paper is called 'A major widespread climatic change around 5300 cal. yr BP at the time of the Alpine Iceman'. Arbon Bleiche is the name of a Late Neolithic settlement on the south side of Lake Constance in Switzerland and it is not too far from *Ötziland*. It is mentioned again many times later in this book. The authors state:

> … Arbon Bleiche 3 stands at the centre of a cold phase, which was detectable globally and which lasted from about 3700 to 3300 BC. In the Alpine region this phase is known as Piora 2 or Rotmoos 2 fluctuation, during which the glaciers advanced and the tree line moved downwards.

Four Swiss scientists led by Martin Grosjean have considered the relevance to climate of the numerous artefacts melted at different periods from the glacier at Schnidejoch, western Swiss Alps, at 2765m. These varied artefacts from several different periods are discussed in Chapter 6. The authors deduce that at that pass there has been permanent ice cover for the last 5000 years until less than 10 years ago.[11]

Vegetation
Because of the great altitudinal range with the marked climatic gradients, the vegetation is strongly zoned, though modified greatly by human activities from prehistoric times until the present (about which more soon). Fig. 2.5 shows the zones in the eastern Alps; this is an important matter because as discussed later these are the zones in the very territory that Ötzi crossed in the last few days of his life. This brief account of the vegetation begins from the lowest ground in *Ötziland* to the highest.

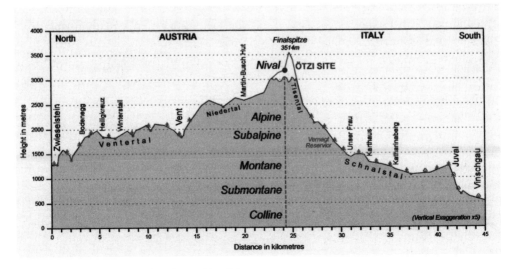

Fig. 2.5 Vegetation zones, altitudes and localities.

Woodland, Meadow, Pasture and Arable Ground; Colline to Alpine Zones (240–2500m)
From Bozen northwards and upwards to middle Schnalstal the climate is mild enough to support warmth-loving, broad-leaved trees and shrubs such as downy oak, hazel, hop horn-beam, snowy mespilus, sweet chestnut, wayfaring tree, small-leaved lime and species of ash and elm. The steep sides of the deep gorge at Juval are densely covered in broad-leaved trees as well as conifers. There is very little woodland even of a semi-natural state left on the valley floor of Vinschgau. Only tiny patches can be found of the alder woodlands that once would have grown extensively along the River Etsch. The hillsides of Vinschgau still carry much coniferous woodland.

There is still some very small-scale cereal growing in Vinschgau, though now the striking feature of that area is the millions of apple trees planted in recent decades. The sunny, low-lying ground of Schnalstal supported cereal growing until very recent agricultural changes (since 1950) as high as 1250mm at Katharinaberg and even about 1900m at the south-facing Finailhof. The woodlands in the valleys closest to the iceman site are dominated by tall conifers. Mainly, there is European larch and Norway spruce. The other tree-forming conifer is Arolla pine which here and there forms the timberline in these valleys. At the northern Ötztal from Sölden northwards is some Scots pine which grows too, but very sparingly, in Schnalstal, as on cliffs near Katharinaberg. These coniferous forests have more Norway spruce in Ötztal but more European larch in Schnalstal.

There are also the low-growing conifers, such as the shrub dwarf mountain pine, locally in large stands on the hillsides at or above the timber line, as well as common juniper, which lives up to its name, and another kind of juniper called savin, which is largely restricted to slopes of southern aspect, sunny and dry, where it can form large circular patches, as on the badly eroding valley side opposite Karthaus. Often, where there are frequent avalanches, there are stands of the shrubby green alder. The highest trees are at about 2200–2300m, depending on aspect as well as present and past land use. Pastures occur from well below the trees to some hundreds of metres above the trees. Today there is much ground grazed by sheep, goats, cattle and horses at 2000–2500m, that is to say just below and above the potential timber line. Often with strongly aquiline noses that confer a snooty appearance, sheep by the many thousand and in a variety of colours from white to brown, black and piebald are everywhere and goats, though less common, are frequently encountered (see Plates 16 and 17). The attractive grey and white cattle are very common and here and there roam to well above the trees, but the beautiful brown Haflinger horses are much less common and graze lower areas such as the boggy ground at Rofenhof and mid Pfossental.

As at the west side of Niedertal between Vent and the Martin Bush Hut, there is deliber-ate burning of dense stands dwarf mountain pine, which like all pines is not palatable to livestock; its dense shade prevents growth of more tempting succulent plant species. Grazing can be too intense and this leads to impoverishment of the vegetation and puddling of the ground.

Bogs and Fens
Like the pastures, peat bogs occur both above the trees and well below the tree limit. Within living memory the valley bottom of Vinschgau was much wetter. The only ground we have seen supporting bog mosses in the flatter parts of Vinschgau lies at the south end of Haidersee

at 1500m, where, amid tall reed fen, there are three species of bog moss. Elsewhere between Haidersee and Naturns, we have noted frequent scattered remnants of reed fens and other marshy ground but no strongly acidic, boggy vegetation. However, there are place names that may well indicate the former presence of such ground; two instances are, at Goldrain, 'Möslweg' (Little Bog Way) and, at Latsch, 'Moosweg' (Bog Way).

Mountain Slopes and Summits, Alpine Zone (2000m–3000m) and Nival Zone (above 3000m)
The alpine zone can support dense if low-growing vegetation with many different, colourful plants including mosses and lichens, but in crossing into the nival zone, in which the iceman lay, it is very different. Casually looking around, the non-botanist standing at the Ötzi site in August or September, when usually there is the least snow, might be forgiven for thinking that nothing grows there. But kneeling shows otherwise. At the great height of the site, at 3210m, well above the timber line, there is only exceedingly sparse vegetation in which few low-growing flowering plants exist, for instance mossy and purple saxifrages, glacier crowfoot, alpine moon daisy, two grasses and a sedge. There is a greater diversity of lichens, mosses and liverworts, all even more diminutive, growing among extensive bare rock outcrops and shattered stone and permanent snow and ice. Immediately around the site only 16 species of mosses and liverworts were to be found after much searching by the author and his skilled helpers. At the summit of the nearby Finail Spitz (3516m) only two mosses have been recorded.

Archaeobotany: Pollen and Seeds
The term archaeobotany will be unfamiliar to very many readers but, as can be readily guessed, it means the science which combines archaeology and botany. The archaeobotanical results from Ötzi, mainly produced by Sigmar Bortenschlager and Klaus Oeggl, have contributed greatly to knowledge of his lifestyle and to elucidation of the events of his very last days. So a basic understanding of the topic is essential. First, there is pollen analysis and then macrofossil analysis.[12] The pollen of oak is very different from that of Scots pine, from that of grasses, from that of ribwort plantain and so on. A good pollen analyst can recognise many different plants (see Fig. 2.6). With care and experience and the use of suitable microscopes, pollen grains of cereals and weeds of arable ground and pastures can be recognised. The identification and counting of pollen grains entombed in peat or lake mud reveals the history of naturally changing vegetation and, cogently in this context, humankind's effects on the environment. Pollen analyses of columns of peat and mud from all over Europe make it very clear that the prehistoric humankind cleared the woodlands to make way for animal husbandry and crop cultivation.

  This powerful technique of pollen analysis has been applied to various peat bogs, which preserve pollen very well, to the north and south of the Ötzi site. One of the most striking results is the demonstration that even before Ötzi's time, according to Sigmar Bortenschlager, there had been developed high-altitude pastures. The peat site at An Soon lies at 2620m only some 5km northeast of the iceman site (see Fig. 2.7). The pollen diagram shows the proportion of pollen of all those plants considered to be indicators of grassland produced by the effects of grazing animals and there is a timescale based on six calibrated radiocarbon dates.

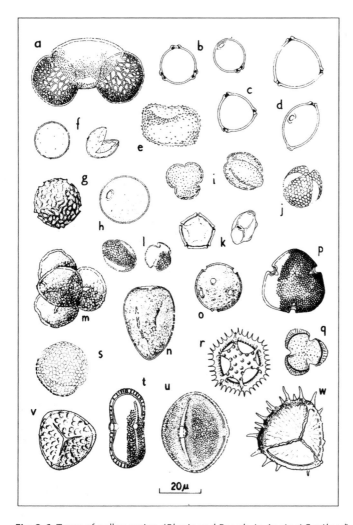

Drawings of pollen
grains and spores
frequently recognised in
samples from British
peats, lake muds and
archaeological layers.
a. Scots Pine, b. Tree
Birch, c. Dwarf Birch,
d. Hazel, e. Yew,
f. Juniper, g. Wych Elm,
h. Poaceae (Grasses),
i. Oak, j. Ash, k. Alder,
l. Willow, m. Heather,
n. Cyperaceae (Sedges
and related plants),
o. Ribwort Plantain,
p. Small-leaved Lime,
q. Mugwort,
r. Dandelion-type,
s. Pondweed, Hogweed-
type, u. Common Rock-
rose, v. Bogmoss,
w. Lesser Clubmoss.
1 micron = one
thousandth of a mm.
From Pigott and Pigott
(1959)

Fig. 2.6 Types of pollen grains. (*Plants and People in Ancient Scotland*)

These pollen types are those of the parsley family, the goosefoot family, the pea family meadowsweet/dropwort, the gentian family, lovages, bird's foot trefoil, plantains, the buttercup family, yellow rattle, the rose family, docks, sorrels and nettles. None of these pollen types need have derived from plants found exclusively in pastures and the low values from some 8500 to 6500 years ago do not relate to such grassland. However, the revealing change is the marked rise in the proportion of such pollen types before 5200 years ago. Sigmar Bortenschlager argued that Stone Age farmers even before Ötzi's time had grazing domestic animals such as sheep and goats at high altitudes. This particular topic, a very important one, is dealt with again in Chapter 5.

At the Botanical Institute of Innsbruck University, Klaus Oeggl's assistants extracted many thousands of macroscopic fossils from the coarse mineral sediments that had accumulated

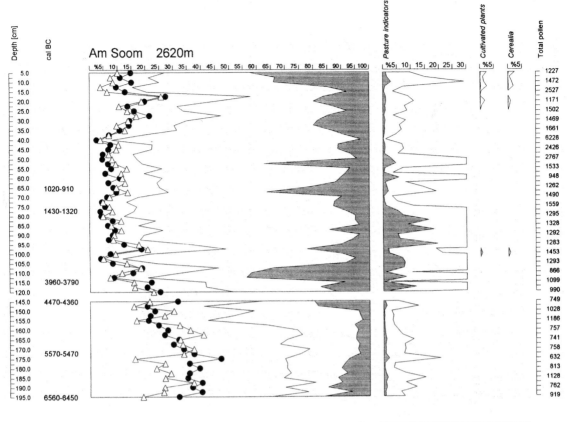

Depth [cm] | **cal BC**

Am Soom 2620m

%5| 10| 15| 20| 25| 30| 35| 40| 45| 50| 55| 60| 65| 70| 75| 80| 85| 90| 95| 100|

Pasture indicators %5| 10| 15| 20| 25| 30|

Cultivated plants %5| *Cerealia* %5| **Total pollen**

Depth [cm]	cal BC	Total pollen
5.0		1227
10.0		1472
15.0		2527
20.0		1171
25.0		1502
30.0		1469
35.0		1661
40.0		6228
45.0		2426
50.0		2767
55.0		1533
60.0		948
65.0	1020-910	1262
70.0		1490
75.0	1430-1320	1559
80.0		1295
85.0		1328
90.0		1292
95.0		1283
100.0		1453
105.0		1293
110.0		866
115.0	3960-3790	1099
120.0		990
145.0	4470-4360	749
150.0		1028
155.0		1186
160.0		757
165.0		741
170.0		758
175.0	5570-5470	632
180.0		813
185.0		1128
190.0		762
195.0	6560-6450	919

Fig. 2.7 Pollen diagram from Am Soom. Note the curve called pasture indicators, just right of middle. (*Sigmar Bortenschlager, University of Innsbruck*)

Fig. 2.8 Coarse remains of plants from the Ötzi site sediments. (*Klaus Oeggl, University of Innsbruck*)

in the hollow for at least 4000 years and were removed in 1992. Such fossils are coarse fragments of plants big enough to be seen with the naked eye (seeds, leaves, wood, charcoal, mosses) as distinct from microscopic ones like pollen. For short they are called macros (see Fig. 2.8).

The bulk of the macros that had become preserved in the hollow provide palaeoenvironmental information about that very high-altitude terrain. The moss northern haircap has been recovered from more than 90 per cent of the mineral sediment samples and it was found adhering to Ötzi's clothes. Clearly, it had been growing within the hydrological catchment. The significance of that particular moss is that it only inhabits areas of late snow lie and so it is certain that, however warm or cold it was during the period of sedimentation, which lasted thousands of years, the area had held snow beds persisting long into summer. Growing on rocks wetted by snow and glacier melt water, the moss water grimmia has been recovered from over 40 per cent of the samples; cold water had flowed into the hollow for much or all of the period of sediment deposition. Another important matter is the recovery of fragments of numerous moss species from low altitudes that could never have grown around the hollow at any time during the last 5000 and more years. How did they get there? This is discussed again in Chapter 5 (see Figs 2.9 and 2.10).

MUMMIFICATION

Ötzi's body is most definitely mummified but exactly what led to this state is poorly understood. Very many people have commented on how well Otzi's body had preserved for over 5000 years. As examples I mention the work on fatty acid composition by Athanasios Makristathis of Innsbruck University with ten others as well as the works of the anatomist Professor Frank Rühli of Zurich University and others, the Italian DNA specialist Franco Rollo and co-authors and also Marek Janko of Munich University and co-authors.[13] Can he be called a wet mummy or a dry mummy? A wet mummy retains some water in the dried-out tissues whereas a dry one does not. Ötzi was a wet mummy, as is dramatically confirmed, according to Eduard Egarter Vigl, by the colour, consistency and aroma of the contents of the lowermost alimentary tract. In Ötzi's body, Eduard Egarter Vigl states there has been 'extensive formation of subcutaneous adipocere'. Adipocere (grave wax) forms when the fats in a corpse are changed by bacteria, water and oxidation to a whitish wax-like substance which is composed of fatty acids. In large amounts it can resemble cottage cheese. The process takes place in wet environments under entirely or partially air-sealed conditions, as when a corpse is submerged or placed in a coffin in dank conditions, lies in waterlogged soil such as peat or in snow in high mountain areas.[14]

It was known at a very early stage that Ötzi's long body and head hair had fallen out, as had the finger and toe nails. Human skin has a very complex structure with three main layers: hypodermis, which is the innermost, then the dermis and the outermost, the epidermis, which itself has several layers. Thomas Bereuter and two colleagues, all of the University of Vienna, obtained a skin sample found beside the damaged left hip region. They produced sound evidence from histology (microscopic examination of a transverse section of the sample) and from spectroscopy that the outer layer of Ötzi's skin is missing. They say that there is 'complete loss of the epidermis'. And continue that there had been 'disintegration of the epidermal basal membrane during water immersion resulting in detachment of the epidermis and its subsequent disappearance'.[15] They demonstrated the presence of adipocere.

The pathologist in the General Hospital in Bozen, Eduard Egarter Vigl oversees the conservation of Ötzi in the Iceman Museum in Bozen. In a paper from 2003, he states, concerning the condition of the skin: 'As the epidermis is destroyed, the outermost layer of the derma appears whitish due to the dry collagenic fibres.'[16] All the soft tissues are very shrivelled. He has written, 'Given the mummy's current weight of 14kg and the body weight of a man when alive, which when calculated on the basis of the body height (approx. 160cm) is about 50kg, a mass of almost 37kg, primarily water, was lost as a result of dehydration.' So the body lost a lot of water but see the several different estimates of live weight as discussed below. In 2006 he wrote, 'The mummification processes have not yet been fully elucidated.' This remains true in 2011.[17]

The corpse was not just well preserved but unfragmented. How it came to remain intact has caused comment. Had Ötzi fallen down a crevasse and become frozen solid then the moving ice would have broken the corpse into pieces. The body was not so much *in* ice as *under* it in the hollow. He was trapped there and the ice moving across – not along the hollow – never moved the corpse or at any rate only an exceedingly short distance. There are no clear signs of any damage to the corpse caused by scavengers such as ravens, which certainly fly well above 3000m today, as around the Similaun hut. They would have pecked the eyes out. However, had the body been lying face down in deep snow or floating in icy water then the eyes would not have been accessible to birds.

Additionally, there is no myasis (a jargon word meaning damage by maggots emerged from fly eggs in the soft tissues). At first thought this may seem hardly a surprise because at the low temperatures encountered above 3000m few if any flesh-eating flies would have lived. However, Claude Wyss and Daniel Cherix, forensic entomologists at Lausanne, Switzerland, have recorded such flies at 2940m at the Glacier des Diablerets, Canton de Vaud, Switzerland, and they feel sure that there could have been flesh-eating flies at the height of the Ötzi site.[18] It seems entirely reasonable to consider that the corpse must have been covered up and so hidden from scavengers very soon after death.

ÖTZI'S TIME AND RADIOCARDON DATING

For the nearly 50 years of his life Ötzi had lived in the period we call the late Neolithic (new/stone) Age, otherwise known as the Chalcolithic (copper/stone) or Copper Age, when copper tools such as axe heads were replacing stone tools. Then came the Bronze Age when bronze, an alloy of copper and tin, which produces harder and so more durable implements, replaced copper. The Neolithic people, with crops and domesticated animals, came after those of the Mesolithic (middle/stone) period. Now recognised more and more as having been sophisticated in many ways, the so-called cavemen lived in the Palaeolithic (old/stone) Age. During the last ice age about 30,000 years ago modern people (Cromagnons) had replaced the earlier Neanderthals in Europe.

Ötzi's life was spent hundreds of years after the farming way of life had spread north-westwards past *Ötziland*. As recounted later in detail, there were cereals in his alimentary tract and adhering to his clothes, some of which were made of domestic goat.

From the 1950s on, the ability to produce a chronology from the decay of the radioactive of the isotope of carbon 14C (decay counting) has been crucial in archaeology. Later came calibration, when counting annual tree rings showed that radiocarbon years were not the same as calendar years. The development in the late 1970s of direct ion counting using accelerator mass spectrometry (AMS) was another very important advance. This technique has the great advantage that much smaller samples are required than for decay counting.[19]

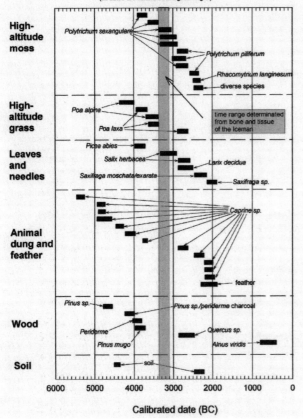

Fig. 2.9 Radiocarbon dates from Ötzi site. (*Walter Kutschera, University of Vienna*)

From different laboratories, there were soon radiocarbon dates made both on plant material (grasses, mosses, wood from the equipment and charcoal) and on samples of Ötzi's bone and skin. They are highly consistent and, when calibrated, they give the most probable period for Ötzi of 5100 to 5370 years ago. There are now many more AMS dates from the body, the gear and from organic materials extracted from the mineral sediments in the hollows. Very often Ötzi is referred to as from 5300 years ago. However, there is a cogent summary by Walter Kutschera, the radiocarbon expert of Vienna University and Wolfgang Müller.[20] They say in their summary that Ötzi had lived some 5200 years ago and that is the figure used throughout this book. This is much older than perceived at first with the recovery team not suspecting the very great age and even the title of the first published archaeological report by Andreas Lippert and Konrad Spindler stated early Bronze Age[21] (see Figs 2.9 and 2.10).

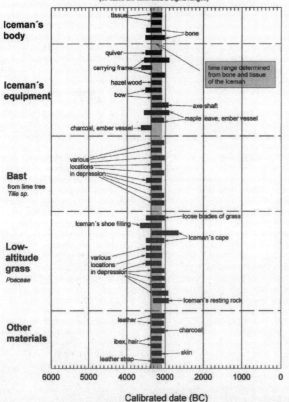

Fig. 2.10 Radiocarbon dates from Ötzi's body, gear and clothes. (*Walter Kutschera, University of Vienna*)

EXCAVATIONS

In the nine days before the forensic team arrived at least 33 people, on a total of 18 occasions, visited the site and inevitably caused damage. This means, according to Elisabeth Rastbichler Zissernig of Innsbruck University, that 'there were at least 41 visits to the site during those nine days'. That is to say between the discovery and the removal of the corpse.

The rough recovery is the very appropriate phrase first used in 1993 by David Roberts in the *National Geographic* magazine for the retrieval of the corpse.[22] However, it has to be borne in mind that the site is at great altitude, perennially icy and snowy with rapidly changing weather and the season was already late when the body was found. Furthermore, the site had already been badly disturbed and some artefacts removed, notably and regrettably the very distinctively ancient axe, before the forensic team could arrive from Innsbruck. These were unhelpful conditions for the retrieval of the corpse. Sadly, however, because the uniqueness and great age of the discovery was not immediately realised with certainty by anyone at the site, the corpse was not carefully removed but torn from the ice and sent to Innsbruck in such a way that the body was badly damaged, as can be seen all too distressingly in the early television films of the process (see Chapter 5, 'Rough Recovery' section).

Conducted by Andreas Lippert, there was a very brief archaeological excavation immediately after the recovery of the body and then a thorough excavation followed in the summer of 1992 which produced much valuable evidence including the hat and two fingernails. In addition and very importantly, coarse mineral sediments were systematically removed from the hollow. In the botanical laboratory of Innsbruck University, these produced an abundance of organic material (seeds, leaves, wood, mosses, mammal droppings). This added greatly to the plant remains, including mosses, already washed from the clothes.

DNA

As in so very many areas of science, DNA analyses have become very important and standard in archaeology. Ötzi's DNA was quickly investigated and the results published in 1994. Mitochondrial DNA analyses were carried out to investigate his geographical origin by a team of no less than 13 people, led by Oliva Handt. Eight samples of muscle, connective tissue and bone were taken from the left hip area, which had been badly damaged during the retrieval of corpse.[23]

The results were compared with those from hundreds of living people from many parts of the world. In the summary of their paper the authors say that the mitochondrial type of the iceman fits into the variation of contemporary Europeans and best matches populations from central and northern Europe. Ötzi's DNA was considered to be badly degraded and so nearly 20 years ago it was very satisfactory to obtain data from such an old corpse but the result was hardly a surprise. In the text they state that Ötzi's DNA was most similar to that of individuals in the Alpine area (16 people from Ötztal). Immediately, however, it must be stressed that does not mean that Ötzi came from Ötztal but merely that that was the best match so far. Their publication was in 1994 and it ends: 'A more precise determination will have to await both more sequence information from the Iceman and a much more extensive survey of genetic diversity among European populations.' It would be most interesting to know how more detailed DNA analyses would fit into the botanical and isotopic results concerning Ötzi's provenance, as discussed in Chapter 8.

Early in 2006, Franco Rollo and five other Italians published about Ötzi's mitochondrial DNA, taken from samples of his intestinal contents.[24] They state that the samples were in a particularly favourable condition. The mtDNA of European populations is divided into nine haplogroups. Ötzi's mtDNA belongs to haplogroup K and to subcluster K1 rather than subcluster K2. K1 has three branches, a, b and c, but Ötzi's DNA does not fit any of the three; 'It rather seems to represent a previously unknown branch of the K1 subcluster'. They found the highest K-haplogroup frequency, 31 per cent, in the Ötztal area, but the frequency was also high, 20 per cent, in the Ladin populations from southern slopes of the eastern Alps. However, only 16 and 20 people from these areas were examined.

In the light of exaggerated statements by the media, a certainly not proven suggestion from this work by the Italians is that Ötzi may have been infertile (reduced sperm mobility). However, Franco Rollo and his colleagues regard the finding as 'intriguing' concerning its possible social implications and as a clue to the so-called 'Disaster'; just what these last claims mean exactly is left unclear by the Italian scientists but the speculation in the media was that he was murdered because he could not have children. Franco Rollo's team's work has been criticised as regards methodology and they responded saying that their project continues.[25]

In 2008 Luca Emiliani of Camerino University with 10 others stated that they had established the complete mitochondrial sequence for Ötzi, the oldest for any member of *Homo sapiens*; they claim in the summary that their results point to the potential significance in addressing questions concerning the genetic history of human populations that the phylogeography of modern lineages is unable to tackle. In July 2010 Albert Zink of the EURAC Institute for Mummies and the Iceman, Bozen, and Carsten Pusch and Andreas Keller announced that they had revealed the complete genetic profile for Ötzi with publication expected in 2011.[26]

AGE, HEALTH AND PHYSIQUE

At about 158 to 160cm (5ft 2in) tall, Ötzi was a small man, as, it seems to me from casual observation, are many men in Schnalstal and adjacent areas today. He was in his mid-forties, an advanced age for people of his time when life expectancy was much lower than today. Othmar Gaber and Karl-Heinz Künzel of Innsbruck University had studied the internal structure of Ötzi's bones (thigh and upper arm) and state he was 45 to 46 years old at the time of his death. Othmar Gaber wrote, 'Using a newly developed combination of macroscopic and microscopic methods a mean age of 45.7 years was established.'[27]

With little technology compared to that of modern times, prehistoric people lived close to nature and so perforce had active lives. Consequently they were fit and tautly muscled and unlikely to be obese. When in his prime, if Ötzi ever cut an impressive figure, at his small height and weighing about 61kg (134.5lb), it would not have been by stature alone, certainly not to modern eyes. Probably, however, he came from a group in which such a short height was more the norm than now. If the figures for the heights of Neolithic populations as listed by Konrad Spindler have remained unchanged by more recent research then Ötzi was of an unexceptional height for his time. Wolfram Bernhard of Munich stated that Ötzi's small stature 'falls well within the range generally found in Neolithic samples of the circumalpine region' (*Innsbruck* 1, p. 184). Had he held his longbow upright and touching the ground it would have reached well above his head (by about 28cm).

Christopher Ruff of John Hopkins University, with seven others, think that the iceman had an active lifestyle 'maintained throughout his life'. Their detailed study included comparison of Ötzi's bones with European male skeletons from the Upper Palaeolithic to the Bronze Age. They paid particular attention to the tibia and concluded that he was used to traversing rough terrain.[28]

Lying on his back in his birthday suit in his frigid cubicle, kept at -6°C in the Iceman Museum, Ötzi appears very emaciated as though he had died of extreme starvation. His skin appears dark brown and very shiny (because of a thin film of ice) and looking tanned like leather. According to Eduard Egarter Vigl, he now weighs 14kg, whereas in life he weighed 50kg (calculated on the basis of approximately 160cm height); 50kg is what Konrad Spindler had claimed. However, in 1998, Othmar Gaber and Heinz Kunzel stated, 'Body height 160cm, living weight 45kg'. In 1999, Luigi Capasso of Chieti, Italy and two others stated: 'Ötzi was an adult man of 1,64m who weighed 40kg.'[29]

So we had estimates of 40, 45 and 50kg. Making no reference to any of the previous estimates and using a height of 158cm, Christopher Ruff and his co-authors gave a body mass of 61kg; this is more than 20 per cent greater than the heaviest of previous estimates. They arrived at that figure by two methods which they explained in detail; this is certainly the most reliable of the estimates. These eight authors think Ötzi was stocky and compare him to modern Olympic wrestlers and decathletes. They say that, although he was small, 'Thus, the Iceman was likely very sturdily built'.[30]

In an unusual congenital anomaly, Ötzi's twelfth ribs are missing, his left ribs were broken but healed and his sixth and seventh right ribs broken and unhealed and right ribcage deformed. Contrary to Konrad Spindler's claim, this last breakage and deformity happened post-mortem, and a fracture of the left humerus also happened sometime after death, probably when the corpse was forced into a coffin to be flown to Innsbruck. Konrad Spindler goes so far as to speculate that the unhealed right ribs might have been broken in a fight with a bear! William Murphy of Texas University MD Cancer Centre and several others published a table giving all the post-mortem bone breakages and other changes.[31] Forensic scientist Peter Vanesis, then of Glasgow University, had shown me radiographs of Ötzi's ribcage and he was adamant that the breakages had occurred after death.

The realisation that these breakages occurred after death disposed of the 'Disaster Theory', with its details so elaborate as to be close to fantasy, proposed by Konrad Spindler. He claimed that Ötzi had fled to safety in the mountains after injury in a fight at his home village. Torstein Sjøvold, anthropologist of Stockholm University, was involved with the Ötzi investigations from the earliest stages and had translated Konrad Spindler's book into Swedish. He told me that Konrad Spindler had inserted the disaster story at the request of the publisher to increase the interest of the book (or as many would say now in 2011 to 'sex it up').

Until 2001 no publication indicated any external signs of violence; an area of missing scalp was considered to have been due to abrasion, not to a blow (as was mentioned at a very

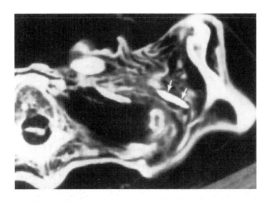

Fig. 2.11 CT scan showing cross section of arrowhead. (*William Murphy, University of Texas*)

Fig. 2.12 Prehistoric arrowheads from South Tyrol (top left and right) and Reggio Emilia (bottom left) with reproduction of arrowhead from Ötzi's back. (*Dal Ri, 2006*)

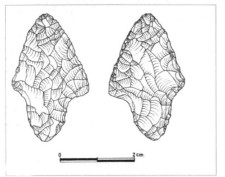

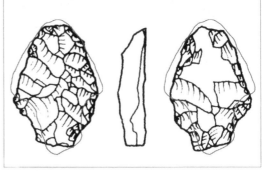

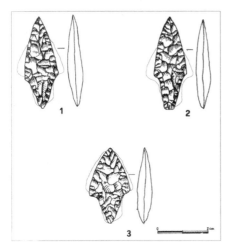

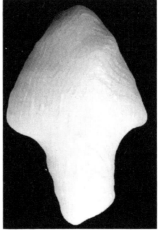

early stage) nor to decay. Neither the arrowhead lodged in back nor the wound in the right palm had then been noticed. How could the Innsbruck medical men have missed them? With the discoveries of these wounds in 2000 and later, the disaster theory was back, this time on a sound basis. It is discussed in full detail in Chapter 5 (see Figs 2.11 and 2.12).

Ötzi's fingers and toes show no injuries bar one. In 2003 William Murphy and his several co-authors published a radiograph showing the little left toe and they state: 'It is surmised that this lone abnormality of the digits represents healed frostbite.'[32] This is an interesting observation because it is important to know that the frostbite did not happen during his last journey and that it at least strongly hints at other forays into the high ground where

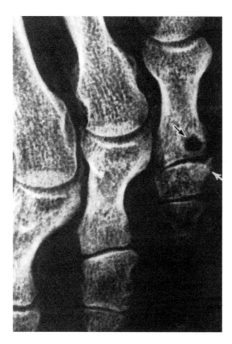

Fig. 2.13 X-ray of Ötzi's left foot showing frostbite. (*William Murphy, University of Texas*)

Fig. 2.14 Ötzi's intestines are mostly very shrivelled. This CT scan shows the transverse colon containing faeces. (*William Murphy, University of Texas*)

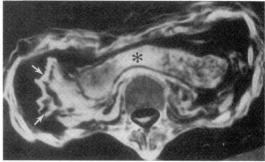

frostbite is a constant risk and, in that regard, the thick long bones of his legs matter too. 'It is speculated that constant climbing and hiking in the Alps would be sufficient to cause such marked muscle and bone development,' say William Murphy *et al.*[33] (see Figs 2.13 and 2.14).

In a paper in volume 3 of the *South Tyrolean Museums Journal* (2006) archaeologist Lorenzo Dal Ri states that Ötzi 'must have felt pain while walking due to a damaged meniscus of the right knee; it is not known whether this derived from a natural degeneration or a trauma'.[34] This radiological finding, perhaps an important one regarding Ötzi's mobility especially if he was indeed fleeing during his last hours, was seemingly unknown to either Bill Murphy *et al.* or to Christofer Ruff *et al.* It was first discussed by Paul Gostner of Bolzano Hospital, Eduard Egarter Vigl and Ulf Reinstadler in the archaeological journal *Germania* in 2004. They state that it was 'eine schmerzhafte behinderung' – a painful handicap.[35] However, Bill Murphy has told me that he has examined the published radiographs and he can see no evidence of a damaged knee.

Ötzi would probably have had little or no access to very sugary food, apart possibly from honey once in a while, and, consequently, had good teeth as prehistoric folk normally did in that there are no cavities (caries/decay). It is pretty sure that he did not consume honey during the period, one to two days or so, represented by the ingesta in his gut. The pollen analyses carried out by Klaus Oeggl on intestinal samples did not show high values of typical honey plants such as lime, clover and meadowsweet or other insect pollinated species.[36]

Fig. 2.15 Ötzi's partially open mouth showing very worn teeth. (*William Murphy, University of Texas*)

However, people living thousands of years ago had their dental problems. Joyce Filler in her book *Disease* states:

> Extremely worn teeth, dental abscesses and advanced periodontal disease affecting gums and bones – a nightmare catalogue of dental problems. Such a picture of poor dental health might be assumed to be that of a poor and inadequately nourished Egyptian peasant but, in fact, this is a picture of the state of dental health of the royal mummy which has been identified as Amenhotep III.[37]

Ötzi's teeth show no decay but he did not have a full set of teeth and the front teeth were much worn. All four third molars (wisdom teeth) are absent, that is to say unerupted, a condition which is 'not at all uncommon in Neolithic skeletal finds', according to Wolfram Bernhard (*Innsbruck* 1, p. 184). He uses that very remark also with reference to the 'medial diastema' – that is to say there is a very obvious gap between the maxillary central incisors, which are right at the front of the upper jaw. The biting surfaces of upper front teeth are worn smooth, perhaps an unsurprising state in view of his age, probable work habits and diet. But the Italian palaeopathologist Luigi Capasso and his colleagues say that the wear of the front teeth is truly remarkable; the crown of one of the teeth had been reduced to a length of a mere 3mm. Dismissive of the idea of Müllner *et al.* that the state of the front teeth could have resulted from clenching a pipe, Luigi Capasso and co-authors state: 'numerous ancient populations, not only in Europe, used the incisors as real tools for the processing of hard materials such as wood, leather, bones, etc.'[38] The 9500-year-old Kennewick Man, mentioned in Chapter 1, had extremely worn teeth, as had Eskimos prior to their adoption of modern ways. Spirit Cave Man, also mentioned in Chapter 1, had front teeth with linear indentations that indicate use for processing sinew. There was especially heavy wear of the maxillary first molars which had exposed the pulp chambers.

A full set of good teeth or no, there is some reason for thinking that Ötzi was not in the best of health. All his finger and toe nails had fallen off but the excavation in 1992 produced one nail, as mentioned above. Luigi Capasso examined the nail which was the wrong shape for a toe nail and too small to have been from a little finger. He could not tell which hand the nail had come from, nor, at first, which finger, but latterly he thought it probably had come from an index finger (*Innsbruck* 2, p. 231). He noted that the nail showed three Beau's lines; these are transverse lines which develop when fingernails stop growing and then start again. The cessation of growth happens during bouts of illness. Robert Baran and his co-editors state that:

> The transverse depression, sometimes involving the whole depth of the nail plate, appears some weeks after illness (e.g. fever). As the approximate growth rate (of nails) is known, it is possible to assess the approximate time of the prior causative disease which has marked the nails, the thumb nail supplies information for the previous 5–6 months, and the big toe nail evidence of disease for up to 2 years. As the thumb and toe nails are the most frequently affected they are the most reliable indicators of previous disease. Markings occur inconsistently on the other digits.[39]

Luigi Capasso concluded that Ötzi had been ill three times in the last six months of his life and the last episode was the most serious and lasted at least two weeks. In 1997 Capasso with three others stated that the lines 'suggest that this Copper Age alpine hunter had a precarious dietary balance, predisposing to periodic nutritional stresses that might have been precipitated by recurrent disease, or by seasonal events that resulted in food shortages and starvation'. Why they thought that the lines had had to do with poor diet and starvation is unclear. In 1999 Capasso thought that the presence of whipworm corroborated the idea of chronic illness but that also is unclear.[40] The matter of Ötzi's occupation, hunter or not, is discussed in Chapter 5, as are Capasso's deductions from the broken, dirty state of the fingernail, and the matter of diet is dealt with in Chapter 4.

Three toenails found inside the left shoe have not been studied for Beau's lines, as far as I know. These particular nails are mentioned only by Konrad Spindler as follows (*Spindler 2*, p. 172): 'Three further toenails were recovered during the restoration of the left shoe at the Römisch-Germanisch Zentralmuseum.' Professor Markus Egg of that museum in Mainz told me that only two toenails were found and they were in the right shoe. Konrad Spindler gave the toenails to Professor Horst Seidler, an anthropologist in the University of Vienna, but no report has ever been published and so we do not know if they showed Beau's lines or not. Lastly, a second fingernail was found by the Innsbruck botanists as they examined the sediment samples; it remains unstudied.

Konrad Spindler (*Spindler 1*, p. 178) wrote that Ötzi 'carried not an ounce of surplus fat on his body … Possibly, given that he had no stored fat reserves, the Iceman had been subjected before his death to an involuntary starvation diet.' He continued: 'However, we cannot rule out degradation of body fats after death.' Later he wrote (*Spindler 2*, p. 190) that the medical men at Innsbruck University 'had revealed slight hardening of the arteries in the area of the base of the brain … a daring hypothesis would be that he had a metabolic susceptibility to early arteriosclerosis, possibly due to high blood cholesterol level.' William Murphy and co-authors make no mention of this particular speculation, perhaps thinking it not worthy of comment, but they do state that there are signs of degenerative arthritis and vascular calcification and, they go on, 'In combination, these calcifications may represent a surprising amount of evidence for arteriosclerotic cardiovascular disease, particularly if we share the perspective that this condition is a modern affliction facilitated by lifestyle, diet, and tobacco use'.

On Ötzi's body there are many simple, soot tattoos (short lines and crosses) which are certainly not decorative, being very inconspicuous, indeed mostly invisible when Ötzi was fully clothed, and are taken to have had a therapeutic purpose. Several are on or close to Chinese acupuncture points and at places where he had suffered from arthritis (the lower spine, right knee and ankle). This has led to claims of treatment by acupuncture. According to Torstein Sjøvold tattoos can be inserted with a needle, a knife or sewing with pigment-soaked thread or sinew. He states that 'So far, no conclusive evidence exists as to how the Iceman's tattoos were applied'.[41] In a long, scholarly article, the Frenchman Luc Renaut accepts that the tattoos were therapeutic but dismisses the 'Tibetan cauterization' proposed by Luigi Capasso and is sceptical of the attempts to link the locations of the tattoos with acupuncture points.[42] Maria Anne Pabst of Graz University with six others examined the tattoos with a whole battery of techniques mainly electron microscopic. They state that the tattoos are in the connective tissue of the epidermis and 'could be identified as soot'. They found silicate crystals such as quartz and almandine between the soot particles and think that they could have come from the fireplace stones from which the soot was removed, a plausible claim.[43]

Among the sparse and badly preserved insect remains found with Ötzi, Wolfgang Schedl of Innsbruck University identified parts of two fleas, in all likelihood the human flea (*Innsbruck* 4). The parts of the heads and had been recovered from the seams of Ötzi's 'upper body clothing'. No ticks were found nor any lice seen, but, as is mentioned fully later, much if not all of his epidermis had been shed and so any body lice may have been lost. However, there were no nits, the eggs of the head louse, on the shed head hair or on hairs from inside the cap. So Ötzi was had fleas, but was neither tick-ridden nor lousy.

In the last few decades, it has become routine for environmental archaeologists to search for the eggs of intestinal parasites such as whipworm, common roundworm and fish tapeworm. The Vienna University parasitologist Horst Aspöck and colleagues (1999) have summarised the topic for prehistoric Central Europe.[44] They found whipworm to be the most commonly encountered. This is so not just in Central Europe but also in Britain, where, for instance, the eggs were found in the midden at Skara Brae, the 5000-year-old Neolithic stone-built village on Orkney and also at many other sites. Petra Dark has found whipworm eggs in a Mesolithic coastal site, Goldcliff in south Wales, and this takes the history of this parasite back a further 2000 years or so. That humans may well have been hosts of whipworm and other parasites for a great deal longer than that is strongly suggested by the discovery of whipworm eggs in 30,000-year-old animal coprolites (fossilised faeces) from Italy.

Horst Aspöck states that (*Innsbruck* 4, p. 131): 'We may conclude that he was rather intensively infested with Whipworm. Consequently at times he had various intestinal problems (abdominal pains, diarrhoea).' In 2000, on the advice of my Glasgow University parasitologist colleague, David Crompton, I wrote that had it been a serious infestation of whipworm, then the effect could have been debilitating, causing diarrhoea and even leading to dysentery. Adult whipworm, 3–5cm long, inhabit the human large intestine and they shed abundant, microscopic eggs which are about 50 microns long, are voided in the faeces and reinfect any human who ingests food contaminated with faeces or put soiled fingers in the mouth. On microscope slides prepared for pollen or other analyses the eggs are easily recognised by their shape, as are the eggs of various other intestinal worms. The Austrian parasitologists had expected to encounter roundworm but did not do so. Nor did they find any other helminth parasite, nor any protozoan pathogen (no copro-antigens of *Giardia lamblia* or *Cryptosporidium parvum*, both of which can cause diarrhoea if contaminated water is drunk).

Konrad Spindler stated (*Spindler* 2, p. 194): 'The enormous infestation with the parasite *Trichuris trichuria*, which also irritated the intestinal mucous membranes, possibly led to impairment of the digestive tract, which caused diarrhoea. It may be cautiously conjectured that the man treated this complaint – as would be done today – with powered charcoal.' It should be added that there are no strong grounds for the use of the word 'enormous'. Other explanations for the charcoal are discussed in Chapter 4 in the section on unintentional ingestions.

So apart from fleas and whipworm, it seems that at the time of his death Ötzi was clear of parasites, external or internal. By contrast, his contemporaries at Arbon Bleiche 3, the Swiss Neolithic lake village, had not just whipworm but a scarily impressive array of other worms: fish tapeworm, beef/pork tapeworm and giant kidney worm (caught from eating fish or frogs and causing the host's death from total kidney failure). There were also two kinds of liverflukes, and *Capillaria*. Furthermore, their ruminant livestock had a different liverfluke, whipworm and *Paramphistomum*.

APPEARANCE, CLOTHING AND EQUIPMENT

Lots of clothing and equipment were found in the hollow immediately beside the body or at the most some 5m away. Everyone takes it for granted that everything had belonged to Ötzi. This may seem plausible enough. However, only two items were 100 per cent certainly his: the shoes, one of which was still on his left foot when the body was torn from the ice, and the leggings which were dimly perceived through the ice before the crude removal of the corpse. The other items, all or some, if only a few or one, could have been belongings of another person or persons. If all the clothing was indeed his then Ötzi was well dressed and shod. If all the gear was indeed Ötzi's it seems that he had carried a great deal of stuff on his last journey. There was a copper-bladed, wooden-handled axe, a longbow, a quiver with 14 arrows, a dagger with its sheath, two cylindrical containers made of bark, a wooden backpack or frame, a belted pouch containing a fire-making kit, a net, a retouching tool (for flaking and so sharpening small flints), thongs on a stone disk and two shaped pieces of a bracket fungus each strung on a thong. Discussed later, important questions are raised by this sheer quantity of gear and also by the precise state of some of the items, such as, outstandingly, the unfinished longbow and mostly headless and featherless arrows, plus the badly cut right hand.

There are many different images of Ötzi's appearance from cartoons in newspapers, to postcards, articles and books, good and not so good. Many are meant just to be fun but many are to be taken seriously. A few, such as the cartoons at the heads of Chapters 4 and 5, are funny with a serious point. There are life-size, fully dressed effigies in various museums, including most importantly the Iceman Museum in Bozen with its many hundreds of thousands of visitors. The first image in the now long series of scholarly publications was that by Lawrence Barfield and his two co-authors in 1992. It was rapidly overtaken by those in Konrad Spindler's book and the very fine drawings in the books by Markus Egg in 1993 and later in 2009. Succeeding the original one in the Iceman Museum, there is now a very lifelike one there. The first full-size reconstruction in the Iceman Museum had Ötzi standing on a boulder which, unfortunately, meant that his diminutiveness was not immediately apparent and may well have been unrealised by some. At 188cm (almost 6ft 2in) I found myself looking directly into his eyes. The clothes seemed to be very ill-fitting (see Figs 2.16 to 2.19).

The new effigy, produced for 2011 by the Kennis brothers, is very different. Almost my first thought on seeing the photographs was 'It's Frodo Baggins in his declining years!' However, more seriously, the fingers and wrist are too thick and the forearm too long. Eduard Egarter Vigl has x-rays showing delicate fingers. Here a comment is necessary about the new reconstruction of Ötzi in the Iceman Museum. This clearly shows Ötzi's fingers as thick. Eduard Egarter Vigl told me in a recent email that 'When I confront the X-ray pictures of the hand and the anatomic reality of the mummified body with the new model I can't find any resemblance'. He thinks the left forearm is too long and the wrist too thick. Angelika Fleckinger, director of the Iceman Museum, told me recently in an email that:

The basis of the work of the Kennis brothers is the skull of the Iceman and CT scans of the body. So we are quite sure about the physiognomy of the head, the proportions of the body and his hair and beard. Also the dark colour of his eyes is a result of the DNA investigations.

Angelika continued: 'The position of the reconstruction is a little bit inclined – that's why the left arm looks long. There are different discussions about his hands. The Kennis brothers saw him as a "worker" with strong muscular body, arms and hands but a graceful skeleton.'

Fig. 2.16 (Far left) Effigy A from *Der Zeuge aus dem Gletscher* 1992. (*Andreas Lippert*)

Fig. 2.17 (Left) Effigy B the original one from the Iceman Museum. (*Iceman Museum*)

Fig. 2.18 (Far left) Effigy C from Egg and Spindler 2009. (*Markus Egg, Roman-Germanic Museum, Mainz*)

Fig. 2.19 (Left) Effigy D from Iceman Museum 2011. (*Iceman Museum*)

The reconstruction of human faces from skulls, or 'facial approximation' or 'craniofacial reconstruction', as it is often now called by sculptors or forensic scientists, is a subject that has been open to criticism as to its sound scientific basis. The practitioners, however, are convinced of the validity of their results. An obvious test is for the sculptors to be given skulls for which there exist portraits or photographs of the deceased faces, kept at first unseen by the sculptors. Then compare sculpted results with the images. This has happened on various occasions.[45]

The late appropriately named, in both English and French, Hungarian Dr Gyula Skultéty, formerly resident in Basel, Switzerland, has reconstructed the faces of homonins such as *Australopithecus boisei*, Neanderthals such as those from La Ferrassie in the Dordogne, France, and modern humans. Especially pertinent are his reconstructions of Hungarians killed in the 1956 anti-communist uprising. He was given skulls but did not see photographs until after completing the project for the Hungarian government. His reconstructions enabled the authorities to give correct names to the skeletal remains. Another such example concerns Egyptian mummy portraits, the 'Fayoum Portraits'. Facial reconstructions of four skulls by a University of Manchester team produced convincing results, though not correct in every detail, as the authors admit.[46]

Now there are many facial approximations to be seen in lots of archaeological publications and on television programmes. There are three in the book *Written in Bones*, edited and partly written by Paul Bahn. One shows 'our first reliable glimpse of a human face of 300,000 years ago', according to Bahn. This approximation is from a skull of an adult *Homo heidelbergensis*, from Burgos, northern Spain. By 2002 there were at least four approximations from Roman England, one of which was that a woman found in a lead coffin, reproduced in the article by David Gill. There are facial reconstructions of Lindow Man and Grauballe Man, two of the famous bog bodies mention in Chapter 1. Finally, in these mere few examples, there is the approximation of Lewis Man, from the Bronze Age of the outer isles of Scotland. The authors Trevor Cowie and Mary Macleod state that 'Obviously, certain features – the shape of the ears and nose, cut of hair and length of hair – are simply guesswork'.[47] They could have added shape of the mouth. There is a very recent one in *Nature* showing the face of 'Myrtis', a young Athenian girl of more than 2000 years ago.[48]

However, that nasal reconstruction is far from guesswork is obvious from the book *Forensic Facial Reconstruction* by Caroline Wilkinson. She states that 'Tangents from the last part of the nasal bone and the nasal spine will determine the nasal projection'. There is also the chapter by Ron Taylor and Pamela Craig of the University of Melbourne who make it clear that nasal approximation, though not without difficulties, has a good basis. Now two more papers by Caroline Wilkinson can be added.[49] My former colleague in Glasgow University but now of the Forensic Science Service in London, Professor Peter Vanesis, with his wife, developed a facial approximation method not based on sculpture but on numerous average measurements of prominent features of the skull and then computerised. But this method seems to me to produce bland images which tend to be rather uniform. At the Iceman Museum the Vanesis reconstruction was on display. There is a facial approximation of Ötzi by the American John Gurche, first published in the *National Geographic* magazine in June 1993 and then again in the November 2006 issue of *National Geographic France*. It gives Ötzi a pleasant demeanour.[50]

Now there is the new face of Ötzi as of 2011 in the Iceman Museum. It gives his face lots of wrinkles. Of course, hair style and beards cannot be deduced from skulls alone but, in the case of Ötzi, dark head hair and even what may very well have been beard hair was found and so the reconstruction is not entirely fanciful in that respect.

When his corpse was recovered Ötzi appeared hairless but he had been far from totally bald; the long hair from almost all over his body had fallen out but much human hair, presumed reasonably enough to have been Ötzi's, was recovered near the body during the excavations, and indeed some was recovered from his clothes. Furthermore, as now can be seen in the photographs in an article by Eduard Egarter Vigl, even some long hair remains on Ötzi's body. Several different investigations at the German Wool Research Institute in Aachen showed that the hair was excellently preserved.[51]

Wearing his hat, little could have been seen of his short head hair which was wavy, dark brown or black and about 9cm long. Angelika Fleckinger states:

> The hair structure indicates that Ötzi wore his hair loose and did not plait it. It is highly proba-
> ble that he also had a beard due to the large number of short, thick hairs found at the site. Other
> hair remains were identified as coming from his armpits, pubic area and other parts of his body.

This is a paraphrase of what Konrad Spindler had said, though he was cautious about the identification of armpit and pubic hair (*Spindler* 1 and 2). Paul Bahn stated that the short length of the head hair must indicate a recent haircut. We cannot know the exact position of his hairline or the precise style of his beard. The new reconstruction has artistic to some degree (see Fig. 2.19).

Archaeologist John Robb of Cambridge University quotes the Iceman Museum in 2006 as stating 'Blue eyes, dark hair, 1.60m tall, 50kg in weight'.[52] However, the colour of Ötzi's eyes as seen in the colour plate in Konrad Spindler's book is dark brown, just as it is in the article by the Italians Marco Samadelli and Terenzo Fabroni. Their article is curiously enti-tled 'The Iceman's True Colour' because it is solely a discourse on the properties of light and says nothing whatever about the original colour of the eyes, or indeed any other part of Ötzi's body.[53] When Ötzi had his mouth wide open the gap between his two first incisors (diastema) would have been obvious.

When completely dressed Ötzi had been covered by three layers of clothes: a hat, a cape, a coat, a loincloth held up by a belt, a belted pouch, as well as leggings and elaborately crafted shoes. So there is little if any suggestion of his apparel having been inadequate for the moun-tains. As Lawrence Barfield in his review article commented, 'Here we have the equipment and clothing of one man in use at one moment of his life (and death). And what a lot there is: it is a contemporary mountain survival kit and more.' In 1995 Markus Egg wrote, 'What the Ice Man wore was very likely not every-day clothing – people in the Copper Age already had woven linen – but rather alpine or winter gear.'[54] In their book Angelika Fleckinger and Hubert Steiner considered the clothes to have been 'very practical and well designed'.

When Ötzi's legs were still in the ice they could be seen to be clad in leggings and one shoe remained on even after the rough recovery. However, after this retrieval the clothes had become a sodden mass of rags and so presented a difficult task for the restorers at the Roman-Germanic Museum in Mainz, Germany. They are precious because clothes and, even more so, full sets of clothes have only very rarely been found from prehistoric Europe and never before from over 5000 years ago. Until the discovery of Ötzi, almost all clothes had been preserved by waterlogging in peat bogs or other submerged sites such as flooded coffins.

However, Ötzi's clothes are by no means the only ones to have come out of a glacier. In 1994, from the Reiser glacier in Pustertal, at 2841m in eastern Südtirol, there emerged clothes, some of them woven: two socks, two stockings and a pair of trousers, as well as the remnants of a pair of shoes. These items, dated at about 2600 years ago, can be seen in the Iceman Museum in Bozen. Whose lower extremities had filled them remains unknown because no body was ever found, despite repeated searches. Similarly, no body has been found at the almost vanished Chilchi glacier at Schnidejoch, southern Switzerland, discussed in Chapter 6, but items of clothing have been found, including a large part of a pair of patched leather trousers and again the owner has never been found.

None of Ötzi's clothes were made of textiles. However, Konrad Spindler (*Spindler* 2, p. 154) states: 'it should be stressed that in the language of scholarship textiles are understood to be all materials produced by knotting, plaiting or weaving. The fibre material can be of vegetable or animal origin.' Therefore, he considers that Ötzi's cape, dagger sheath, cords from his shoes and also his net are textiles. However, I prefer to use the definition as used by the American expert Elizabeth Barber of Occidental College, who says:

> I have chosen to write this book about those objects which come under the broad category of cloth – large thin sheets of material made from fibre, which are soft and floppy enough to be used as coverings for people and things. Technically the word *textile*, which comes to us from the Latin *texere* 'to weave', refers exclusively to woven cloth.

Weaving has a history going back to the seventh millennium BC, according to Barber.[55]

When reading the various books and papers that deal with Ötzi's clothes I have found myself confused, at least at first, about which part of his apparel was leather or merely unprepared skins or fur or what. What exactly was leather at Ötzi's time, 5200 years ago? For modern times leather can be defined as 'the skin of animals dressed and prepared for use by tanning, tawing or other processes'. Tanning is 'to convert into leather, as animal skins, by steeping them in an infusion of oak or some other bark, by which they are rendered firm, durable, and in some degree impervious to water'. And tawing is 'to dress with alum and other matters and make into white leather'.[56] However, all that is too narrow a definition with reference to Ötzi or even to recent ethnic practices in various parts of the world where tanning with oak, or even with other plants, is not or seldom used. Daniel Moerman of the University of Michigan in his volume on Native American ethnobotany lists various plants as used in preparing hides; examples are wormwoods (sagebrushes), docks and crookneck squash.

For the study of the early history of tanning using fat, there is the oft quoted passage from Homer's *Iliad*, Book 17, about stretching a hide after it had been soaked in fat to allow the fat to penetrate the pores. This statement comes from not less than 750 years BC.

The Dutch Professor Willy Groenman-van Waateringe of Amsterdam University, who was involved in the study of Ötzi's clothes from the beginning, wished to know the precise nature of the tanning process that had been used for the clothes and equipment. With two others she carried out experiments to try to settle the matter.[57] They mention that the earliest known

European leather from a waterlogged site, prior to the discovery of Ötzi, is a leather bag from the late Iron Age site of La Tène in Switzerland and so, as in many other ways, the discovery of Ötzi pushes the matter of producing leather much further back into prehistory. These Dutch experimenters state: 'In the find from the Hauslabjoch … we have, for the first time, the possibility of establishing the prehistoric curing methods.' Joachim Lange of Reutingen, Germany, had been the first to investigate this matter. He supposed that vegetable tanning had been used but thin-section chromatography showed only weak fluorescence, whereas it should have been a strong reaction if plants had been the agents used (*Spindler* 1).

In the early 1990s, Willy Groenman-van Waateringe had extracted pollen from some loose animal hairs found with Ötzi and she noticed two sizes and colours of pollen: some of normal size and colour and some (44 per cent) of about half the normal size and paler than usual. She considered that the abnormal grains were those that had become attached to the skin in the first place – when the animal was still alive – and then some kind of tanning process made the pollen smaller and paler. The Dutch archaeologists carried out a series of tests using differing tanning methods on modern skins and they conclude: 'Pollen [size] data from the Iceman's clothing and data from the tanning experiments with fresh pollen point to a process of smoke-drying in combination with the use of fat. The yellow-brown colour of the material points in the same direction.'[58]

In recent times the fat used has usually been from brains. As for instance, by the Zulus of South Africa, by inhabitants of northern Asia and North America and by the Japanese. Lynne Sageflower Pennington, a Native American, states online that 'Brains are used because they contain oils which do not separate when used with water. These oils will coat the hide but not saturate into it which is what the tanner wants.'[59]

Now there are the investigations by Joachim Lange (pp. 221–45 in the 2009 volume by Markus Egg and Konrad Spindler). He calls the clothing 'fell leder' meaning fur leather. Using the three techniques, absorption spectroscopy, infrared spectroscopy and x-ray fluorescence, he did not find evidence for any tanning agents in the strict sense (tannins, metallic salts and the like). The fat of land animals was probably used and this replaces the water, a process which is speeded up by the use of brains. The fur leather might have been smoked and then greased. But no traces of smoke were found, only traces of fat. Now there is the even more recent paper by the Swiss Alois Pütener and Serge Moss.[60] They state: 'This allows us to conclude that tanning of the Iceman's clothes partly consisted of saponified land animal fats, which had been physically incorporated in the form of calcium stearate.'[61] If all the items worn by Otzi had been especially treated skins then they can be called leather.

Hat
Ötzi wore a conical fur cap with leather straps for tying under the neck. The straps had been broken in antiquity (see Fig. 2.20).

Fig. 2.20 Özti's fur cap. (*Markus Egg, Roman-Germanic Museum, Mainz*)

Cape

Unfortunately, the cape was in a very fragmentary state when found and this leaves room for disagreement about its reconstruction. This elaborate garment was made mainly of tall grass which was made into vertical bundles. Bast (bark) fibres arranged horizontally held the grass bundles together. Only some fragments of the cape had survived under Ötzi's body, though one of them is quite substantial. That the cape was worn as the reconstruction in Fig. 2.18 shows has been questioned and indeed that it was even a cape at all has been disputed. Rolf Barth has claimed that it may have been the bag for the backpack frame or that is was a simple mat. Why the bag came to be detached from the frame of the backpack and ended up under Ötzi's body is left unexplained[62] (see Fig. 2.21).

Fig. 2.21 Özti's cape. (*Markus Egg, Roman-Germanic Museum, Mainz*)

On this topic the German experimental archaeologist, Anne Reichert, wrote a long article which has photographs of ethnological parallels from Japan and New Guinea and even Schnalstal. She states that:

> Remnants of a mat made in weft-twine technique were partially frozen to the rock on which the Iceman 'Ötzi' was found. They were thought to be fragments of a cape. However, experiments have shown that a backpack and a quiver like Ötzi's could neither be worn underneath nor above such a cape. Besides, careful examination of the original fragments did not reveal enlargements. These enlargements, however, would have been necessary to widen a cape from the relatively narrow neck opening to an appropriate width for the shoulders. The pieces of weft-twined grass are in fact fragments of a straight sided mat which, knotted together at the top with small cords, could have been worn as a long hood covering the head, shoulders and back. As a protection against rain, wind and sun similar mats are still known throughout the world. Possibly the Iceman Otzi had also worn his mat as a long hood.[63]

In their 2009 volume Markus Egg and Konrad Spindler stick to the interpretation as a cape and show a New Zealand Maori cape to back up their case.

Coat/Jacket

Beneath his cape Ötzi wore what some of the German literature calls 'Oberkorperbekleidung' (upper-body clothing) because, not being complete, there is uncertainty whether there had been sleeves or not. So to use a term like jacket or jerkin may be thought misleading. Angelika Fleckinger and Gudrun Shulzenbacher use 'coat'. Whatever its pristine state, it was made of stitched leather. The upper-body clothing clearly shows make-do-and-mend stitching crude by comparison with the beautiful, tightly neat, original stitchwork, as can be seen in the fine photographs in Markus Egg *et al*. Lorenzo Dal Ri refers to the coat/jacket as 'probably sleeveless (a kind of poncho)'; this is strange because by definition a poncho slips

Fig. 2.22 Özti's upper-body clothing. (*Markus Egg, Roman-Germanic Museum, Mainz*)

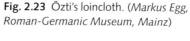

Fig. 2.23 Özti's loincloth. (*Markus Egg, Roman-Germanic Museum, Mainz*)

over the head and has no frontal opening. All the reconstructions show a frontal opening (see Fig. 2.22).

Loincloth

Unlike the cape, coat/jacket and shoes, there is nothing controversial about the rectangular leather loincloth, apart from its original length. Made of stitched pieces of leather and 33cm at the widest, the loincloth was about 180cm long according to Konrad Spindler, but only about 100cm according to Angelika Fleckinger and Hubert Steiner. However, the caption at the display in the Iceman Museum (October 2007) stated 'at least 1.5m long' (see Fig. 2.23).

Belt

The loincloth was held up by a belt found in two pieces. Together they make a length of about 133cm and an irregular width of 1.5 to 4.3cm.

Leggings

Tight-fitting and attached to the belt by suspenders, the leggings closely resemble those in use by some Native Americans until the nineteenth century. Attached to the lower ends were tongues which could be pushed into the shoes. The leggings were made of pieces of leather and show patches, a clear indication of hard use.

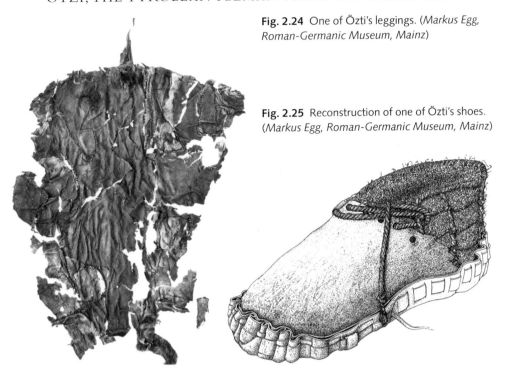

Fig. 2.24 One of Özti's leggings. (*Markus Egg, Roman-Germanic Museum, Mainz*)

Fig. 2.25 Reconstruction of one of Özti's shoes. (*Markus Egg, Roman-Germanic Museum, Mainz*)

Shoes

There are various rival versions of Ötzi's complex shoes which were in a poor state when found: the original one of Roswitha Goedecker-Ciolek, that of Willy Groenman-van Waateringe, that of Donja Malhotra and that of Anne Riechert[64] (see Fig. 2.25).

In 2003 in the journal of the South Tyrolean Archaeological Museums, Donja Malhorta published a detailed paper about the shoes. It is well worth quoting her summary extensively:

> The badly damaged shoes of the Iceman consisted each of a sole and an upper part composed of three layers: An upper layer of two pieces of hide, a mesh-like woven net of lime-bast, and a grass cushion between the two. The shoes came up over the ankle, were lined and had extra grass which served as 'socks' between the foot and the shoe. The right shoe is in a better state of conservation than the left. In the case of both shoes, the heel section is more damaged than the front. The revised reconstruction of the Iceman's shoes presented here takes as the basic form the one piece shoe bound around the instep with a leather string passing through slits in the raised margins of the shoe.

Ötzi's shoes are not the only footwear to have emerged from a European glacier. From the melting ice at Schnidejoch, discussed in Chapter 6, came a large fragment of a Neolithic leather shoe, but a very different in design from Ötzi's shoe. The reconstruction shows that it resembled a North American moccasin. Now, very recently, there has been discovered the oldest shoe in Eurasia. It was found well preserved in dry state in a cave in Armenia. It had been worn on the right foot of someone about 5500 years ago and so is slightly older than Ötzi's shoes, which it resembles in the use of grass.[65]

In Full Fig

On suitable outdoor occasions, which seem quite frequent in those parts of Tyrol with which I am familiar, modern Tyroleans love to dress up in bright, fancy clothes with plumed hats and various other decorations and so can be very striking. Some sport musical instruments or guns and other weapons. Could this love of conspicuousness possibly be a very ancient tradition? No large decorative objects, like boar tusks, were found with Ötzi and so there is little to support my speculation, even if it is thought an appealing one. However, boar tusks were found when a late Neolithic burial from near Gratsch, Austria, was exposed (*Spindler* 1 and 2). Furthermore, Ötzi's jacket was very carefully stitched together in such a way as to appear striped. This leads Gudrun Sulzenbacher in her book to claim that 'The variety of colours on the strips that made up Ötzi's hide coat indicates a certain degree of fashion-consciousness on his part'. In this she was following Konrad Spindler who stated that (*Spindler* 1, p. 138) 'Immediately after it was made this garment must have been splendid to look at'. John Robb is also impressed by Ötzi's coat/jacket, which he calls a 'tunic'.[66] Furthermore, he wonders if the bearskin cap could have been more than a mere head warmer but homage to 'the largest, most dangerous carnivore in the area'.

Axe

The axe head was made of virtually pure copper, weighing 174g, and was 9.5cm long with a cutting edge of only 3.7cm. The maximum thickness is less than 10mm and there are very low flanges which do not extend to the apex or base. Only a quarter of this small blade protruded from the wooden handle, which is 60cm long and slightly curved at the proximal end and the distal end is a forked shaft with a deep groove into which the blade was slotted. There are bindings of narrow leather strips. Glue was also used to fix the axe head into the shaft. The haft had an internal crack at the top. Now it is a very visible crack, as can be seen in the Iceman Museum and in the book by Angelika Fleckinger and Hubert Steiner and also that by Markus Egg and Konrad Spindler (see Fig. 2.26).

Gerhard Sperl of Leoben, Austria, gives the exact analysis of 0.22 per cent arsenic, 0.09 per cent silver and the rest copper (*Innsbruck* 1). In 1992, Raffaele De Marinis of Milan (*Innsbruck* 1, p. 454) wrote of the copper axes of the north Italian copper age: 'The axes are practically all of pure copper ... the daggers and halberds are of copper with high percentages of arsenic. The marked difference tends to support the use of arsenic alloys.' In 1998, Mark Pearce of the University of Nottingham repeated this statement in somewhat stronger terms. He noted that such a deliberate choice seems the wrong way round, because arsenical copper (with a few to several per cent arsenic) makes the harder product and one would have expected the user of an axe for, for instance, cutting down trees would have liked as hard a blade as possible.[67]

Fig. 2.26 The head of Özti's axe and the copper blade. (*Markus Egg, Roman-Germanic Museum, Mainz*)

Using crystallographic techniques, Professor Gilberto Artioli of the University of Padua, Italy, has investigated the axe head. He has kindly summarised his findings as follows (personal communication): the axe head was produced by casting in a bivalve mould and was never work-hardened, so that it was used in the soft metal state. This is common to most investigated chalcolithic axes. The axe was used extensively as shown by the recrystallisation of copper grains and cracks in the back. He considers that the axe was fully functional for wood working, tree felling or smashing a skull. A soft-copper replica was used to fell a tree of 30cm diameter in 15 minutes.

Bow, Quiver and Arrows

Another marvellous discovery, unprecedented in ancient prehistory in its completeness, was the evidence for archery. At the site there was an unfinished longbow, which, sadly, was broken during an overhasty attempt at removal from the ice. However, the two pieces have been neatly put back together, as can be seen at the Iceman Museum. It measures 182cm long. The bow is clearly not smoothed down, there being many obvious shallow cut marks from the maker's tool. There are no notches for the string but that need not be another

Fig. 2.27 (Right) The longbow with detail showing cut marks. (*Markus Egg, Roman-Germanic Museum, Mainz*)

Fig. 2.28 (Far right)The quiver and contents. (*Markus Egg, Roman-Germanic Museum, Mainz*)

indication of incompleteness; some Neolithic and Bronze Age bows had them and others did not, as is made clear by Jurgen Junkmanns.[68] Ötzi's quiver was of a complex design and made of hide with a wooden stiffener. Its closing flap had been torn off and found away from the main part of the quiver, which contained 14 wooden arrow shafts but 12 had neither heads nor feathers. Nor did the quiver include any nocks (sleeves to go over the ends of the bow and hold the string in place). According to Angelika Fleckinger, a mass of bast cord (fibre from bark) found inside the quiver is unlikely to have been the string for the bow because of 'its irregular and inelastic nature'. In contrast, Konrad Spindler was inclined, though not strongly, to regard the ball of string as intended for the bow (*Spindler* 2). Also inside the quiver were four fragments of deer antler tied with bast into a bundle about 13cm long, as well as a single carved piece of deer antler narrowly pointed and two strips of sinew about 20cm long tied together with bast (see Figs 2.27 and 2.28). The arrow shafts vary somewhat in length being 84 to 87.5cm and are 8 to 9.5mm in diameter. A broken one is only 69cm long. Klaus Oeggl and Werner Schoch (*Innsbruck* 4, p. 29) discuss the suitability of the shafts and say that some appear unfinished and incapable of being shot. Only two have flint tips and feathers.

Dagger and Sheath

His slim dagger had a flint blade lacking the tip. (Lost in antiquity or during the rough recovery?) The wooden handle was crudely carved. It is a small, one might almost say tiny, implement a mere 12.8cm long and 2.2cm wide in all, with the blade 6.3 x 2.2 cm but protruding only 4.5 or perhaps 5cm when intact. So hardly a very deeply penetrating weapon, though no doubt very sharp indeed, as flint can be, if it was meant as weapon rather than a cutting tool. According to Angelica Fleckinger and Hubert Steiner, 'The flint blade had multiple uses. The Iceman probably used it for the precision work on the bow.' (See Figs 2.29 and 2.30).

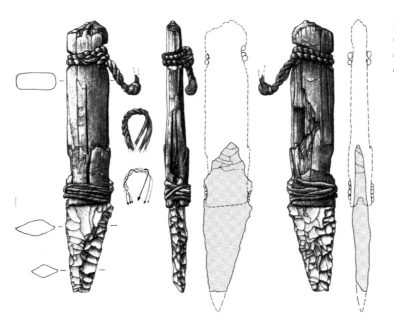

Fig. 2.29 The dagger. (*Markus Egg, Roman-Germanic Museum, Mainz*)

Fig. 2.30 The dagger sheath.
(*Markus Egg, Roman-Germanic Museum, Mainz*)

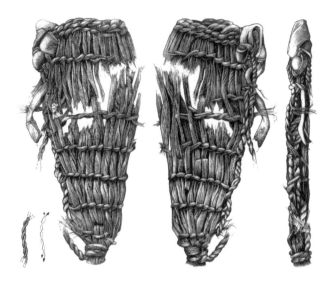

The dagger had been carried in a 12cm-long sheath made of a mesh of bast, which Konrad Spindler (*Spindler* 1, p. 102-103) calls 'a minor masterpiece of plaiting technique', and he goes on 'Did the Iceman with his coarse hands make it himself? One would be more inclined to ascribe such delicate work to gentler hands.' This begs the question of coarse hands or not. These statements about craftsmanship by Angelika Fleckinger and Hubert Steiner and Konrad Spindler raise the question: 'How can we possibly know who made the bow and the sheath?'

Bark Containers

Two cylindrical containers made of bark were found, one close to the body and other further away. Originally they were about 20cm tall and about 15 to 18cm in diameter. Stitching had been used to make the cylinders and attach the base but none of the material has survived. One at least, in all likelihood, had held both charcoal and green leaves; this is Container 1 as discussed by Konrad Spindler. Its remnants were found lying on the ice, about 2m south-west of Ötzi's head. It had been badly broken by being trampled during the rather unfortunate, if inevitable, visits by about 28 people in the nine days before the body was removed so roughly from the ice.

Already in a fragmentary condition, Container 2, as discussed by Spindler, was found on a rock

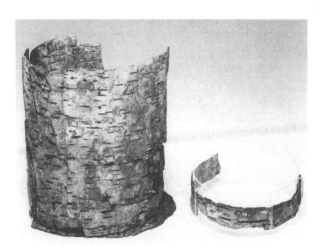

Fig. 2.31 Birch bark Container 1. (*Markus Egg, Roman-Germanic Museum, Mainz*)

shelf 5m or so away from the body and, he thought, may have been tied to the 'backpack' or even in it. In contrast, the inner surface of Container 1 was darkened from having held embers; when first found, Container 1 had held 'wet hay' (see Fig. 2.31).

Torstein Sjøvold has visited the Ötzi site many times. During a visit in 1994 he recovered some missing pieces of Container 2, a finding which he thought 'sensational' and Brenda Fowler thought 'miraculous'. Both these adjectives strike me as more than a little on the hyperbolic side. 'Useful but depressing' would be better: 'depressing' in that the fragments had been unnoticed by the excavators but 'useful' because the container could be better reconstituted. However, Brenda Fowler's description of the finding of Container 1 by Helmut Simon is well worth quoting in the light of new interpretations of events after Ötzi's death:

> Not far from the [Ötzi's] head, Helmut noticed something lying on the ice, and he stooped to pick it up. It was a flattened bundle wrapped in white birch bark and apparently tied up with leather laces. As he turned it in his hands, he noticed how fragile and soggy it was.

Konrad Spindler's account (*Spindler* 1, p. 10–1) is 'Not Far from the body we [The Simons] saw a piece of birch bark which used to be a tube but had been squashed flat, wound round with string or leather and open at both ends. Helmut picked it up, looked at it carefully and put it back.' It seems very likely that the container had not been upright when it melted from the ice shortly before the discovery.

Konrad Spindler wanted the inner surface of Container 2 to be examined. He stated (*Spindler* 2, p. 100): 'At the moment nothing can be hazarded about the contents of the container from the rock ledge, since examination of the inner surface for micro-traces has not produced any positive results.' Now, in his last published article on Ötzi, Konrad Spindler has speculated that perhaps it had been used in the preparation of cheese.[69] In contrast, the inner surface of Container 1 was darkened from having held embers. When first found, Container 1 held 'wet hay' which proved to be the purple moor grass, as identified by Peter Acs. Konrad Spindler stated (*Spindler* 1, p. 100): 'Embedded in these maple leaves were needles of spruce (*Picea abies*) and juniper (*Juniperus* sp). Traces of grain also adhered to the leaves, fragments of glume and husk of einkorn (*Triticum monococcum*) and wheat (*Triticum*).'

Backpack/Frame

What exactly was the object he carried on his back is a matter of controversy because all that is certain of its structure is the u-shaped piece of wood and the two narrow wooden cross boards. The English version of Konrad Spindler's books uses the word 'pannier', which is certainly not appropriate because by definition a pannier is a container made of basketry, no remains of which were found at the site, but plenty of string was. So, was it a frame for tying up a partial or whole carcass? According to Angelika Fleckinger, 'A few pieces of hide and clumps of hair tend to indicate that a hide sack was attached to the frame to carry the Iceman's possessions.' Yet a third interpretation is that of Rolf Barth, who contemplated that the remnants which most people have accepted as a cape had been 'the missing bag that was attached to the backpack frame'.[70] How the missing bag came to be separated from the frame and then ended up under Ötzi's prone body far from the remains of the frame is not even mentioned let alone any explanation offered (see Fig. 2.32).

Fig. 2.32 The frame of the backpack. (*Markus Egg, Roman-Germanic Museum, Mainz*)

There has been yet another interpretation of the wood pieces that most
people accept as having been a backpack.
This is that it was not a backpack at all
but the remnants of a snowshoe, as suggested Biba Teržan of Berlin.[71] In *Archaeo
News*, 27 Feb 2005, that idea was taken
up by the British archaeologist Jaqui
Wood. She thinks that for Ötzi to have
worn snowshoes was 'the obvious thing
to have done'. I wonder if it was obvious
to have snowshoes if he was travelling
over rough and in places very steep terrain, as he would have to have done to
reach the spot where his body lay. She
does not explain why there should have
been remains of only one snowshoe;
though, of course, the frame of the other
snowshoe might have been lost. These
claims by Biba Teržan and Wood seem
to have gained little if any acceptance,
probably rightly so. Angelika Fleckinger
and Gudrun Sulzenbacher make no mention of this claim in their books. Nor do Anne
Reichert or Donja Malhotra in their papers on the shoes. However, Markus Egg with
Konrad Spindler in a footnote dismiss the claim on the grounds of unsuitability for climbing and snowshoes from North America have a more elaborate structure.

Net

Fragments of a net of very thin strands and of 5cm mesh were found in 1991, during the
first excavation after the recovery of the body. Konrad Spindler thought that the net could
have been used for catching birds and only quite large fish and not for carrying things.

Retouching Tool

Ötzi had carried a tool resembling a fat pencil which at first, perhaps not surprisingly, puz-
zled Konrad Spindler and other investigators. Its dimensions are 12 x 2.6cm and inside there
is a splinter of antler 6.2cm long, like the lead in the pencil, and protruding by 4mm. The
antler point had been hardened by fire. Without such hardening antlers are too soft for such
use. Experimental archaeologists quickly showed the usefulness of such a tool. As already
pointed out by Konrad Spindler, using such a tool and starting from a suitable small flake, it
is possible to make a flint arrowhead in a matter of minutes. This I have seen for myself dem-

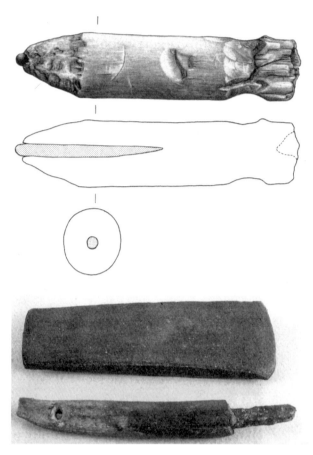

Fig. 2.33 The retouching tool. (*Markus Egg, Roman-Germanic Museum, Mainz*)

Fig. 2.34 The retouching tool and copper axe blade from Fontaine-le-Puits, Haute-Savoie, France. (*Aimé Bocquet, France*)

onstrated at the Mammutheum at Siegesdorf, southern Bavaria, by Bernard von Bredow, and at ArcheoParc in Schnalstal by Valentin Müller, both of whom are skilled flint knappers. (See Figs 2.33 and 2.34.)

So, Ötzi's retouching tool had been used for re-edging flints. Konrad Spindler stated that (*Spindler* 2, p. 105): 'To start with, no similar – let alone identical – object was then known from prehistoric or from historical or ethnographic finds.' We now know, however, that Ötzi's retouching tool is not the only one to have been found but is the only one of its precise construction to have come down to us from ancient times. The previous one, found more than a century ago (1908), lay in one of three of the principal late Neolithic tombs at Fontaine-le-Puits, Savoie, France. It has a handle of deer antler into which had been inserted a long narrow piece of copper to be 'the lead in the pencil'. The tool, with the copper inserted in the handle, is about 12 to 13cm long and so is very similar in size to Ötzi's tool. Frenchman Aimé Bocquet was impressed by the similarities between the grave goods buried with the Fontaine-le-Puits man and Ötzi's equipment.[72]

Belted Pouch and Contents

These together make yet another marvellous discovery with no parallel from such ancient times. As they say, there is nothing new under the sun and, as Konrad Spindler first related engagingly, closely similar items are worn today to protect small important objects. They are called bum-bags by the British and bananas by the French and bananas and blisters by Germans, while Americans would say fanny packs.

Ötzi carried a flint-pointed small dagger and two arrows, both flint-tipped, as well as, in his pouch, three small flints, two of which could very well have been used to make sparks. The largest flint is about 7cm long with rounded ends and the second largest is somewhat dagger shaped; these bear striking resemblances to Upper Palaeolithic Danish and

Fig. 2.35 The belted pouch. (*Markus Egg, Roman-Germanic Museum, Mainz*)

Fig. 2.36 Shaped pieces of bracket fungus on thongs. (*Markus Egg, Roman-Germanic Museum, Mainz*)

Fig. 2.37 Stone disk and thongs. (*Markus Egg, Roman-Germanic Museum, Mainz*)

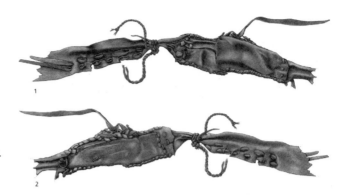

Dutch flints illustrated by Dick Stapert and Lykke Johansen and considered to be 'strike-a-lights'.[73] Also in the pouch were tiny fragments of pyrites which, with the flints, constituted a fire-making kit. (See Chapter 3.)

Strips of Hide with Bracket Fungus
An intriguing discovery was two strips of hide, each threaded through a small piece of a bracket fungus which had been cut from a whole bracket. Konrad Spindler thought that they had been fastened to Ötzi's clothing, belt or wrist (*Spindler 2*, p. 117). (See Fig. 2.36).

Stone Bead with Tassel
The bead is a pierced disk 2.26cm in diameter and 3.7mm thick and attached to nine twisted hide strips giving the appearance of a tassel. Konrad Spindler thought it might be considered as an ornament but also that, entirely reasonably, the strips had a practical function as a spare supply of thongs, useful for various purposes (*Spindler 2*, p. 120). (See Fig. 2.37.)

'Stick'
Fig. 1.8 shows an extraordinary stick-like object apparently projecting from Ötzi's upper right leg. When thawed out and unravelled, this proved to be several strips of leather twisted together. Perhaps they were spare thongs or a wiper for cleaning the bow and arrows. How they came to be stuck together and to the hip in such a fashion is a puzzle. (See Fig. 1.8.)

Notes

1   Baroni, C. and Orombelli, G. 1996. 'The Alpine "Iceman" and Holocene Climatic Change'. *Quaternary Research* 46, pp. 78–83.

2   Müller, W. *et al*. 2003. 'Origin and Migration of the Alpine Iceman'. *Science* 302, pp. 862–6.

3   Hays, J.D., Imbrie, J. and Shackleton, N.J. 1976. 'Variations in the Earth's Orbit: pacemaker of the Ice Ages'. *Science* 194, pp. 1121–32. Sigman, D., Hain, M.P. and Haug, G.H. 2010. 'The polar ocean and glacial cycles in atmospheric CO concentration'. *Nature* 466, pp. 47–55.

4   Ibid.

5   Schlüchter, C. and Jörin, U. 2004. 'Alpen ohne Gletscher?' *Die Alpen* 6, pp. 34–47. Breu, M. 2005. 'Green Alps instead of perpetual ice?' *ETHlife international web*.

6   Grove, M.J. 1988. *The Little Ice Age*. Cambridge University Press. Ladurie, E.L.R. 1988. *Times of Feast, Times of Famine: A History of Climate since the Year 1000*. London, George Allen and Unwin.

7   Henson, R. 2008. *The Rough Guide to Climatic Change*. London, Penguin. Schmidt, G. and Wolfe, J.D. 2009. *Climatic Change Picturing the Science*. New York, W.W. Norton. Collins, W. *et al*. 2007. 'The Physical Science behind Climate Change'. *Scientific American*, pp. 48–57.

8   Ruddiman, W.F. 2003. 'The anthropogenic greenhouse era began thousands of years ago'. *Climatic Change* 61, pp. 261–93. Ruddiman, W.F. 2005. 'How did humans first alter global climate?' *Scientific American* 292, pp. 34–41. Smith, F.A., Elliot, S.M. and Lyons, S.K. 2010. 'Methane emissions from extinct megafauna'. *Nature Geoscience online*, pp. 1–2. But see also Nogués-Bravo, D. *et al*. 2010. 'Climate Change, Humans, and the Extinction of the Woolly Mammoth'. *Plosbiology online*. Kurbatov, A.V. *et al*. 2010. 'Discovery of nano-diamond-rich layer in the Greenland ice sheet'. *Journal of Glaciology* 56, pp. 747–57.

9   Bortenschlager, S. 1970. 'Waldgrenz- und Klimaschwankungen im pollenalaytischen bild des Gurgler Rotmooses'. *Mitt. Ostalp-din. Ges f. Vegetkde* 11, pp. 19–26. Bortenschlager, S. 1991. 'Die Waldgrenze im Postglazial'. *Proceedings of the Pan-European Paleootanical Conference Vienna*, pp. 9–13.

10 Baroni, C. and Orombelli, G. 1996. 'The Alpine "Iceman" and Holocene Climatic Change'. *Quaternary Research* 46, pp. 78–83.

11 Magny, M. and Haas, J.N. 2004. 'A major widespread climatic change around 5300 cal. yrs. BP at the time of the Alpine Iceman'. *Journal of Quaternary Science* 19, pp. 423–30. Magny, M. *et al*. 2005. 'Quantitative reconstruction of mid-Holocene climatic variations in the northern Alpine foreland based on Lake Morat (Swiss Plateau) and Lake Annecy (French pre-Alps) data'. *Boreas* 34, pp. 434–44. Magny, M. *et al*. 2005. 'Tripartite climate reversal in Central Europe 5600–5300 years ago'. *Quaternary Research* 65, pp. 3–19. Arbogast, R-M. *et al*. 2006. 'The significance of climate fluctuations for lake level changes during the late Neolithic (4300–2400 BC) in central Europe'. *Vegetational History and Archaeobotany* 15, pp. 403–18. Grosjean, M., Suter, P.J., Trachsel, M. and Wanner, H. 2007. 'Ice-borne prehistoric finds in the Swiss Alps reflect Holocene glacier fluctuations'. *Journal of Quaternary Science* 22, pp. 203–7.

12 Jacomet, S. and Kreuz, S. *Archäobotanik*. Stuttgart, Eugen Ulmer. Bortenschlager, S. 1999. 'Die Umwelt des Mannes aus dem Eis und sein Einfluss darauf'. *Schriften des Südtiroler Archäologiemuseums* 1, pp. 81–95.

13 Makristathis, A. *et al*. 2002. 'Fatty acid composition and preservation of the Tyrolean Iceman and other mummies'. *Journal of Lipid Research* 43, pp. 2056–61. Rühli, F.J., Chem, R.K. and Böni, T. 2004. 'Diagnostic paleoradiology of mummified tissue: interpretation and pitfalls'. *Journal of Association of Canadian Radiologists* 55, pp. 218–27. Rühli, F.J. 2007. 'Non-invasive spatial tissue discrimination in ancient mummies and bones in situ by portable nuclear magnetic resonance'. *Journal of Cultural Heritage* 8, pp. 257–63. Janko, M *et al*. 2010. 'Nanostructure and mechanics of mummified type 1 collagen from the 5300-year-old Tyrolean Iceman'. *Proceedings of the Royal Society B* 277, pp. 2301–9.

14 Bereuter, T.L., Mikenda, W. and Reiter, C. 1997. 'Iceman's Mummification implications from Infrared Spectroscopical and Histological Studies'. *Chem. Eur. Journal* 3, pp. 1032–8. Egarter Vigl, E. 2006. 'The Preservation of the Iceman Mummy'. *Schriften des Südtiroler Archäologiemuseums* 4, pp. 45–70. Ambach, E., Tributsch, W., Henn, R. and Ambach, W. 1992. 'Is mummification possible in snow?' *Forensic Science International* 54, pp. 191–2.

15 Ibid.

16 Ibid.

17 Ibid.

18 Wyss, C. *et al.* 2003. 'Pontes de *Calliphora vicina*, Robineaux-Desvoiody et de *Calliphora vomitoria* (Linné) (Diptères, Calliphoridare) sur un cadavre humain enseveli dans la neige'. *Revue intenationale de criminologie et de police technique et scientifique* LVI, pp. 112–1146.

19 Taylor, R.E. 'Radiocarbon Dating'. In Brothwell, D. and Pollard, A.M. (eds) 2001. *Handbook of Archaeological Sciences*. Chichester, John Wiley & Sons, pp. 23–34. Kutschera, W. and Müller, W. 2003. '"Isotope language" of the Alpine Iceman investigated with AMS and MS'. *Nuclear Instruments and Methods in Physics Research B* 204, pp. 705–19. Lippert, A. and Spindler, K. 1991. 'Die Auffindung einer frühbronzezeitlichen Gletschermumie am Hauslabjoch in den Ötztaler Alpen (Gem. Schnals)'. *Archäologie Osterreicheichs* 2/2, pp. 11–7.

20 Ibid.

21 Ibid.

22 Roberts, D. 1993. 'The Iceman Lone Voyager from the Copper Age'. *National Geographic*, June, pp. 36–57.

23 Brown, T.A. 2001. 'Ancient DNA'. In Brothwell, D. and Pollard, A.M. 'DNA analysis – a tool to help reconstructing the past'. *Handbook of Archaeological Sciences*. Chichester, John Wiley & Sons. Nørby, S. 2003. 'DNA analysis – a tool to help reconstructing the past'. In Lynnerup, N., Andreasen, C. and Berglund, J. (eds) *Mummies in a New Millenium*. Copenhagen, Danish Polar Centre, pp. 121–5. Renfrew, C. 2006. 'Archaeogenetics'. In Renfrew, C. and Bahn, P. *Archaeology The Key Concepts*. London, Routledge, p. 1620. Handt, O. *et al.* 1994. 'Molecular Genetic Analysis of the Tyrolean Iceman'. *Science* 264, pp. 1775–8.

24 Rollo, F. *et al.* 2000. 'Analysis of Bacterial DNA in Skin and Muscle of the Tyrolean Iceman Offers New Insight into the Mummification Process'. *American Journal of Physical Anthropology* 11, pp. 211–9. Cano, R.J. *et al.* 2000. 'Sequence Analysis of Bacterial DNA in the Colon and Stomach of the Tyrolean Iceman'. *American Journal of Physical Anthropology* 112, pp. 297–309. Rollo, F. *et al.* 2006. 'Fine characterisation of the Iceman's mtDNA Haplogroup'. *American Journal of Physical Anthropology* 130, pp. 557–64. Endicott, P *et al.* 2007. 'The Unresolved Location of Otzi's mtDNA within Haplogroup K'. *American Journal of Physical Anthropology* 132, pp. 590–3. Rollo, F. *et al.* 2007. 'The Resolved Location of Otzi's mtDNA within Haplogroup K'. A reply to Endicott *et al.* 2007. *American Journal of Physical Anthropology* 132, pp. 590–3.

25 Ibid.

26 Ermini, L. *et al.* 2008. 'The Complete Mitochondrial Genome Sequence of the Tyrolean Iceman'. *Current Biology* 18, pp. 1687–93. 'Ötzi's Secrets About to be Revealed'. *ScienceDaily*, 27 July 2010.

27 Gaber, O. and Künzel, K-H. 1998. 'Man from Hauslabjoch'. *Journal of Gerontology* 33, pp. 655–60. Gaber, O. 1999. 'Medizinische Forschungen am Mann aus dem Eis am Institut für Anatomie der Universität Innbruck'. *Schriften des Südtiroler Archäologiemuseums* 1, pp. 39–44.

28 Ruff, C.B. *et al.* 2006. 'Body size, body proportions, and mobility in the Tyrolean Iceman'. *Journal of Human Evolution* 51, pp. 91–101.

29 Capasso, L., La Verghetta, M. and D'Anasasio, R. 1999. 'L'Homme du Similaun: Une Synthèse Anthropologique et Paletpathologique'. *L'Anthropologie* 103, pp. 447–70. Luigi Capasso and two colleagues have written, p. 464, supported by a photograph: 'The microscopic examination of the skin fragments have permitted Gino Fornaciari to highlight the very well preserved eggs of diptera on the epidermis. Because of the condition of weak dehydration we can suppose these eggs have been laid quite recently, perhaps at the time of one of the periodic emersions of the mummy out of the ice. Then we must exclude the possibility that the eggs have been laid when the Iceman was alive (myasis).' However, neither Claude Wyss nor Daniel Cherix are convinced by Luigi Capasso's claim which they feel is very inadequately explicit to be sure that the eggs are invertebrate eggs, let alone dipteran eggs, or even eggs at all.

30 Ruff, C.B. *et al.* 2006. 'Body size, body proportions, and mobility in the Tyrolean Iceman'. *Journal of Human Evolution* 51, pp. 91–101.

31 Murphy, W.A. Jr. *et al.* 2003. 'The Iceman: Discovery and Imaging'. *Radiology* 2003, pp. 614–29.

32 Ibid.

33 Ibid.

34 Dal Ri, L. 2006. 'The Archaeology of the Iceman'. *Schriften des Südtirorler Archäologiemuseums* 3, pp. 17–44. Gostner, P., Egarter Vigl, E. and Reinstadler, U. 2004. 'Der Mann aus dem Eis. Eine paläoradiologisch-forensische zehn Jahre nach der Auffindung der Mumie'. *Germania* 82, pp. 83–107.

35 Ibid.

36 Oeggl, K. 2000. *Innsbruck* 3, p. 89. Oeggl, K. *et al.* 'The reconstruction of the last itinerary of "Ötzi",
    the Neolithic Iceman, by pollen analysis from sequentially sampled gut extracts'. *Quaternary Science
    Reviews* 26, pp. 853–61.

37 Filler, J. 1995. *Disease*. London, British Museum Press. As early as 7500–9000 years ago in early
    Neolithic Pakistan, caries may have been drilled with palliative intention using flints. Coppa, A. *et al.*
    2006. 'Early Neolithic tradition of dentistry'. *Nature* 440, p. 755.

38 Capasso, L., La Verghetta, M. and D'Anasasio, R. 1999. 'L'Homme du Similaun: Une Synthèse
    Anthropologique et Paletpathologique'. *L'Anthropologie* 103, pp. 447–70.

39 Capasso, L. 1999. 'La Mummia della Val Senales: rilievi paleopatologici'. *Schriften des Südtiroler
    Archäologiemuseums* 1, pp. 51–9. Baran R. *et al.* 2001. *Diseases of the Nails and their Management*. Third
    edition. Oxford, Blackwell Science. Capasso, L. 1994. 'Ungueal Morphology and pathology of the
    human mummy fround in the Val Senales (Eastern Alps. Tyrol, Bronze Age)'. *MUNIBE* 94, pp. 123–32.
    Readers should note that in the papers by Capasso and his associates there is frequent reference to the
    'Val Senales mummy' and 'Val Senales Glacier'. There is no such glacier and the mummy lies in the
    uppermost drainage basin of Ötztal. Being south of the frontier, legally the mummy was found in Italy
    but it was not in Val Senales (Schnalstal). Capasso, L. *et al.* 1997. 'The Health of the Tyrolean Ice Man:
    Evidences from Nail, Skin and Hair'. *Journal of Paleopathology* 9, pp. 153–8.

40 Capasso, L., La Verghetta, M. and D'Anasasio, R. 1999. 'L'Homme du Similaun: Une Synthèse
    Anthropologique et Paletpathologique'. *L'Anthropologie* 103, pp. 447–70.

41 Capasso, L. 1993. 'A preliminary report on the tattoos of the Val Senales mummy (Tyrol, Neolithic)'.
    Journal of Palepopathology 5, pp. 171–82. 'Are Ötzi's Tattoos Acupuncture? Skin markings on the
    Tyrolean Iceman may have been treatment for his ills'. *Discovering Archaeology*, Jan/Feb 1999, pp. 16–7.
    Sjøvold, T. 2003. 'The Location of the Iceman's Tattoos'. *Schriften des Südtiroloer Archäologiemusems* 3,
    pp. 111–22. Renaut, L. 2004. 'Les tatouages d'Ötzi et la petite chirurgie traditionelle'. *L'Anthropologie*
    108, pp. 69–105. Pabst, M.A. 2009. 'The tattoos of the Tyrolean Iceman: a light microscopical,
    ultrastructural and element analytical study'. *Journal of Archaeological Science* 36, pp. 2335–41. Pabst,
    M.A. and Hofer, F. 1998. 'Deposits of Different Origin in the Lungs of the 5,300-Year-Old Tyrolean
    Iceman'. *American Journal of Physical Anthropology* 107, pp. 1–12.

42 Ibid.

43 Ibid.

44 Aspöck, H. 2000. 'Paläoparasitologie: Zeugen der Vergangenheit'. *Nova Acta Leopoldina* 83, pp. 159–81.
    Aspöck, H., Auer, H. and Picher, O. 1999. 'Parasites and parasitic diseases in prehistoric human
    populations in Central Europe'. *Helminthologia* 36, pp. 139–45. Aspöck, H. *et al.* 2000. 'Parasitological
    examination of the Iceman'. In *Innsbruck* 4, pp. 127–36. Dickson, C. and Dickson, J. 2000 *Plants and
    People in Ancient Scotland*. Stroud, Tempus. Dickson, J.H. *et al.* 2000. 'The omnivorous Tyrolean Iceman:
    colon contents (meat, cereals, pollen, moss and whipworm) and stable isotope analyses'. *Philosophical
    Transactions of the Royal Society* 1404, pp. 1843–51. Dark, P. 2004. 'New evidence for the antiquity of
    the intestinal parasite Trichuris (whipworm) in Europe'. *Antiquity* 78, pp. 676–82. Ferreira, L.F. *et
    al.* 1991. '*Trichuris*-eggs in animal coprolites dated from 30,000 years ago'. *Journal of Parasitology* 77,
    pp. 491–3. Jacomet, S., Leuzinger, U. and Schibler, J. 2004. *Die Jungsteinzeitliche Seeufersiedlung Arbon
    Bleiche 3 3.* Frauenfeld, Huber & Co. Gostner, P. and Egarter Vigl, E. 2002. 'INSIGHT: Report of
    Radiological-Forensic Findings on the Iceman'. *Journal of Archaeological Science* 29, pp. 323–6. Nerlich,
    A. *et al.* 2003. 'Ötzi had a wound on his right hand'. *The Lancet* 362, p. 334.

45 Mackenzie, D. 2003. 'Putting a face to a skull'. *New Scientist* 3, June, pp. 26–7. Wilkinson, C. *et al.* 2003.
    'The Facial Reconstruction of Egyptian Mummies and Comparison with the Fayum Portraits'. In
    Lynnerup, N., Andreasen, C. and Berglund, J. *Mummies in a New Millenium*. Copenhagen, Danish Polar
    Centre, pp. 141–6.

46 Ibid.

47 Bahn, P. 2003. 'Pit of Bones'. *Written in Bones*. Toronto, Firefly Books, pp. 136–9. Gill, D. 'A Woman
    from Roman London: In a Lead Coffin'. In Bahn, P. 2003, pp. 144–7. Cowie, T. and Macleod, M. 'Man
    Lewis Man: A Face from the Past'. In Bahn, P. 2003, pp. 32–5. Papagrigorakis, M. 2011. 'Facing the
    past'. *Nature,* 471, p. 35.

48 Ibid.

49   Wilkinson, C. 2004. 'Forensic Facial Reconstruction'. Cambridge University Press. Taylor, R. and Craig, P. 2005 'The Wisdon of Bones: Facial Approximation on the Skull'. In Clement, G.C. and Murray, K.M. (eds) *Computer-Graphic Facial Reconstruction*. Amsterdam, Elsevier, pp. 33–55. Wilkinson, C. 2010. 'Facial reconstruction – anatomical art or artistic anatomy?' *Journal of Anatomy* 216, pp. 235–50. Rynn, C., Wilkinson, C.M. and Peters, H.L. 2004. *Forensic Science and Medical Pathology*. Online 19 November. Roberts, D. 1993. 'The Iceman Lone Voyager from the Copper Age'. *National Geographic* 183, 36–67.

50   Ibid.

51   Wortmann, G., Wilrich, C. and Wortmann, F.-J. 1996. 'Ötzi – the Mummy from Hauslabjoch. Investigation of archaeological keratin material'. *European Fine Fibre Network Occasional Publications* 4, pp. 71–84. Bahn, P.G. 1997. *The Story of Archaeology*. London, Weidefield & Nicholson. Bahn, P.G. 1998. *Tombs, Graves & Mummies*. London, Weidenfield & Nicholson.

52   Robb, J. 2009. 'Towards a Critical Ötziography: Inventing Prehistoric Bodies'. In Lambert, H. and McDonald, M. (eds) *Social Bodies*. New York, Berghahn Books, pp. 100–28. Samadelli, M. and Fraboni, T. 2006. 'The Iceman's True Colour'. *Schriften des Südtiroler Archäologiemuseums* 4, pp. 143–50.

53   Ibid.

54   Egg, M. 1995 'Secrets of the Ice Man'. *Science Spectra* 2, pp. 26–31.

55   Barber, E.J.W. 1991. *Prehistoric Textiles*. Princeton University Press.

56   Annandale, C. 1920. *The Concise English Dictionary Literary Scientific and Technical*. Glasgow, Blackie.

57   Groenman-van Waateringe, W., Kilian, M. and van Londen, H. 1999. 'The curing of hides and skins in European prehistory'. *Antiquity* 73, pp. 884–90. *The History of Brain Tan*. Web pages adapted from *Deerskins into Buckskins* by Matt Richards. Pennington, L.S. 2002. 'Craft Series – Tanning – Preparing a Hide for Clothing – Part Two'. *Cantu Ota* 54 (Online Newsletter). Püntener, A.G. and Moss, S. 2010. 'Ötzi the Iceman and his Leather Clothes'. *Chimia* 64, pp. 315–20.

58   Ibid.

59   Ibid.

60   Ibid.

61   Ibid.

62   Barth, R. 2003. 'Neurer Deutungsversuch zu den beim Mann aus dem Eis gefundenen mattenar-tigen Grasfragmenten'. *Schriften des Südtiroler Archäoolgiemuseums* 32, pp. 3–26. Reichert, A. 2006. 'Umhang oder Matte? Versuche zur Rekonstruktion des Grasgeflechts des "Mannes aus dem Eis"'. In *Experimentelle Archäologie in Europa Oldenberg*. Isensee Verlag, pp. 7–23.

63   Ibid.

64   Malhotra, D. 1998a. 'Zur Rekonstruktion der Fussbekleidung des Mannes vom Tisenjoch'. *Experimentelle Archäologie* 19, pp. 75–88. Malhotra, D. 1998b. 'Zu den Beschädigungen der Schuhe des Mannes vom Tisenjoch'. *Experimentelle Archäologie* 24, pp. 57–67. Malhotra, D. 2003. 'Die Beschädigungen der Schuhe des Mannes suf dem Eis'. *Schriften des Südtiroler Archäologiemuseums* 3, pp. 65–74. Reichert, A. 2001. Keine kalten Füsse in der Steinzeit? – Ein Experiment zur "Rheumassole" von Zug'. *Anzeiger AEAS* 1, pp. 4–5. Reichert, A. 2002. 'Weich und warm auf Moossohlen. Experimente zur Rheumasole von Zug'. *Jahrbuch der Schweizerischen Gesellschaft für Ur- und Frügeschichte* 85, pp. 50–4. Teržan, B. 1994. 'Bemerkungen zu dem sogenannten rucksack des Ötztaler mannes'. *Archäologisches Korrespondenzblatt* 24, pp. 265–8. Groenman-van Waateringe, W. 'The Reconstruction of the Iceman's Shoes Revised'. http://home.hccnet.nl/willy.groenman. Pinhasi, R. et al. 2010. 'First Direct Evidence of Chalcolithic Footwear from the Near Eastern Highlands'. *PLoS ONE* 5, 6, pp. 1–5.

65   Ibid.

66   Robb, J. 2009. 'Towards a Critical Ötziography: Inventing Prehistoric Bodies'. In Lambert, H. and McDonald, M. (eds) *Social Bodies*. New York, Berghahn Books, pp. 100–28. Samadelli, M. and Fraboni, T. 2006. 'The Iceman's True Colour'. *Schriften des Südtiroler Archäologiemuseums* 4, pp. 143–50.

67   Pearce, M. 1998. 'Reconstructing prehistoric metallurical knowledge; the northern Italian Copper and Bronze Ages'. *European Journal of Archaeology* 1, pp. 51–70. Pearce, M. 2003. 'Excavations at the Fourth Millenium Cal BC Copper Mines at Monte Loreto (Liguria – NW Italy)'. In *Archaeometullurgy in Europe Proceedings Volume 1*, pp. 587–96. Artioli, G. et al. 2003. 'Crystallographic Texture Analysis of the Iceman and Coeval Copper Axes by Non-invasive Neutron Powder Diffraction'. *Schriften des Südtiroler*

Archäologiemuseums 3, pp. 9–22. Pearce, M. 2005. 'Mid fourth-millenium copper mining in Liguria, north-west Italy: the earliest known copper mines in Western Europe'. *Antiquity* 79, pp. 66–77. Sperl, G.O. 2005. 'Metallography for the Euopean Copper Age; Research on the Axe-Blade of the Glacier Mummy from the Ötztaler Alps in Tyrol'. *Microscopy Today* 13, 6 pages. Artioli, G. 2007. 'Crystallographic texture analysis of archaeological metals; interpretation of manufacturing techniques'. *Applied Physics A* 89, pp. 899–908. Dolfini, A. 2010. 'The function of Chalcolithic metalwork in Italy: an assessment based on use-wear analysis'. *Journal of Archaeological Science xx*. Dolfini, A. 2010. 'The origins of metullargy in central Italy: new radiometric evidence'. *Antiquity* 84, pp. 707–23.

68 Junkmanns, J. 2001. *Arc et Flèche Fabrication and Utilisation au Neolithique.* Bienne, Éditions Musée Schwab.

69 Spindler, K. 2005. 'Der Mann in Eis und das Wanderhirtentum'. In Holzner, J. and Walde, E. (eds) *Brüche und Brücken.* Wien, Folio Verlag, pp. 22–41.

70 Barth, R. 2003. 'Neurer Deutungsversuch zu den beim Mann aus dem Eis gefundenen mattenartigen Grasfragmenten'. *Schriften des Südtiroler Archäoolgiemuseums* 32, pp. 3–26. Reichert, A. 2006. 'Umhang oder Matte? Versuche zur Rekonstruktion des Grasgeflechts des "Mannes aus dem Eis"'. In *Experimentelle Archäologie in Europa Oldenberg.* Isensee Verlag, pp. 7–23.

71 Teržan, B. 1994. 'Bemerkungen zu dem sogenannten rucksack des Ötztaler mannes'. *Archäologisches Korrespondenzblatt* 24, pp. 265–8.

72 Whittaker, J.C. 1994. *Flintknapping: making and understanding stone tools.* Austin, University of Texas Press. Bocquet, A. 1997. 'Les Alpes occidentales français au temps de l'homme du Similaun vers 3000 av. J.-C'. *Dossiers d'Archeologie* 224, pp. 44–51. Stapert, D. and Johansen, L. 1999. 'Flint and pyrite: making fire in the Stone Age'. *Antiquity* 73, pp. 765–77.

73 Ibid.

3

Use of Resources:
Clothing, Equipment and
Fire-making

That prehistoric people across Europe and elsewhere obtained materials from far afield has been known to archaeologists for a very long time. However, only recently has it been realised that in Africa, as early as 140,000 years ago, humans indulged in long-distance exchange.[1] In Britain and elsewhere in Europe, this long-distance movement has been especially clear in the case of materials such as Neolithic axe heads made of types of stone specific to particular regions and found far from their origins. Being imperishable, they have come down to us in large numbers, have been studied for many years and can be seen in diversity of size and rock type, polished or not, in many archaeological museums. With regard to distant transport of perishable items like foodstuffs there is a striking recent discovery. About 3500 to 4000 years ago at Waynuna, in the southern Peruvian Highlands at 4475m, the inhabitants obtained arrowroot, a root vegetable which grows only to about 1000m in tropical forest. It came, most probably, from the Amazonian forest some 300km to the east.[2]

However, with one exception, everything Ötzi had carried on his last journey could have been found in the near vicinity of his home. His flints (two arrowheads, dagger point and little flints from the pouch) were the exception that must have come from outside *Ötziland*.

The animals, fungi, lichens, mosses, vascular plants (ferns, conifers and flowering plants) and rocks and minerals, discussed in this and later chapters, all have great significance for the understanding of the lifestyles of Ötzi and Kwäday Dän Ts'inchí Man. It is possible to deduce with a greater or lesser degree of certainty the location of homelands, details of last journeys, season of deaths, diets, uses of different woods for equipment and fuel, uses of fungi and lichens for tinder and medicine. To do all that as thoroughly as possible, leading to the fullest understanding, a prerequisite is detailed knowledge of the present and past occurrences of all these different organisms in relation to climate, altitude, soils, human activities and other factors.

The ways in which people now living close to nature exploit plants, fungi, animals and rocks and minerals may aid our understanding of the prehistoric uses. The survival of prehistoric people was ensured by a very intimate knowledge of their surroundings. Few Europeans now live close to nature but the indigenous peoples of North America did so until very recent times and the practices and substantial memories remain. Many North American plants, fungi and also animals are akin to those of Europe and so it is appropriate to make use, if cautiously, of the comparisons. In the case of plants, the multitude of uses by the Native Americans has been compiled in the large tome by Daniel Moerman (also online). The uses by the First Nations of Canada have been written about engagingly by Nancy Turner of the University of Victoria in various colourful books. There are also numerous publications by native peoples themselves, of which only a very few are listed here.[3]

There has been a great flourishing of archaeobotanical work all over Europe in recent decades that demonstrates, for instance, clearly that almost all the trees, tall shrubs and non-woody plants discussed here have had importance, often great importance, to prehistoric and historic people. No matter if it is the French Palaeolithic, the Scottish Mesolithic, the Tyrolean Neolithic, the Scandinavian Bronze Age or medieval times in the Czech Republic, woody plants have been economically indispensable in many ways, just as they are today. The different woody plants found with Ötzi have been identified by their anatomy by the Swiss Werner Schoch.[4] As pointed out first by Konrad Spindler, using information from the Innsbruck botanists and Werner Schoch, Ötzi made use of a great many trees and shrubs.

The late Neolithic lake village at Arbon Bleiche 3, in Switzerland, near the eastern extremity of Lake Constance (Bodensee), was occupied at just the time that Ötzi lived. Highly detailed and varied science has been applied successfully to the organically rich layers, including archaeobotany and archaeozoology relevant to Ötzi.[5] Almost all the plants and animals connected with Ötzi were found at Arbon Bleiche 3 with the noteworthy exception hop hornbeam; that place lay beyond the natural range of this small tree. I have quoted freely from the large volume of results produced by Professor Stefanie Jacomet of the University of Basel and her numerous collaborators. What is badly needed is a similarly rich, waterlogged settlement site excavated from somewhere nearby to the south of Schnalstal; sadly, such a site is unlikely ever to be found.

Until 2008, none of the publications dealing with which animals had been used to make clothing for Ötzi had mentioned sheep. Deer, chamois, goat, calf and brown bear had all been claimed but now Klaus Hollemeyer of Saarland University and three others state that sheepskin had been used for his jacket/coat and leggings.[6]

PLANTS AND ANIMALS FOR CLOTHING

Grasses: Cape and Shoes

Just as elsewhere in Europe, grasses, large and small and in a diversity of habitats, grow in *Ötziland* and Ötzi exploited several of them for his clothing. Peter Acs, working under Klaus Oeggl, has identified the numerous pieces of stems and leaves found with Ötzi and recovered from the sediments around him. To a large extent, this was careful microscope work on the different patterns that the cells of the epidermis show.[7] With only such material to go on it can be very difficult to identify grasses with certainty but at least seven different grasses were found. The species recognised the most often were tor grass, purple moor grass and mat grass, all three of which are common today in *Ötziland* and there is no sound reason to think that they would not have been at Ötzi's time too.

The vertical bundles of Ötzi's cape were made of tor grass, which can grow over 1m in height, and the bundles were held together by lime tree bast. Tor grass has never been recorded in Schnalstal by botanists and so if that were the case 5000 or so years ago, the cape may well have been made somewhere outside that valley.

Only one sample of the insulating plant material in the shoes was made available to Klaus Oeggl for study. It came from the left shoe and proved to be composed entirely of several types of grass and a sedge. Among the grasses were tor grass, a bent grass (or related grass), mat grass and three types of fescues and related grasses. This insulation could have been gathered from upper Ötztal or Schnalstal, probably at no higher than 2500m in sub-alpine grass lawns, say Peter Acs *et al.*[8]

Mosses: Shoes

No matter how much mosses might seem suitable for insulating the shoes no mosses were found in Ötzi's shoes; none of the iceman books nor any of my articles on the mosses mention a moss or mosses in the shoes. However, some people think mosses had been used. The author of an elementary text on mosses, Robin Kimmerer, citing my work, even goes so far as to specify flat neckera and she compounds the mistake by making a further misleading statement about the importance of that moss in the iceman studies. Gail Vines of the *New Scientist* states that the 'boots' were packed not just with one moss but with 'mosses'. In an engaging article in the *New Yorker*, Burkhard Bilger writes about Professors Petr Hlavacek and Vaclav Gresak of the Czech Republic reconstructing the shoes and using hay and moss.[9] (See Figs 3.1 and 3.2.)

In the hope (probably vain) of no more such misleading statements getting into print, I repeat that there were no mosses, not even the merest scrap of a moss, in Ötzi's shoes. Thankfully, there is no

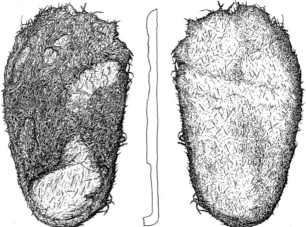

Fig. 3.1 Glittering wood moss in woodland near Bergün. Switzerland.

Fig. 3.2 Insole of crisp neckera from Zug.

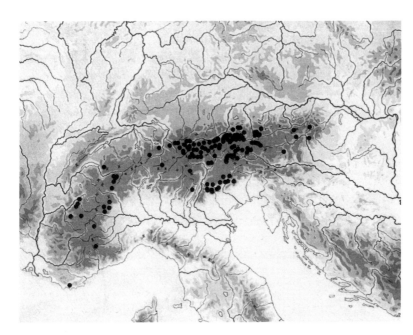

Fig. 3.3 Copper deposits in the Alps. (*Endrizzi and Marsatio, 1997*)

mention of mosses in the Canadian national newspaper *Globe and Mail* for 5 July 2005, in which there is a report that Professor Hlavacek says that his replicas 'are very comfortable' and that they beat modern footwear in many respects other than keeping out water; that, I would think, is surely a bad defect.

It is worth stating that no mosses were in the recently discovered Armenian shoe slightly older than the iceman's shoes. However, at least one Neolithic shoe had a moss insole. The site is at Zug, Switzerland, and the period is the same as that of Ötzi. It has to be emphasised that no actual shoe was found but a foot-shaped pad of the moss crisp neckera was recovered, with what looks very like the impression of a heel and big toe. Comparison was made with Ötzi's shoes.[10] (See Fig. 3.2).

Lime Trees: Cape and Dagger Sheath
Widespread in Europe as a whole, the two limes that are native in *Ötziland* are small-leaved and large-leaved lime. Common at lower altitudes in southern *Ötziland*, the former grows in lower Schnalstal as far up as Neurateis, but not the latter, which seems to be much the scarcer in the general vicinity. Both can grow into large trees which flower in early/mid-summer, producing an abundance of nectar. Bees make the nectar into honey, a prized food for many thousands of years, all the more so before the advent of cane sugar. The flowers are made into a tisane in Central Europe and from Denmark, as well as Scotland and from other places in prehistory, there is Lime pollen evidence from containers used in making alcoholic drinks. See section on drink in Chapter 4.

The inner bark, called bast, is very fibrous and those fibres can be readily extracted. However, the two species cannot be separated by the anatomy of the bast fibres alone. Fritz Schweingruber reports that on many Neolithic and Bronze Age sites in Central Europe the high percentages of lime bark are the debris from extraction of the bast fibres. Such remains have been noted as especially common in Switzerland and Czech Republic. Archaeological objects made of lime wood or bast include sculpture, shields and scabbards, thread and cordage, fishing nets, plough parts, boatbuilding, spindles, coffins, mummy portraits and toys.

The vertically arranged bundles of tor grass, composing Ötzi's cape, were tied together by lime bast, as identified microscopically by Klaus Pfeifer and Klaus Oeggl. They stated (*Innsbruck* 4, p. 71): 'For his binding materials, the Iceman used the best raw material available in his environment. In the Neolithic – and presumably in the Palaeolithic too – the bast of the lime was the material of choice for binding materials in Central Europe.' All the many other plant fibres associated with Ötzi that they studied proved to be lime. So the limes are highly useful trees in various ways and have been exploited for a very long time across Europe.

The natives of the Pacific North-west Coast of North America had no access to lime trees but they had the even better bark of yellow cedar and red cedar, which was made into capes and other clothing. The Ainu of Hokkaido, the northern island of Japan, also had bark clothing made of ohyo, a species of elm, and, in more recent times, of shinanoki, a kind of lime.[11]

Brown Bear: Hat and Shoes
On his head Ötzi had had a stitched cap of brown bear fur with leather straps and, at the opposite end of his person, the soles of his shoes were brown bear skin. This is the same species as the famous grizzly bear of North America. Formerly widespread in Europe and presumably common at Ötzi's time, the brown bear is now much reduced, being, for instance, long extinct in Britain (for at least 1000 years).[12] There are scarcely any left in the Spanish Cantabrian Mountains and the Pyrenees, though bears from Slovenia have been introduced on the French side. There are fewer than 3000 in the eastern Alps, Italy and the Balkans, as stated on the web by the conservationist William Alex Wall. There had been none in *Ötziland* for a long time but in 2005 two have appeared near the south-western fringes of *Ötziland* where, perhaps not surprisingly, it is claimed, they have been enjoying the sheep.[13] In 2006 a bear, thought to have wandered north from Slovenia, appeared in southern Bavaria but, sadly, was shot after failed attempts to capture it. Bears have been of interest to humans long before Ötzi as the Palaeolithic cave art from France abundantly demonstrates. An outstanding example are the representations at Chauvet Cave, Ardèche, where there are the 'World's Oldest Paintings'.[14]

Goat and Sheep: Jacket/Coat, Leggings, Loincloth and Shoes
There is direct connection between goats and Ötzi because much of his clothing is made of goatskin. The uppers of his shoes were of goatskin, as were the leggings and jacket/coat. Descended from the bezoar of south-west Asia, the goat, a browser rather than a grazer, was domesticated more than 9000 years ago and had been taken across Europe before Ötzi's time. In *Ötziland* today, small herds of goats are to be seen here and there in the hills.

According to Michael Ryder, there are four kinds of wild sheep, the bighorn of North America, the argali of central Asia, the urial of south-west Asia and the mouflon, also of south-west Asia.[15] The husbanded sheep, a grazer rather than a browser, was domesticated from the urial in south-west Asia at least 9000 years ago, and, like goats, were being taken through Europe before Ötzi's time.[16] In the early days of domestication, sheep were kept for mutton or milk, not wool.

Deer: Shoes and Suspenders

Ötzi's leggings were held up by suspenders tied to the belt. Deerskin strips were used to tie the leggings to the shoes. The uppers of the shoes were made of deerskin. The two kinds of deer in *Ötziland* are the red and the roe, both of which are widespread in Europe. Red deer are gregarious and both graze and browse in woodlands which are the preferred habitat. The stags can weigh up to nearly 300kg, with a height at the shoulder of 1.2m and impressive antlers, being large and branched.

Since ancient times humankind has been interested in red deer. Franco Rollo *et al.* state:

> The strict connection between Neolithic man and red deer is witnessed by the wealth of artistic representation of this animal among archaeological finds in the central and eastern Alps; the polished and carved stones of the Val Camonica, in particular, evidence how the red deer was central to the interests of the prehistoric populations along the Alpine arc.[17]

Just how very important red deer were in the diet of Neolithic peoples of the Alpine region has been made very clear by the detailed studies of bone remains by Jörg Schibler and Stefanie Jacomet; during periods of poor climate, unhelpful for growing cereals, hunting of deer was more intense. That the excellence of the venison was appreciated long before the Neolithic is made clear by red deer bones being 75 per cent of all the approximately 20,000 bones recovered from La Grotte du Lazaret, near Nice, France. This was a cave inhabited by Acheulians, some 160,000 years ago.[18]

Roe Deer

Roe deer is much smaller than red deer, the largest stags being little more than 65 to 75cm at the shoulder and 15 to 30kg in weight. They occur as small family parties and rest up in dense shrubbery. The meat makes very good eating.

PLANTS, ANIMALS AND ROCKS FOR EQUIPMENT

In the hollow where Ötzi's body was found were an axe, a longbow, a quiver with arrows, two containers made of bark, a backpack and fragments of a bast net. He had worn a belted skin pouch with a variety of small contents. He had carried a dagger with a bast sheath, a retouching tool, a pierced disk of white dolomite through which had been threaded a hide strip to which a further nine strips had been tied. The disk could have been attached to the belted pouch, as could the dagger and the retouching tool.

Ash Tree: Dagger

The crudely crafted handle of Ötzi's dagger was made of ash. There are two species of ash trees that could have been exploited in *Ötziland*: ash and manna ash. The former is very widespread in Europe, where it favours alkaline soils, but the latter is from the south, not reaching very far north. In *Ötziland* they grow on warm, moist slopes to an altitude of 1200m or 1300m.

As the wood of ash does not splinter readily it is good for making handles for tools such as hammers. The wood of ash is well known from the Mesolithic, Neolithic and Bronze Age sites. Rowena Gale and David Cutler, scientists at the Royal Botanic Garden, Kew, list the wood as having been used for hurdles, mouldings, statuary, boxes, bowls, toggles, shoes, bungs, spoons, caskets, furniture, fuel, tools, ladder bungs, barrel bindings, paddles, wheels, boat building, arrows and spears. Eight twigs of ash were recovered from Arbon Bleiche 3.

At Karthaus in Schnalstal, not far from the Ötzi site, pollarded ash trees can still be seen immediately to the north of the village. Pollarding (cutting the top off) and shredding (severe cutting off of boughs) makes the trees sprout numerous new leafy shoots. After a few years, these are then gathered in late summer, dried and kept for winter fodder for stalled animals. This is an ancient practice at least 6000 years old in the Alps.[19] In 2005 in mid Schnalstal at Saxalbhof, a farm inaccessible by road, the aged farmer still had a few ash trees that he had pollarded in the last few years. So this venerable custom has lasted into the twenty-first century but surely it will die out in Schnalstal very soon because modern irrigation allows two grass hay crops each summer and consequently tree leaf fodder is not needed. Ötzi may well have been familiar with such pollarded and shredded trees.

Birch: Containers and Glue

Being white and with dark, horizontally elongate lenticels (breathing pores), the two bark containers were very obviously made of birch, as can be seen in numerous photographs and at the Iceman Museum. The bark is most easily detached from birch if cut logs have been allowed to dry out.

The glue for Ötzi's axe and arrowheads was a pitch prepared by heating a tar obtained by pyrolysis (distillation) of birch bark. This was very convincingly shown by Fritz Sauter and colleagues of Vienna University of Technology who isolated the characteristic terpene fraction, betulin, in large quantities. They had compared the bark of birch with that of alder, hazel and hornbeam, all members of the birch family, Betulaceae. This use of birch bark to make glue has an ancient history from the Middle Palaeolithic to the Iron Age and even to the present.[20]

As it happens, the birch which I have seen in Ötziland has all been silver birch, not downy birch, which is the other tree birch widely spread in Europe; the former goes further south (to Sicily). Recording by Thomas Wilhalm of the South Tyrol Natural History Museum and others clearly shows that silver birch is much the commoner of the two. In Ötziland, neither silver birch nor downy birch is a major woodland-forming tree. Silver birch is a pioneer of ground opened by avalanches or rock falls, as in Pfossental, a side valley of Schnalstal, and elsewhere.

The two species cannot be separated on the basis of their wood anatomy. Wood of birch has been found rarely in late Palaeolithic, Mesolithic, Neolithic and Bronze Age sites. This wood was practically never used in Switzerland during the Neolithic and Bronze Age, according to Fritz Schweingruber, but he says that the bark was rolled to make candles and extracts of bark were used as glue. Rolls of bark have been found in England as early as the Mesolithic period at the famous site at Starr Carr, Yorkshire. On the 2005 expedition to the site of Kwäday Dän Ts'inchí Man, Bill Hanlon found a small roll of birch bark under a rock, a long way from any birch trees (see Chapter 7).

For tree birches, I wrote in *Plants and People in Ancient Scotland*: 'The wood can be made into household utensils, the bark into containers and into glue …There are records of the bark being eaten in Kamchatka and Fennoscandia and infusions of leaves have been made in Europe …' Additionally, birch has been made into paddles, weapons, cult figures, bowls, roofing, ovens, hearths, boats, clothing and writing material. There have been two discoveries of birch bark made into hats in Iron Age Europe: in the rich burial of the prince at Hochdorf in south-western Germany and at Mardié, Loiret, south of Paris. The native peoples of North America made much use of birches, especially paper birch, the bark of which was made into baskets and even into beautifully crafted canoes.[21] And not just there, because the Oroquen of Inner Mongolia make birch bark boxes for keeping sacred objects and other more utilitarian things such as barrels for boiling meat. The Nanais in far eastern Siberia make lures made of birch bark, household articles and boats as well as peaked hats and aprons. Now, a quiver, from perhaps as much as about 4800 years ago, can be added to this long list; it was recently recovered from the disappearing lobe of the Chilchli glacier at Schnidejoch, as mentioned in Chapter 6.

Lime Tree: Net and Retouching Tool

The handle of Ötzi's retoucher is roughly carved lime wood. Why he chose this particular wood is not clear. Perhaps he just happened to have a suitably sized piece handy. Konrad Spindler says that the net was made of grass (*Spindler* 1, p. 118). However, not just the horizontal binding of the cape, but all the many other plant fibres associated with Ötzi studied by Klaus Pfeifer and Klaus Oeggl proved to be lime bast (*Innsbruck* 4). Angelika Fleckinger follows Konrad Spindler in stating that the net was 'probably used for catching birds' but then she goes on to discuss rabbits. She shows a hunting scene from a bronze receptacle of the Late Iron Age from near Bologna, Italy. Certainly, it depicts a club-wielding hunter and two mammals that are clearly lagomorphs (the group that includes rabbits and hares). However, they could easily be meant to be hares. Rabbits are native to Spain and southern France and did not spread through Europe until after the Neolithic.

Wayfaring Tree: Arrow Shafts

This tall shrub, a member of the genus *Viburnum*, has a southerly distribution in Europe as a whole and a preference for limy soil.[22] In Schnalstal, where the soils are not limy, it grows at Altrateis (at 844m) and there are a few bushes at the roadside just below Karthaus at about 1100m, but perhaps it has been planted there. It is common in southern *Ötziland*. The wood has more uses than I listed in *Plants and People in Ancient Scotland*. According to Geoffrey Grigson, the name twistwood came from twisting into whip handles.[23] Glue can be made from the bark of the roots. I had not realised that arrow wood is a common name for *V. dentatum* of eastern North America, though I did mention *V. edule* probably not being used by the First Nations of the Pacific Northwest for arrow shafts because of unsuitable growth. However, the Native Americans of North Carolina used *V. dentatum* for shafts in the early eighteenth century, as recorded by John Lawson , Surveyor General of that region.[24]

In their clean straightness, hardness and inflexibility, the 1 or 2-year-old shoots of both wayfaring tree and the guelder rose, which is another *Viburnum*, are highly suitable for quickly turning into arrow shafts and have been used as such by Mesolithic Danes, prehistoric Scots and Iron Age Germans. Now we have three arrow shafts of *Viburnum* from Switzerland; they were found at the melting lobe of the Chilchli glacier at Schnidejoch and two come from the late Neolithic, a few centuries after the time of Ötzi, and one from the early Bronze Age (see Chapter 6). In view of this growing indication for the ancient use of *Viburnum* for arrow shafts and the very great suitability of the straight shoots for that purpose, one may well wonder if it was ever deliberately coppiced. Seemingly there is no evidence of such. The first book in English about toxophily (love of archery), written in the sixteenth century, lists no less than 15 types of wood suitable for shafts but *Viburnum* is not one of them.[25] Fritz Schweingruber mentioned that the thin branches were made into combs and that twigs are recovered occasionally from Neolithic sediments. At Arbon Bleiche *Viburnum* wood was rarely found.

Cornelian Cherry/Dogwood: Composite Arrow Shaft

One of Ötzi's arrow shafts was partly made of *Cornus* wood. Cornelian cherry (*Cornus mas*) grows to 1200m in *Ötziland*, where it is southern and central, in dry woods and woodland edges, but it does not inhabit Schnalstal. This tall shrub is native in southern and Central Europe. The dogwood from *Ötziland* is *Cornus sanguinea* which is common at low altitudes. These two species are difficult to separate on wood anatomy and so we do not know which the arrow maker had used. Some twigs of *Cornus* are known from Neolithic sediments in Switzerland. Cornelian cherry fleshy fruits are edible and fruit stones were found at Neolithic Arbon Bleiche 3. Remains of cornelian cherry have been found many times in European sites, especially in Italy, but not in Britain or northern Europe, where it is not native. The very small flowers of cornelian cherry appear very early in the year and seldom if ever develop into fruits in Britain and never in my garden near Glasgow. Dogwood fish traps and barbs have been recognised from the Mesolithic and Neolithic of Denmark, a lance from Neolithic France and dogwood fruit stones have been found at two Danish Mesolithic sites.[26] There were 11 twigs excavated at Arbon Bleiche 3. Archaeological remains have been recovered many times especially in France and Switzerland.

Nettle: Fibres for Binding

There are only two types of nettle that grow in *Ötziland*: the perennial stinging nettle and the annual small nettle. Stinging nettle can grow in large patches that flourish where the soil has been enriched in phosphate and nitrate. This happens where human excretory waste and that of domestic and wild mammals and birds has landed and so stinging nettles are very common around settlements and farms. Stinging nettle has long, strong fibres around the stems under the epidermis and these can be extracted to make very strong string, cords and even ropes. The aboriginal peoples of Pacific Northwest coast of North America exploited the stinging nettle for its fibres. According to Hilary Stewart, many different styles of fishing nets were made of the fibres. In a process, involving much time and skill, the nettles were 'cut, split, dried, peeled, beaten, shredded and spun into a fine two-strand twine of exceptional strength'. They even used nettles to make tumplines, which are straps to put round the forehead or chest to assist with carrying heavy loads on the back.[27] 'In fact, the word *net* is derived from *nettle*.'

Prehistoric people throughout the greater part of Europe would have had no difficulty finding stinging nettles. A Neolithic arrowhead from Somerset was bound to the shaft with nettle fibres and a hoard of Bronze Age axes were secured with such fibres; there are also prehistoric Danish textiles. That the feathers on two of Ötzi's arrows had been bound on with stinging nettle fibres has been claimed by Angelica Fleckinger. I know of no publication where this has been microscopically proven and certainly the Innsbruck botanists have not been involved. So, however plausible it may be, it remains an assertion, in the eyes of the archaeobotanist, not a fact.

Hazel: Quiver Stiffener and Backpack

Ötzi had a quiver stiffener, already broken when found, specially crafted from hazel. The U-piece for his backpack was also hazel. There are stands of hazel in Schnalstal, as at Altrateis (884m) and from Neurateis to Karthaus there are very large stands on the lower slopes to about 1300m, closest to the iceman site. This tall shrub, widespread in Europe from northern Norway to Sicily, has been of varied use to modern, historic and prehistoric people because of the nutritious and tasty nuts and the straight poles, produced by coppicing. According to Fritz Schweingruber relatively few pieces of charcoal have been found from the Mesolithic but remains are more frequent from the Neolithic and Bronze Age, particularly of twigs. It had been rarely used for posts and tools.

For its English history, Oliver Rackham of the University of Cambridge, states:

> From Neolithic times onwards it has been the normal tree for wattle-work – hurdles, wattle-and-daub, woven fences, thatching wood. Its specific advantage is that it can be twisted to separate the fibres and then bent at a sharp angle without breaking: thatching broaches and the rods at the ends of hurdles need to be bent through 180°, and faggot ends are tied in knots.[28]

This great usefulness has applied to vast areas of Europe far back into prehistory, certainly to the Mesolithic if not even earlier. Bowls, ropes, fuel, tools, caulking rope, fish spears and traps, long bows and arrows have all been made from hazel.

European Larch: Backpack

Having been split from a massive trunk according to Klaus Oeggl, the two thin cross boards of Ötzi's pack frame were made of larch. A third board was found during the 1992 excavation. Wood of this tall conifer would have been readily available to Ötzi and his tribe. Larch wood has seldom been recovered from archaeological sites.

Yew: Longbow and Axe Handle

Archaeological objects of Yew, in whole or in part, include sculpture, knives, pins, coffins, tankard and bucket staves, writing tablets, bungs, spatulas, spoons, bowls, withies and ropes, tool handles, mallets, boats, boat stitching, anchors, treenails, spears, clubs, arrows and bows. From the mainland of Orkney there is even a sword made of Yew. As I stated in *Plants and People in Ancient Scotland*, Yew has been written about over and over again because of its great longevity, its association with churchyards, its connections with folklore, myths and superstitions and its use in making bows, both long and short. It is widespread in Europe and North Africa and often grows on shallow, limy soils; P.A. Thomas and A. Polwart have given a detailed account of the ecology of this rather low-growing tree.[29] Thomas Wilhalm of the South Tyrolean Natural History Museum thinks that the northernmost stand in Südtirol is at Passeiertal, where it may be relict in a natural habitat. It is often planted and the seeds are dispersed by birds and consequently new trees grow up as escapes from cultivation. I have never noticed it in Schnalstal as such an escape, far less as a native. Nor have I seen it in Vinschgau.

Konrad Spindler states (*Spindler* 1, p.87): 'As late as the sixteenth and seventeenth centuries major quantities of yew bows were exported from Tyrol to England for the English army – which is why yew has become a rarity in the Tyrol and is now protected.' According to Brenda Fowler, Klaus Oeggl and his associates searched for yews in Vinschgau and wrote, 'During the Middle Ages, the yew had been harvested far and wide, and they had been largely depleted'. But it had 'recolonised the valley bottom of Vinschgau' since then. This latter statement is not correct. Klaus Oeggl found it not in Vinschgau but in the Etsch valley to the south-east, at places such as Andrian and Tisens.

European prehistoric people were entirely familiar with the excellent properties of the wood, hard, fine-grained and springy, for the making of bows especially, but also handles, as in Neolithic Somerset and the Neolithic Netherlands. The anatomically very distinctive wood and charcoal have been recorded many times from archaeological sites from many periods and places. From a site, Horgen Scheller, in north-eastern Switzerland, not too far from *Ötziland*, and from a period close to that of Ötzi, were hundreds of branches, a quarter of which were yew; the interpretation was that the inhabitants specialised in obtaining yew and that they had traded the timbers. Of the horizontal timbers 5 per cent were yew. The smaller leafy branches could have been used for bedding, insulation or even winter fodder. Wooden tools from the same site numbered 43, of which 8 were of yew.[30] There is a claim that the Celtic peoples planted yew trees extensively. Attractive and even plausible as this idea may be, how one could ever be sure is difficult to know.[31]

The qualities of the wood which make yew so suitable for longbows are the high tensile strength of the sapwood and the resistance of the heartwood to compression. Most historic and prehistoric bows in Europe were made of yew, as I know very well having helped my late wife in the early 1960s to confirm by microscopy that the two Neolithic longbows from Somerset were made of that tree. But yew was certainly not the only tree used for bows in prehistoric times, as claimed very surprisingly by Konrad Spindler in the English editions of his book. For instance, there are Mesolithic bows made of elm from Denmark. However, the fault lies with the translator or perhaps the printer or proofreader because a crucial omission was the word 'fast', which is German for 'almost'. What Konrad Spindler had written was that *almost* all prehistoric bows were made of yew.

In modern times and probably since the medieval period if not before, the making of a longbow was a complex matter involving long seasoned wood and skilled craftsmanship, certainly not undertaken in any rough and ready way. Just how far back does the complexity go? Ötzi's longbow had been carved from a trunk or bough of at least 9cm in diameter and consists entirely of very dense heartwood with about 16 annual rings per centimetre (Walter Oberhuber and R. Knapp, *Innsbruck* 4, p. 63). This is a very different approach to bow making to that by Harm Paulsen, a German experimental archaeologist. Konrad Spindler stated that 'With a replica of the Iceman's copper axe, it would be possible to chop down a yew tree with a diameter of about 20cm in just under 45 minutes'. According to

Jürgen Junkmanns of the Museum Schwab in Switzerland in his thorough little book *Bow and Arrow*, it took Harm Paulsen only 5 hours and 20 minutes to make a bow like Ötzi's using only appropriate Neolithic tools.[32]

Ötzi's bow is certainly not the only one to have melted out of a Central European glacier. In the 1930s and 1940s, no less then three bows of yew have been recovered from a glacier at the Lötschenpass in southern Switzerland. Much more recently a bow was found melted out of the now almost vanished glacier lobe at Schnidejoch, also in southern Switzerland. Switzerland is something of a treasure house of Neolithic bows. Mostly coming from lake-shore settlements, no less than about 70 have been listed by Jürgen Junkmanns.

Arolla Pine
A small piece of arolla pine was found in the washings from his fur cap. Why it is there and what use Ötzi may have had in mind, if any, will remain obscure matters. This handsome pine is prominent here and there at the upper edges of the forests in *Ötziland* and elsewhere in the Alps.

Field Horsetail: Smoothing the Bow
Angelika Fleckinger states in her little book that 'The finished bow would have been rubbed down and polished using field horsetail –a poisonous herb – to achieve a smooth surface'. This is conjecture because, as far as I am aware, there are no traces of the silica-rich plant on the bow surface to prove the point. Has anyone looked? In any case, Dutch rush, which despite the name is another horsetail, would have been better for such a purpose.

Mosses: Wrapping
The flat neckera that Ötzi had carried was probably wrapping for provisions, or so I have published as a plausible explanation. Whatever may have been the intended purpose (or purposes) of the low to moderate altitude mosses Ötzi had carried is, however, unclear and it hard to see how it will ever be known for sure.

Birds: Fletching
The feathers of the two finished arrow shafts have not been closely identified. Konrad Spindler listed the following birds as possibly having been used: Alpine chough, Cornish chough, black woodpecker, golden eagle, common raven and three types of vulture (black, Egyptian and griffon), mountain cock and hermit ibis. That bird species can be identified from fragments of feathers is clearly shown by the work of the well-named Carla Dove *et al.* They list northern flicker, white-tailed ptarmigan, gyrfalcon and short-eared owl, as well as the less precise eagle and duck.[33] These fragments had come from the ancient and now disappearing ice patches in the southern Yukon (see Chapter 7).

Chamois: Quiver
The quiver that held the 14 arrows had been elaborately constructed and showed damage, which gave Konrad Spindler much food for thought. It was made of the hide probably of chamois, which is a common, goat-sized, antelope-like animal of mountainous areas: Alps, Vosges, Jura, Carpathians, Apennines and Asia Minor. In the Pyrenees and mountains

of Cantabria there is the closely related isard. The meat makes good eating and has been consumed by humankind for many thousands of years as bones at Lazeret and drawings at Cosquer Cave show.

Deer: Antler Pieces
Inside the quiver were four antler tips bound by Lime bast and also a separate slightly curved tip.

Copper: Axe Head
The map of copper deposits shows many sources of ores scattered throughout the Alps from the Alpes Maritmes, France, in the west as far as the Styrian Alps, Austria, in the east.[34] There is a dense concentration of copper ores in and around *Ötziland* and so, had Ötzi collected and smelted ores himself, he would, perhaps, not have had to go too far to get the raw material. Praising the skill of the maker of the axe head, Konrad Spindler thought the source of the ore to be 'probably local' (*Spindler* 1, p. 90). However, considering the absence of antimony in the axe head to be important, Gerhard Sperl thought that the source of the ore was the area near Trento, south of *Ötziland*.[35] (See Fig. 3.4.)

Dolomite: Disk with Tassel
Named after a French eighteenth-century geologist, Déodat Gratet de Dolomieu, dolomite is a kind of altered, hardened limestone, composed of the carbonates of both calcium and magnesium.

FIRE-MAKING WITH FUNGI, PLANTS AND ROCKS

Cattle: Belted Pouch
The pouch contained Ötzi's fire-making kit. Inside were tinder, tiny traces of pyrites and little flints as well as an awl made of bone. The identification of the skin as that of calf was made by the Dutch archaeologist Willy Groenman-van Waateringe. The calf skin could be that of either that of aurochs or European domestic cattle.

Cattle are descended from the aurochs and had been domesticated by the Neolithic period.[36] That cattle were of interest to late Neolithic people across very wide areas is well shown by numerous bones at the famous stone-built Neolithic village at Skara Brae in the Orkney Islands and the low-relief sculptures on the large stones of the Neolithic temple at Tarxien on the Mediterranean island of Malta. Furthermore, there are three engraved representations of aurochs from an Upper Paleolithic rock shelter (around 18,750 years ago) in Calabria, Italy.[37]

Fungi
Unlike pollen grains and the spores of ferns, the spores of fungi, though often found, are seldom recognised with useful precision in archaeological contexts. For the most part, being soft and quickly decaying, the large bodies of fungi are seldom found in archaeological contexts with the striking exception of some bracket fungi, which can be hard and therefore durable.

3.4 Pieces of true tinder fungus from the belted pouch. (*Markus Egg*)

The discovery of bracket fungi in prehistoric contexts has a long history, going back to the first investigations of the Swiss lake villages in the mid-nineteenth century. Later, in 1882, the Regius Professor of Botany in the University of Glasgow recognised two bracket fungi from a crannog (prehistoric lake dwelling) in Ayrshire, south-west Scotland. They were oak daedalea and false tinder fungus.[38]

Ötzi's intimacy with the environment is very well illustrated by his tinder kit. As well as pyrites and flints for making sparks, the pouch contained the true tinder fungus. The 'black matter', which filled the major part of the pouch, was found to be this fungus, which had been pounded to make a material of wad-like consistency. There were traces of pyrites in the wad (*Innsbruck* 4). When sparks set such tinder alight what happens is that it glows and continues to do so slowly. Aboriginal groups in North America used the inner tissue of bracket fungi as 'slow matches' (see Fig. 3.4).

The use of the true tinder fungus for fire-making may well have a very ancient history, long before the Neolithic, as the discovery of that species at the famous Mesolithic site at Starr Carr, Yorkshire, shows. It was identified by the Cambridge botanist John Corner, who thought that the abundance at the site was significant, meaning that it had probably been used as tinder. He stated: 'In the British Isles *F. fomentarius* occurs mainly, if not entirely, on living birch in Scotland, where it is often very common.'[39] The same preference for birch is found in North America. Nevertheless, this long-lasting bracket fungus grows on a variety of trees. It has a great geographical spread in Europe, which may very well be a distribution of long standing and so this economically valuable fungus would have been widely and readily available to prehistoric people.

Pounded to soften it or shaved into thin pieces to receive the sparks, it readily glows. Based on the work of Norbert Nieszery, Konrad Spindler gives an extended account of how to use the true tinder fungus (*Spindler* 2). Norbert Nieszery recommends that flames be produced with the use of reedmace 'wool', hammered willow bark, mosses, down feathers, thistledown, reedmace or juniper pith, dry grass and small twigs. Despite Nieszery's statement, it is improbable that Ötzi used mosses for tinder. If he had tried he would have found that mosses simply do not work well for that purpose. What happens is that a spark applied to moss such as flat neckera quickly produces flames which immediately go out, leaving only the briefest glow. Ötzi would better have used dry grass as kindling. The two French archaeologists, Bertrand Roussel and Paul Boutié, in their 2006 book, *La Grande Aventure du Feu*, recommended the hairy seeds of poplar and reedmace, as well as three bracket fungi. In 2002, Bertrand Roussel and three others published a detailed account of the many uses of the true tinder fungus, which the French call *amadou*.[40]

The true tinder fungus has medical uses discussed in Chapter 4, but it is convincingly part of Ötzi's fire-making kit. Before leaving this account of fungi and fire-making it should be mentioned that birch bracket fungus can be used as tinder; Reinhold Pöder *et al.* were aware of this but they say (*Innsbruck* 4, p. 147): 'This polypore has never been reported to be a useful tinder material.'

Flint

Ötzi's flints had been obtained from the Monti Lessini, about 20km east of Lake Garda, which lies some 150km to the south of *Ötziland*. This is by far the furthest distance that any of Ötzi's resources need have come from and that distance is no great surprise. Brenda Fowler has recounted at length how the source of Ötzi's flint was found and how the behaviour of the people involved spoiled what could have been fruitful co-operation between the Austrians, Germans and Italians. There is no scientific publication in English but the German Alexander Binsteiner published two papers in 1995.[41] He also thought that the precise place was Ceredo in the Monti Lessini but it might be wondered if Monte Baldo further to the west was also possible as the source.

Throughout human prehistory and history, flints, with their edges of great sharpness, have been of enormous importance; a usefulness, which, even today in our highly advanced technological world, has not entirely vanished. A form of quartz, flint is found as large nodules in layers in calcareous (limy) rock, chalk and limestone. The nodules can be worked into implements, large and small, used for a variety of cutting purposes. Such was the importance of flint to prehistoric people that they did not just rely on what they could gather lying exposed on the ground or sticking out of outcrops, but they mined it. They dug circular shafts up to 9m deep with radiating galleries, nowhere better seen than at Grimes Graves near Brandon in East Anglia; these particular mines are of later Neolithic and early Bronze Age.[42]

Pyrites: Sparks

There were tiny pieces of pyrites in Ötzi's belted pouch. When yellow in colour it is sometimes called fool's gold, because incompetent prospectors mistook it for the precious metal. This mineral can be a sulphide of iron, copper, arsenic and other elements. The mineral called marcasite is copper pyrites, which is the commonest copper ore and Ötzi would have encountered it frequently had he been seeking copper ore for smelting into axe heads. When pyrites is struck with a hard stone sparks are produced.

Norway Maple: Keeping Embers Aglow

This tree, which can reach 30m in height, is native over much of Continental Europe, including the Tyrol. However, it does not reach quite into Vinschgau, let alone Schnalstal; it grows no nearer than Marlinger Berg, to the west of Meran. Nor does it inhabit Ötztal. So if

Fig. 3.5 Norway maple leaves, Milngavie, Scotland.

the geographical spread has not changed significantly since Ötzi's lifetime then he plucked the leaves before he entered Schnalstal on his final journey.

Regarded as wrapping having been used to keep embers aglow, the leaves were still green and with the stalks deliberately removed. They were found beside the birch bark Container 1, as discussed by Konrad Spindler; this is a discovery without parallel in European archaeobotany. There appears to be only one other known prehistoric site in Europe where containers may have held embers. This is mentioned by Marcus Egg and Konrad Spindler in their 2009 book:

> Cylindric bark containers turn up frequently in Swiss lakeshore settlements. With their more or less cylindrical shape with a tendency towards an elliptic base area and sewn bottom largely correspond to the specimen from Tisenjoch. They were however not made of birch bark but (as far as recognizable) of lime (Tilia). Of special significance is R. Wyss' observation that bark containers from Egolzwil 5 held charcoal and ashes …

Jean Nicolas Haas has told me that Tibetans are known to carry charcoal embers in little containers on a belt and there are leaves of a kind of maple around the embers.

Fritz Schweingruber states that Norway maple cannot be separated from sycamore on wood anatomy and that acer is relatively abundant in Neolithic and Bronze Age levels, especially as wood chips. 'Maple' wood has been made into many artefacts, including bows and arrows and furniture. There were 28 twigs of maple found at Arbon Bleiche 3 and two buds were field maple (see Fig. 3.4).

Fuel: Charcoal

Charcoal of several woody plants was found with Ötzi. Needles of spruce and juniper were found with the Norway maple leaves.

Elm Trees: Elm charcoal was found with the Norway maple leaves. The elms in *Ötziland* are wych elm and small-leaved elm. The former grows up Schnalstal as far as the gorge below Karthaus and the latter only to lower down the valley. Wood anatomy cannot separate European species of elm. Wood of elms has been made into posts, roof beams, water pipes, piles, brushes, stelae, tools and handles, chariot wheels and bodies, boatbuilding and bows. Thirty Elm twigs and 23 buds were recovered from Arbon Bleiche 3. Just like those of ash, leafy twigs of elm are very palatable to cattle and other large herbivores.

Green Alder: With Ötzi were an isolated wood chip of green alder and charcoal among the maple leaves. There are three species of alder in *Ötziland*: alder, grey alder and green alder. The last named is shrubby, reaching a few metres tall and it grows in the hills where it can form large stands on slopes, often where avalanches are so recurrent as to prevent the growth of larch and spruce.

Snowy Mespilus (Juneberry): The tentatively identified charcoal, found with 'grass and leaf remains' associated with Ötzi, may be the first archaeobotanical record of this plant; no other finds are listed in any of the sources I have consulted. Inhabiting southern and Central Europe, this shrub which can reach about 3m grows on cliffs and banks in hilly areas, especially in open oak and pine woods and it reaches 1700m in Südtirol. I have seen it at 1400m at Tappeiner above Schlanders, but have never noticed it in Schnalstal, apart from in the gorge below Juval.

Willow: Some charcoal fragments of reticulate willow type were found with the maple leaves. As elsewhere in Europe and other parts of the world, there are lots of species of willow in *Ötziland*, at least 30 species, from tall trees to dwarf, creeping shrubs. Even with good living specimens, the identification of one willow from another can be a tricky business because willows hybridise freely. Remains of willows are often found in archaeological contexts but, unsurprisingly, not often precisely identified. Reticulate willow is a very low-growing shrub that favours limy soils high in the mountains, as in the mountain avens heath on outcropping marble at about 2250m at the western end of Pflederertal.

Mountain Pine: Charcoal of a pine (mountain pine type) was found with remains of grasses and cords and with birch bark fragments.

Notes

1   McBrearty, S. and Brooks, S. 2000. 'The revolution that wasn't: a new interpretation of the origin of modern human behaviour'. *Journal of Human Evolution* 39, pp. 453–563. Wong, K. 2006. 'The Morning of the Modern Mind'. *Scientific American Special Edition* 16, pp. 74–83.

2   Perry, L. *et al.* 2006. 'Early maize agriculture and interzonal interaction in southern Peru'. *Nature*, 440, pp. 76–9.

3   Moerman, D. 1998. *Native American Ethnobotany*. Portland, Timber Press. Turner, N.J. 1995. *Food Plants of the Coastal First Peoples*. Vancouver, UBC. Turner, N.J. 1997. *Food Plants of the Interior First Peoples*. Vancouver, UBC Press. Turner, N.J. 1998. *Plant Technology of First Peoples in British Columbia*. Vancouver, UBC Press. Turner, N.J. 2004. *Plants of Haida Gwaii*. Winlaw, Sononis Press.

4   The sources used in listing the archaeobotanical discoveries of plants are: Schweingruber, F.H. 1978. *Microscopic Wood Anatomy*. Zug, Edition Zürcher AG. This book deals mostly with Switzerland. His 1990 book, *Anatomy of European Woods*, Bern, Paul Haupt, is a comprehensive guide to the anatomical identification of the woody plants of Europe. The book by Schoch, W.H., Pawlik, B. and Schweinergruber, F.H. 1988. *Botanical Macro-remains*, Berne, Editions Paul Haupt, again deals mainly with Switzerland and surrounding countries. Oeggl, K. and Schoch, W. 1995. 'Neolithic plant remains discovered together with a mummified corpse (Homo tyrolensis) in the Tyrolean Alps'. In Kroll, H. and Pasternak, R. (ed.) *Res archaeobotanicae*. Kiel, Oetker-Voges-Verlag, pp. 229–38. Oeggl, K. and Schoch, W. 2000. 'Dendrological analyses of artifactsand other remains'. In *Innsbruck* 4, pp. 29–61.

By contrast, the book by Gale, R. and Cutler, D. 2000. *Plants in Archaeology*, Otley, Westbury Publishing, covers the perhaps too enormous an area of all of Europe and the Mediterranean. Helmut Kroll's European Archaeobotanical Database has been very useful: www.archaeobotany.de/. The importance of archaeobotanical studies is cogently summarised by Stefanie Jacomet. 2007. 'The use of plant macrofossils in environmental archaeology'. *Encyclopedia of Quaternary Sciences*. Amsterdam, Elsevere.

5   The tome on the late Neolithic site, contemporaneous with Ötzi at Arbon Bleiche 3 is an outstanding source for comparison of exploitation of plants and animals: Jacomet, S., Leuzinger, U. and Schibler, J. 2004. *Die jungsteinzeitliche Seeufersiedlung Arbon Bleiche 3*. Frauenfeld, Huber & Co.

6   Holleymeyer, K., Altmeyer, W., Heinzle, E. and Pitra, C. 2008. 'Species identification of Oetzi's clothing with matrix-assisted laser desorption/ionization time-of-flight mass spectrometry based on peptide pattern similarities of hair digests'. *Rapid Communications in Mass Spectrometry* 22, pp. 2751–67.

7   Acs, P., Wilhalm, T. and Oeggl, K. 2005. 'Remains of Grasses found with the Neolithic Iceman "Ötzi"'. *Vegetation History and Archaeobotany* 14, pp. 198–206.

8   Ibid.

9   Kimmerer, R. W. 2003. *Gathering Moss. A Natural and Cultural History of Mosses*. Corvallis, Oregon State University Press. Vines, G. 2004. 'Dreaming of a green Christmas?' *New Scientist* 25, December. Bilger, B. 2005. 'Sole Survivor'. *New Yorker*, 14 & 21 February, pp. 152–67.

10   Pinashi, R. *et al.* 2010. 'First Direct Evidence of Chalcolithic Footwear from the Near Eastern Hihghlands'. *PloS ONE* 5, pp. 1–5. Hochuli, S. 2002. 'Teil eines neolithischen Shuhs aus Zug'. *Jahrbuch der Schweizerischen Gesellschaft für Ur- und Frügeschichte* 84, pp. 45–9. Reichert, A. 2002. 'Weich und warm auf Moossohlen. Experimente zur Rheumasole von Zug'. *Jahrbuch der Schweizerischen Gesellschaft für Ur- und Frügeschichte* 85, pp. 50–4. Reichert, A. 2001. 'Keine kalten Füsse in der Steinzeit? – Ein Experiment zur "Rheumassole" von Zug'. *Anzeiger AEAS* 1, pp. 4–5. Malhotra, D. 1998a. 'Zur Rekonstruktion der Fussbekleidung des Mannes vom Tisenjoch'. *Experimentelle Archäologie* 19, pp. 75–88. Malhotra, D. 1998b. 'Zu den Beschädigungen der Schuhe des Mannes vom Tisenjoch'. *Experimentelle Archäologie* 24, pp. 57–67. Malhotra, D. 2003. 'Die Beschädigungen der Schuhe des Mannes suf dem Eis'. *Schriften des Südtiroler Archäologiemuseums* 3, pp. 65–74.

11   Anonymous. 1997. *Les Ainu Aborigienes du Japon*. Besançon, Musee des Beaux-Arts et D'Archeologie.

12   Yalden, D. 1999. *The History of British Mammals*. London, T & A.D. Poyser. Anonymous. 2005. 'Seltener Gast auf leisen Tatzen' (p. 2) and '"Sommerfrischler" fühlt sich wohl' (p. 5). *Vinschger Dolomiten* 17, June.

13   Ibid.

14   Clottes, J. 2003. *Return to Chauvet Cave*. London, Thames & Hudson. Clottes, J. 2008. *Cave Art*. London, Phaidon Press.

15   Yalden, D. 1999. *The History of British Mammals*. London, T & A.D. Poyser. Anonymous. 2005. 'Seltener Gast auf leisen Tatzen' (p. 2) and '"Sommerfrischler" fühlt sich wohl' (p. 5). *Vinschger Dolomiten* 17, June. Ryder, M.L. 1983. *Sheep and Man*. London, Duckworth.

16   Rollo, F *et al.* 2002. 'Ötzi's last meals: DNA analysis of the intestinal content of the Neolithic glacier mummy from the Alps'. *Proceedings of the National Academy of Sciences* 99, pp. 12594–9. Schibler, J. and Jacomet, S. 2010. 'Short climatic fluctuations and their impact on human economies and societies: the potential of the Neolithic lake shore settlements in the Alpine foreland'. *Environmental Archaeology* 15, pp. 173–82.

17   Ibid.

18   Ibid.

19   Haas, J.N., Karg, S. and Rasmussen, P. 1998. 'Beech leaves and Twigs used as Winter Fodder: Examples from Historic and Prehistoric Times'. *Environmental Archaeology* 1, pp. 81–6.

20   Sauter, F., Jordis, U., Graf, A., Werther, W. and Varmuza, K. 2000. 'Studies in Organic Archaeometry: identification of the prehistoric adhesive used by the "Tyrolean Iceman" to fix his weapons'. *ARKAT USA*. Stacey, B. 2004. 'Evidence for the Use of Birch-Bark Tar from Iron Age Britain'. *Past* 47, pp. 1–2.

21   Gidmark, D. 1988. *The Algonquin Birchbark Canoe*. Aylesbury: Shire Publications.

22   Kollmann, J. and Grubb, P.J. 2002. '*Viburnum lantana* L. and *Viburnum opulus* L. (*V. lobatum* Lam., *Opulus vulgaris* Borkh)'. *Journal of Ecology* 90, pp. 1044–70. Grigson, G. 1987. *The Englishman's Flora*. London, J.M. Dent & Sons. André, M. 2002. *La Flora de la Montagne Jurassienne*. Besançon, NEO.

Lawson, J. 1709. *A New Voyage to Carolina; Containing the Exact Description and Natural History of that County*. He suffered the sad fate of being burnt to death by the local inhabitants in 1711. Ascham, R. 1545. *Toxophilus, The Schole, or Partitions of Shooting*. Wakefield, S.R. Publishers (1968).

23 Ibid.

24 Ibid.

25 Ibid.

26 Kubiac-Martens, L. 1999. 'The plant food component of the diet at the late Mesolithic (Ertebolle) settlement at Tybrind Vig, Denmark'. *Vegetation History and Archaeobotany* 8, pp. 117–27.

27 Stewart, H. 1982. *Indian Fishing Early Methods on the Northwest Coast*. Vancouver, Douglas & MacIntyre. Turner, N.J. 1998. *Plant Technology of the First Peoples of British Columbia*. Vancouver, UBC Press. Pojar, J. and MacKinnon, A. 1994. *Plants of the Pacific Northwest Coast*. Vancouver, Lone Pine Publishing.

28 Rackham, O. 2003. *Ancient Woodland*. Dalbeattie, Castlepoint Press.

29 Bevan-Jones, R. 2002. *The Ancient Yew*. Macclesfield, Windgather Press. Thomas, P.A. and Polwart, A. 2003. '*Taxus baccata* L. Biological Flora of the British Isles'. *Journal of Ecology* 91, pp. 489–524. Spindler, K. 2004. 'The Yew Bow of the Man in the Ice'. *Austrian Journal of Forestry Science* 121, pp. 1–24. Favre, P. and Jacomet, S. 1998. 'Branch wood from the lake shore settlements of Horgen Scheller, Switzerland: evidence for economic specialization in the late Neolithic period'. *Vegetation History and Archaeobotany* 7, pp. 167–72. Lyubenova, M. and Nedelchev, R. 2001. 'Influence of human factors on population of *Taxus baccata* L'. *Journal of Balkan Ecology* 4, pp. 382–8. Junkmanns, J. 2001. *Arc et Flèche Fabrication and Utilisation au Neolithique*. Bienne, Éditions Musée Schwab. Bellwald, W. 1992. 'Drei spätneolithischen/frübronzezeitliche Pfeilbogen aus dem Gletschereis am Lötschenpass'. *Archéologie Suisse* 15, pp. 166–71.

30 Ibid.

31 Ibid.

32 Ibid.

33 Dove, C.J., Hare, P.G. and Heacker, M. 2005. 'Identification of Ancient Feather Fragments Found in Melting Alpine Ice Patches in Southern Yukon'. *Arctic* 58, pp. 38–43.

34 Endrizzi, L. and Marzatio, F. 1997. *Ori del Alpi*. Trento, Ufficio Beni Archeologici. Sperl, G. *Innsbruck* 1, p. 454. Sperl, G. 'Metallography for the European Copper Age'. *Microscopy Today* 13, pp. 1–4.

35 Ibid.

36 Clutton-brock, J. 1999. *A History of Domesticated Animals*. Cambridge University Press. Second edition. Yalden, D. 1999. *The History of British Mammals*. T & A.D. Poyser, London. Bonanno, A. 2003. *Malta An Archaeological Paradise*. Valletta, M.J. Publications. Malone, D., Bonanno, A., Gouder, G., Stoddart, S. and Trump, P. 2005. 'The Death Cults of Prehistoric Malta'. *Scientific American Special Edition* 15, pp. 14–24. Bahn, P. 2002.

37 Ibid.

38 Dickson, C. and Dickson, J. 2000 *Plants & People in Ancient Scotland*. Stroud, Tempus. Corner, E.J.H. 1950. 'Report on the Fungus-brackets from Starr Carr, Seamer'. In Clark, J.G.D. 'Preliminary Report on excavations at Starr Carr, Seamer, Scarborough, Yorkshire (Second Season, 1950)'. *Proceedings of the Prehistoric Society* XVI, pp. 109–29. Rousell, B. and Boutié, P. 2006. *La Grande Aventure du Feu*. Aix-en-Provence, Édisud.

39 Ibid.

40 Ibid.

41 Binsteiner, A. 2005. 'Ausgewalte Silexlagerstätten in deren Abbau in den Porvinzen Trient und Verona'. *Archäologisches Korrespondenzblatt* 24, pp. 255–64. Binsteiner, A. 1994. 'Silexlagerstätten in den Provinzen Trient und Verona und die Fuerstein-Gruben des "Mannes im Eis"'. *Der Anschnitt: Zietschrift für Kunst und Kultur im Berhau* 46, pp. 6, 208. Stapert, D. and Johansen, L. 1999. 'Flint and pyrite: making fire in the Stone Age'. *Antiquity* 73, pp. 765–77.

42 Topping, P. 2003. *Grimes Graves Norfolk*. Thetford, English Heritage.

4

Use of Resources:
Food, Drink and Medicine

In 1993, concerning Ötzi's last journey, Konrad Spindler could write (*Spindler* 1, p.131): 'Finally, his food supplies were not exactly optimal. All we can prove is a single measly sloe and probably a chunk of meat, perhaps pemmican.' This statement is a tendentious argument. He wanted to make out that Ötzi had arrived at his last resting place in a poor state, exhausted and very hungry. He conveniently forgot or ignored that Ötzi's food supplies might have been largely lost to us. The often quoted maxim 'Absence of evidence is not evidence of absence' applies here as well as to various other statements about Ötzi (and not just assertions by Konrad Spindler). Additionally, he could have stated that examination of the gut contents might give a better assessment of the energy content of the food consumed

"C'mon, Oetzi...try some...at least it was a vegetarian goat"

Fig. 4.1 Cartoon from *The Herald*.

during his last few days. Since then we have come a very long way in understanding Ötzi's diet and know in some considerable detail the precise nature of his last meals. We even know now that his stomach, in the strict sense, was full but not yet what it contained; samples were taken in November 2010 and so soon we shall know.

FOOD FOUND BESIDE THE BODY AND ON THE CLOTHES

Three different foodstuffs were found close to the body or on the clothes: Alpine ibex, blackthorn (sloe) and remains of three cereals which were einkorn wheat, barley and common millet. There were also seeds of opium poppy and a seed of flax (linseed).

Alpine Ibex

Neck bone splinters of a male of this massively horned wild goat were discovered beside Ötzi's corpse and so it was likely that meat of this eye-catching animal had been eaten during the last meals, perhaps even the very last meal. Following Konrad Spindler, in their large book Angelika Fleckinger and Hubert Steiner claim that the iceman had probably taken smoked or dried ibex meat with him on his last journey.

Alpine ibex is both a grazer and browser. Living up to 12 years and weighing up to 120kg, it roams to an altitude of about 3000m and more. It inhabits the Alps and other mountains, such as the Pyrenees, where the populations are sometimes regarded as a distinct species. Close to the Ötzi site today, it inhabits Pfossental, where it had to be introduced after having been shot out during the Second World War.[1] The small Swiss town of Bergün, near the site of the Porchabella Shepherdess, discussed in Chapter 6, has as its emblem an Alpine ibex rampant holding a sword. However, soon after the year 1500, Apine Ibex had been exterminated by overhunting throughout Switzerland and in other parts of the Alps. This very fine creature has now been reintroduced at many places in the Alps including nearly 40 localities scattered over north Tyrol. (See Plate 15.)

The strikingly large, curved and transversely ribbed horns can reach 85cm long. They have been dramatically depicted in engravings and a charcoal drawing that may be as old as about 32,000 years, in the Chauvet Cave in the Ardèche region of France.[2] They were also depicted in an incised rock sculpture at Abri Pataud, Perigord, France, by a Solutrean artist of about 18,000–19,000 years ago. The somewhat later Magdalenians of about 15,000 years ago also cleverly drew this creature on bones and on cave walls. Further afield than France, at Dalmeri rock shelter near Trento, south of *Ötziland*, the inhabitants lived during late glacial times (about 13,300 years ago). They ate principally Alpine ibex, which comprised about 90 per cent of the mammal bones. They also drew the ibex in red ochre on stones.[3]

That it was a favourite source of meat for Palaeolithic people is dramatically shown by the contents of La Grotte de la Vache, in Ariège, France, which had been lived in by Magdalenians. There were 71,451 ibex bones, derived from a minimum number of individuals of 1,831; this was far many more bones than those of reindeer, chamois and other large mammals. That the meat of ibex was appreciated much earlier than that is well shown by La Grotte du Lazaret, near Nice, France. This was a cave inhabited by Acheulians, some 160,000 years ago, and a quarter of all the approximately 20,000 bones studied belonged to ibex.[4]

So, just like the extinct woolly mammoth and woolly rhinoceros and other large mammals such as reindeer, bison and horse, the Alpine ibex was of interest to humankind, both artistically and gastronomically, long before Ötzi's time. It is not just in Europe where ibex has caught the artistic attention of ancient people. From the first century AD a beautifully made statuette of an ibex, in gold and a mere 5.2cm high, was found in a tomb (Tillia tempe) along with many other magnificently fashioned gold objects. It is beautifully illustrated on the cover of the January 2007 edition of the French magazine *Archéologia*. Coming from ancient Iran, this statuette is one of many splendid gold representations of ibex that derive from the Achaemenid dynasty of the first millennium BC. This would have been the Siberian ibex, not the Alpine ibex.

Konrad Spindler gives a highly engaging account of this animal and discusses its excellent, highly nutritious meat, the use of its droppings as medicine and the great difficulties faced by hunters because of its precipitous habitats. The meat could have been cold-smoked into long-keeping pemmican. Indeed, he goes so far as to say that the worn state of Ötzi's teeth might be explainable by his chewing such dry, tough meat (*Spindler 2*).

Blackthorn (Sloe)

A solitary but whole sloe fruit (the stone with surrounding flesh) was found by the corpse and so the question arises had Ötzi been carrying dried or fresh sloes as provisions. The fruit was not certainly inside one of the birch bark containers as stated by Paul Bahn,[5] as is clear from Spindler's book (*Spindler 1*, p. 117):

> When the two Alpine archaeologists Sölder and Lochbihler visited the Hauslabjoch in a gale, they recovered a sloe … near where the corpse was found. Lying as it was on the surface of the ice, it had almost certainly been moved from its original position by the tumultuous events of the previous day or by the meltwater.

In addition, Klaus Oeggl and Werner Schoch state: 'A further fruit find was made in the vicinity of the no more existing birchbark receptacle. This is a fruit of sloe *Prunus spinosa*.'[6] (See Plate 19.)

Often forming thickets, blackthorn is a densely branched, thorny, tall shrub, to 3m or more high and is closely related to the plum tree and its fruits, though small (1–1.5cm), are indeed structurally identical to plums (in botanical terminology called drupes) (see Plate 21). The name in French, *prunelle*, means 'little plum'. Blackthorn flowers in spring before the leaves are expanded and if the flowers are not damaged by frost, a not infrequent occurrence in Western Europe, the drupes develop through the summer. Common at low altitudes in the southern part of Ötziland, it ascends to an altitude of about 1400m, as above Tappeiner, on the south-facing slopes north-east of Schlanders. Its habitats are forest margins, bushy places and hedgerows.

The ripe fruits are very bitter and Konrad Spindler tells the amusing story that there is in Tyrol is a saying that if you eat them fresh they will draw your shirt tails in at the back (*Spindler 2*). However, it is not entirely 'sour fruit at the best of times', as stated by Lawrence Barfield in his review, because, if the drupes are dried, then they are much more palatable, though not very tasty, at least to the modern palate if my reaction is typical. After being frosted they are less bitter too.[7] That prehistoric folk used sloes is very well attested by the common occurrence of the stones in archaeological sites over much of Europe. Apart from the frequent fruit stones, twigs have been found rarely in Neolithic and later sites. However, 170 twigs, probably of this species, and nine buds were found at Arbon Bleiche 3.

It always has to be remembered that information was lost by the rough recovery and that an unknowable amount of material may have been scattered at the time of the death or later and has never come down to us. However, to say that Ötzi's rucksack had been full of sloes and cereals, as claimed by Richard Rudgley in a Channel Four television programme, is unjustifiable. Three pieces of shaped wood are all that certainly survive of the 'rucksack'. As discussed above, we do not know that it was indeed a rucksack rather than, say, merely a frame for strapping on a carcass of a mammal, and we do know that both Alpine ibex and red deer meat were in his gut. To be completely fair, there may also have been sloes in his gut because Klaus Oeggl has on pollen slides unidentified stone cells and other plant tissues that may be the partly digested remains of these fruits or other edible plants or both. The point about the sloe having been fresh or dried is a far from unimportant one because it bears on the season of death, a contentious topic which is considered thoroughly in Chapter 5.

Cereals

Humankind may have been collecting and processing wild grasses, including the progenitors of barley and possibly wheat, for food as early as about 20,000 years ago (Upper Palaeolithic) in what is now Israel.[8] In the Middle East, by some 10,000 years later, cereals had come into cultivation.

Cereals are grasses domesticated in ancient times in various continents: rice in the Far East, maize in the Americas and barley, wheat, oats and rye in the Middle East and common millet perhaps in Central Asia or China.[9] Two types of cereals, einkorn wheat and barley, were found with Ötzi's clothes and gear and also inside his body, and a third, common millet, was found close to the mummy.

Einkorn Wheat: Seven spikelets (parts of a cereal head) of einkorn wheat were removed from the clothes. Remains of this primitive wheat were also found with the Norway maple leaves. Furthermore, bran has been recovered all the small samples taken from Ötzi's innards. The two first wheats to be domesticated were those called einkorn and emmer. The domestication took place in the Fertile Crescent of the Middle East some 10,000 years ago and its cultivation spread through Europe:

> Einkorn is a small plant, rarely more than 70cm high, with a relatively low yield, but it can survive on poor soils where other wheat types fail. The fine yellow flour is nutritious, but gives bread of poor rising qualities. Thus einkorn has been consumed primarily as porridge or as cooked whole grains.

So say David Zohary and Maria Hopf.[10]

Naked Six-row Barley: Along with the primitive wheats, barley came very early into cultivation. Eleven rachis segments of naked six-row barley were found with the clothes. The colon sample examined by English archaeobotanist Tim Holden contained remains of this barley.[11]

Common/Broomcorn Millet: This small-seeded cereal is familiar to modern lovers of small cage birds as a staple for their pets but it has been used as human food for over 6000 years by the inhabitants of Eurasia. According to Daniel Zohary and Maria Hopf, it 'ranks among the hardiest cereals. It is a warm season plant which stands up well to intense heat, poor soils, and severe droughts, completing its life cycle in a very short time (60–90 days)'. The grains are 'quite rich (10–11 percent) in proteins'.[12] Andreas Heiss and Klaus Oeggl discovered two grains of millet, one close to Ötzi, the other a bit further away. They stated: 'the carbonised grains could not be identified with certainty as broomcorn millet (cf. *Panicum miliaceum*), as they were in a very bad state of preservation, and no chaff remains could be observed.'[13] David Zohary and Maria Hopf said that millet came during the late fifth and fourth millennia BC to Eastern and Central Europe. 'The seeds … become more common in the late Neolithic and in the Bronze Age cultures.' 'In northern Italy, the millet appears in the early Bronze Age (1700–1500 BC) settlements.'[14] So the discovery with Ötzi is a good deal earlier than that.

Two seeds of the notorious plant, opium poppy, were found in the hollow. This does not, repeat not, constitute sound evidence that Ötzi was a junkie. The latex (juice) from the walls of the unripe fruits contains the opium but the seeds do not. For well over 100 years remains of this cultivated and weedy plant have been recovered from Neolithic sites in Central Europe and so, while good to know that Ötzi had likely carried them, it is no great surprise. Think of the seeds on some kinds of bread; they are opium poppy. At present opium poppy is cultivated under licence on a small scale in Südtirol. One linseed was recovered from 2m west of the corpse. Like opium poppy, linseed is well known from European Neolithic and later sites. It was 'probably the earliest plant used for weaving clothes', according to Daniel Zohary and Maria Hopf.[15] Apart from the strong fibres rotted from the stems (a process called retting), linseed is useful too. Oil can be extracted and used for cooking and other purposes. In recent decades once again flax has become extensively cultivated in Europe.

MICROSCOPY REVEALING FOOD

Some 1800 years ago on the mainland of Orkney, lumps of human excrement began to be preserved by mineralisation in a well. While investigating these lumps in the 1980s in my laboratory in Glasgow University, the late Camilla Lambert, a highly skilled archaeobotanist, found 33 types of flowering plants and mosses, as well as fragments of bone, feathers and mammalian hair.[16] These plant remains included barley bran, fragments of linseed and seeds of chickweed and other weeds. All this recognition of pollen and coarser remains of plants and animals was achieved by light microscopy. These lumps tell us about the diet at brief moments but precisely unknowable moments in the lives of the producer or producers.

For the contents of expelled and then fossilised faeces (known as coprolites) this type of investigation using traditional light microscopes has been done for many decades and not just human coprolites but those of other mammals, such as bats and packrats.[17] For mummies that have not been eviscerated, there are ways to establish the very final aspects of the deceased's diet, that is to say the very last few days of life. By examining microscopically the food residues through the alimentary canal the composition of the last meals can be deduced to a greater or lesser degree. Even minute scraps of the indigestible parts of both plants and animals may have distinctive features which allow very detailed recognition.

However, for the gut contents of mummies, microscopy has seldom been carried out and, certainly in the case of glacier mummies, never until the investigations of Ötzi and Kwäday Dän Ts'ìnchí Man. From the late 1960s onwards, scanning electron microscopy, which reveals very tiny objects beautifully in three dimensions, has been used for investigating Ötzi. Klaus Oeggl published images of some of the colon contents: einkorn, conifer wood, mineral particle, whipworm egg and muscle fibre (*Innsbruck* 4, p. 152). Earlier Franco Rollo produced an image of a grass epidermis (*Innsbruck* 2, p. 101). The more recent development, called environmental scanning electron microscopy, has been applied to Kwäday Dän Ts'ìnchí Man's stomach contents by Petra Mudie and colleagues (see Chapter 7). Such uses for both traditional and electron microscopy retain great importance but there are now additionally other very cogent techniques that reveal diet. These are the measurement of stable isotopes and DNA assays.

Most of the samples of food residues from Ötzi have so far been obtained by computer tomographic scanning and then endoscopy (the insertion of specially instruments into the body cavity and the gut). Ötzi's intestines are very shrivelled and because the human alimentary tract is many metres long and the different organs are closely packed together, it has been difficult sometimes for the medical investigators to be sure just which organ they were sampling.

As yet, there is no sample taken from Ötzi's stomach (in the strict sense), which CT scans reveal as probably being empty, though we cannot be sure if there are slight remains of his last meal there or not. Konrad Spindler had written (*Spindler* 2, p. 193): 'no food remains whatsoever were found in the stomach.' I had written these sentences before March 2009 but at a mummy conference in Bozen that month the radiologist Dr Patrizia Pertner of the Bozen General Hospital showed evidence that his stomach was full. Very surprising! The important significance of that discovery is discussed in Chapter 5.

From a colon sample taken in 1996 and weighing a mere 40mg, Klaus Oeggl and his co-researchers found abundant bran of einkorn and that cereal appeared in all the other gut samples obtained later. The cereal debris is in such a minute state that it may well have been ground into flour for baking bread rather than having been made into a gruel for which such fineness would have been unnecessary. That Ötzi had eaten other plants is shown by microscopic debris of as yet unidentified types. Meat fibres were found. These may have come from Alpine ibex; splinters of the neck bones of that tasty animal were found close to the corpse, as mentioned above. However, there was nothing to exclude other animals having been consumed as well, as was revealed by the DNA studies.

The Edinburgh-based archaeobotanist, Tim Holden, was given a sample from the colon of approximately 0.25cc and he recognised cereal bran, wood charcoal, charred vesicular material and grit/sand, one hair, meat fibres and possible animal connective tissue, as well as one whole spikelet fork and one fragmentary one of einkorn and two fragments of barley, one being 4mm long.[18]

In 2005 Klaus Oeggl *et al.* published on new aspects of the Ötzi's diet.[19] The two very interesting additions to the plants in Ötzi's gut are a seed of a chenopod and sporangia of bracken and both need explanation. Chenopods are plants belonging to the family Chenopodiaceae, a name that means goose foot. The familiar vegetables beetroot and spinach are both chenopods, as is fathen, a common weedy plant, up to a metre tall but usually less, that grows on arable ground across Europe. The seed from Ötzi's gut may well be fathen but it is impossible to be sure because the details of the seed coat could not be seen. A weed it may be, but the leaves and seeds are edible and there is good evidence to suggest that the seeds were deliberately consumed in ancient times elsewhere in Europe.[20] Bracken is a robust, creeping, tall fern with fronds often poisonous to livestock. It grows the world over and can form enormous clones, that is to say large patches composed of one individual. In the upland parts of Britain, where it is abundant, it is loathed by hill farmers and by conservationists, though it is a native plant. In Ötziland it is not unruly and is seldom if ever found outside the lower woodlands, never grows in enormous stands and does not reach anywhere near the timber line. In Schnalstal, for instance, it grows in moderation in the roadside woodland at Altrateis (844m) and as high as Karthaus (1500m). It is a plant which has had many uses, including medicinal. It has also been used as fuel and dunnage (material used to protect cargo). The important matter to be considered here is that bracken is edible. Klaus Oeggl et al. state: 'The young fronds and the starchy rhizomes were and are eaten by natives in Australia, Japan, New Zealand and North America.'[21]

Ferns produce their spores, which are individually much too small to see with the naked eye, in structures called sporangia which can be seen without a microscope and very clearly with a hand lens. The point is that Klaus Oeggl found both spores and sporangia in all the gut samples and is convinced that the consistent presence and large numbers of both spores and sporangia must indicate intentional consumption. But the question is for what exactly – food or medicine? See the section on drugs and dressings later in this chapter for more discussion.

Klaus Oeggl is also convinced that some pollen types found in the gut samples indicate deliberate consumption. The chenopod pollen from the ileum sample and the colon (sample 1) could well be fathen as just mentioned, but it is not so easy to say anything very firm about the pollen of primulaceae, papilionaceae and Caltha-type (all in colon sample 2). Primulaceae (primrose family) is not a family noted for edible plants; but like so many other families it has medicinal uses, for a sedative infusion, for instance. Papilionaceae includes many edible peas and beans but there are also many species of wild-growing vetches and similar plants. Caltha belongs to ranunculaceae (buttercups), which is a family much more noted for its toxicity (alkaloids) than for edibility. Again, however there are medicinal uses.

DNA

The microscopy had shown conclusively that Ötzi had eaten a diversity of food, both plant and animal, during his last few days. Then came Franco Rollo of the University of Camerino and three colleagues. They studied Ötzi's diet by investigating the DNA extracted from the ingesta.[22] They obtained a sample from the ileum and one from the colon. Their most interesting finding was that the ileum sample contained meat of red deer and the colon sample contained meat of Alpine ibex. So it is satisfactory to know that Ötzi had eaten the very palatable meat of these wild large mammals. None of Franco Rollo's other findings add much to the results obtained by microscopy, nor is there any significant discrepancy between the two types of investigation.

STABLE ISOTOPES

The important elements in this context, a very important one for archaeology, are Sr (the metal strontium which is sixteenth most abundant element in the Earth's crust), N (the gas nitrogen which comprises 78 per cent of the air and is the thirtieth most abundant element in the Earth's crust), O (the gas oxygen which comprises 21 per cent of the air and is the most abundant element in the Earth's crust) and C (the solid carbon, the fifteenth most abundant element in the Earth's crust).[23] Famous for the unstable radioactive isotope 14, carbon has two stable isotopes 12 and 13. Nitrogen has two stable isotopes, 14 and 15. Oxygen has threes table isotopes, 16, 17 and 18. All the isotopes of strontium are stable, 84, 86, 87 and 88.

Different foods have different isotopic signatures. These are come up through the food web and are registered in the consumer's body. Analysing archaeological remains for their abundances of the stable isotopes of carbon and nitrogen ($\delta^{13}C$ and $\delta^{15}N$) can provide information about the individual's diet, if there is sufficient additional data to make the $\delta^{13}C$ and $\delta^{15}N$ data interpretable. In addition, the remains must be sufficiently undegraded for there to be confidence in the results of the analyses. $\delta^{15}N$ can reveal the extent to which the individual relied on animal or plant protein. $\delta^{13}C$ can reveal whether the individual relied on food plants having a C_3 or C_4 form of photosynthesis. For instance, wheats and many other cereals are C_3 plants; that is, they first combine carbon into a three-carbon acid, but maize combines a four-carbon acid. Also, $\delta^{13}C$ can reveal whether seafood or terrestrial carbon were substantial parts of the diet, not an issue of any real importance for Ötzi, but a crucial one for Kwäday Dän Ts'ìnchí Man (see Chapter 7).

Various analyses can be applied to human and other hair from archaeological sites with worthwhile results and the estimation of arsenic and copper in Ötzi's hair is discussed in a later chapter, but here it is stable isotopes and diet. Cautionary statements have been made, with warnings that change to the hair chemistry after deposition may happen. Diagenesis is the jargon word for this environmentally induced change.

In 1999, after the initial but not fully published microscopy of the ingesta had revealed a varied diet, Stephen Macko of the University of Virginia was the lead author of two papers on stable isotopes and Ötzi's diet. He had obtained samples of Ötzi's hair from a German source: 'several strands of hair of different lengths' (FASEB, p. 560). From these he produced one set of results which were then discussed in the two papers, not cross-referenced, but with different conclusions.[24] In one the iceman had 'a diet which is essentially vegan' and in the other the diet had been merely 'a primarily vegetarian diet'.

In the late 1970s and much of the 1980s, with my wife Camilla in the lead, I helped investigate the abundant plant remains preserved in a defensive ditch of the Roman fort at Bearsden near Milngavie, Glasgow. It turned out that the waste products from the troops' latrine had been allowed to flow into the ditch and had stayed in waterlogged clay for nearly 2000 years until the excavation. From the archaeobotanical findings, such as wheat bran and fig pips, we suspected that we were investigating a sewage-impregnated layer, but we wished confirmation from some other technique. We enlisted the help of a chemical colleague who recognised coprostanol (found in mammalian faeces) in the clay. At that time, 30 years ago, this was one of the first attempts to reveal ancient diet by chemical means. After the chemical investigation had been added to our botanical discoveries, we concluded that the

Romans had had a largely 'vegetarian' diet.[25] I now regret that use of that adjective and take the line that, in trying to assess ancient diets, it is best to avoid using such terms as 'vegetarian' and 'vegan', which imply lifestyle choices of a philosophical/religious nature. We do not know what our ancient prehistoric forebears deliberately chose not to eat, although omnivory might seem to most of us to have been by far the most likely behaviour.

So surprised was I by this extraordinary, indeed unprecedented, claim concerning Ötzi having had an essentially vegan diet that, with five others including three isotope chemists, I published a rebuttal. If there has ever been a proof that any prehistoric person had been a vegan then it is unknown to me and presumably to Stephen Macko too, because he makes no mention of any other such conclusions. The sparse data produced by Stephen Macko and his seven co-authors are not just for Ötzi's hair, but for 'associated' goat's hair and for a 'grass-like-plant'. These were inadequate as controls.[26]

Amino acid analyses of the hair indicated possible N loss and/or replacement since Ötzi's death, making the accuracy of the $\delta^{15}N$ value suspect. Taking into account these possible problems, the $\delta^{15}N$ data suggest that Ötzi obtained about 30 per cent of his dietary nitrogen from animal protein and the remainder from plants. This is consistent with the similar values found for modern subsistence peoples. $\delta^{13}C$ confirmed that seafood was probably not a component of Ötzi's diet, a finding consistent, not surprisingly, with the great distance of Ötzi's homeland from the sea. $\delta^{13}C$ further confirmed that C_4 plants were not a substantial part of his diet, hardly a major discovery because there is no evidence for C_4 plants in prehistoric Central and Northern Europe. Ötzi undoubtedly ate a mixed animal and plant diet, and the very limited isotopic data produced so far confirms this conclusion.[27]

For Ötzi there would also have been readily available edible wild resources, to be gathered at the appropriate times, such as the nutritious nuts of hazel and fruits such as raspberries and blackberries. Remains of all these and many others have been found repeatedly at prehistoric and later sites across Europe and so it is certain that they were exploited for food, just as one would expect, by Neolithic people. However, it has to be said that we have no direct evidence that Ötzi consumed them, though, of course, it is very likely that he would have done so. Neither microscopy nor DNA analysis of the ingesta has revealed as yet peas, apples, lentils, wild plum, nor 'edible fungi', as listed by Gudrun Sulzenbacher in her pages on 'Plants and Ötzi's Diet'.

UNINTENTIONAL INGESTIONS AND INHALATIONS

Inevitably when we breathe we take in through the nose and mouth not just the air we need but also the numerous types of minute particulate matter it contains. Apart from dust, water vapour and bacteria and viruses, there are the spores of fungi, ferns and mosses, but also pollen grains from conifers and flowering plants, as all sufferers of hay fever know only too well. We also breathe in tiny pieces of charcoal in smoke. The plants we eat can have pollen, spores and small fragments of charcoal sticking to them and small mineral particles too – clay, silt and sand. Similarly, when drinking water, we take in unintentionally such particles of organic and inorganic origins. These do not, of course, reveal diet but they do

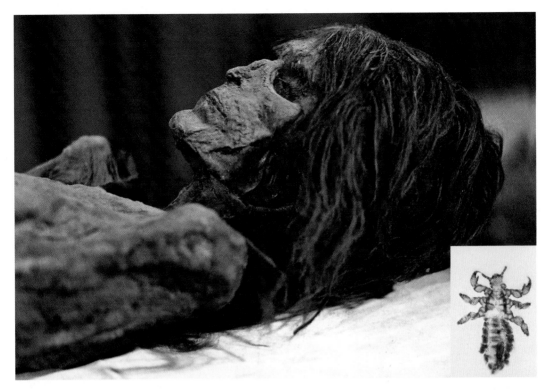

1 The Beauty of Loulan (with inset of a body louse). She lived some 4000 years ago in what is now Xinjiang, China. (*Wang Binghua*)

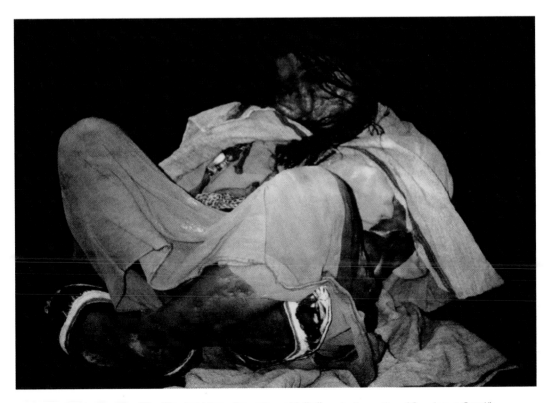

2 Mummified by freezing, sacrificed girl from the volcano Llullaillaco in Argentina. (*Constanza Ceruti*)

Above: 3 Constanza Ceruti cleaning the face of a just excavated mummy from Llullaillaco. (*Constanza Ceruti*)

Opposite above: 4 A kurgan, boulders placed over a tomb, in the Altai Mountains of Siberia. (*Wouter Gheyle, University of Gent*)

Opposite below: 5 A body mummified by freezing from a kurgan at Ak-Alaka in the Altai Republic. Note the decorative tatoos. (*Wouter Gheyle, University of Gent*)

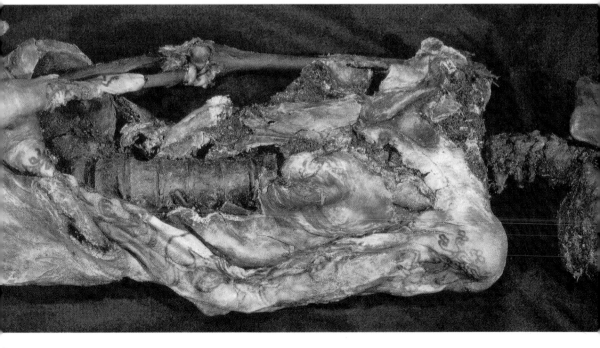

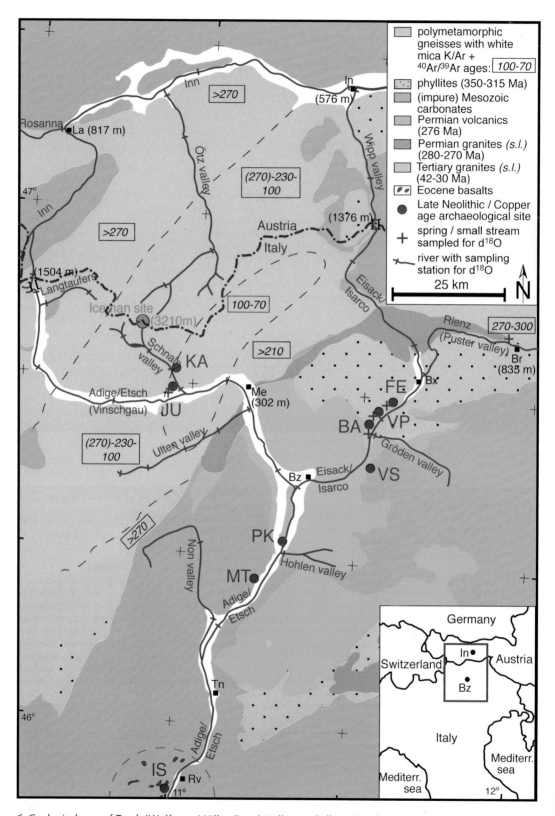

6 Geological map of Tyrol. (*Wolfgang Müller, Royal Holloway College, London*)

7 In the nival zone at about 3250m in the Ötztal Alps, 17 September 2007, looking north-westwards with the Ötzi site in the middle distance.

8 At the Ötzi site, 2210m, late August 2000, looking south-east with the memorial conspicuous in the background.

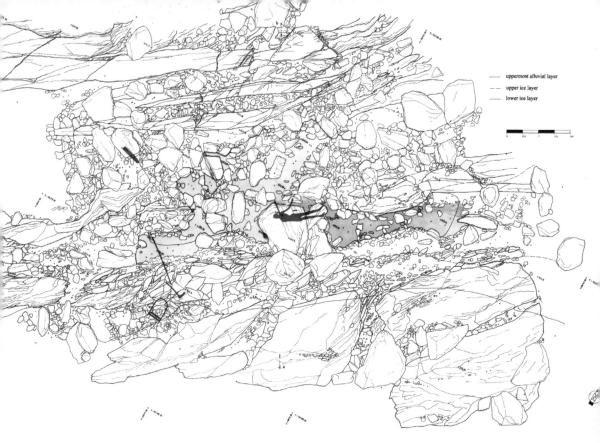

Opposite top: 9 Three bryologists (moss scientists) in the alpine zone and ascending but still quite a way below the Similaun Hut, 1 September 2001.

Opposite bottom: 10 Larch woodland with moss boulders in Schnalstal in the montane zone.

Above: 11 Plan of the Ötzi site showing the positions of the mummy and gear. (*Markus Egg*)

Below: 12 The moss flat neckera growing on a shady wall, Wharfedale, England. (*Michael Lueth*)

13 The moss crisp neckera growing on a rockface, Wharfedale, England. (*Michael Lueth*)

14 A bog moss growing in moist woodland near Glasgow, Scotland.

15 A male alpine ibex in the Alpine Zoo in Innsbruck, Austria.

16 Goats in Niedertal at about 2230m in the alpine zone.

17 Sheep returning to Italy in mid-September in the alpine zone at about 2600m above the Martin Busch Hut. The Similaun Hut is on the right of the skyline.

18 Hop hornbeam with young fruits and old male catkins (the narrow brown structures) near Meran, south Tyrol.

19 Birch bracket fungus on birch trunk near Glasgow, Scotland.

20 True tinder fungus on a trunk near Glasgow, Scotland.

Above: 21 Sloes, the fruits of blackthorn, at Chemilly, Vesoul in Haute- Saône, France.

Below: 22 The Porchabella glacier, near Bergün, Switzerland.

Opposite top: 23 The Chilchi glacier, Schnidejoch, north of Sion, Switzerland.

Opposite bottom: 24 Ice patch in the Yellowstone area, USA. (*Craig Lee*)

25 Mount St Elias from Yakutat, south-east Alaska, USA

26 The Kwäday Dän Ts'ìnchí site, British Columbia, Canada, August 2002. Note the helicopter as a scale object.

27 Coniferous forest at Yakutat. Note the mosses abundant on the tree trunks and the large mass of a bog moss in the foreground.

28 Sparse coniferous trees on sandy ground at Carcross, the Yukon Territory, Canada.

29 Beach asparagus in the flower (the tiny, pale protruding objects near the tips) at Gustavus, south-east Alaska, USA.

30 Red glasswort near Whitehorse, the Yukon Territory, Canada. The flowers are inside the stem tips.

help in various important, even crucial, ways in the understanding of the last few days of life of the unfortunates who became glacier mummies (see Chapters 5 and 7).

Modern people deliberately eat pollen but only in very small amounts. Pollen can be bought in health shops and when we eat honey there is always some pollen at least as an admixture because the nectar collected by bees inevitably has pollen therein. Also bees intentionally collect pollen from plants such as that of meadowsweet. Some Native Americans deliberately ate pollen. The Navajos collected pollen of maize as food and the Californian natives collected reedmace (cat-tail) pollen and made it into a kind of bread. The Yuma of Arizona also ate reedmace pollen raw or stored it for further use, boiled it into a thin gruel, baked it into cakes and used it as a flavouring. On the other side of the Pacific, the Maoris of New Zealand ate reedmace pollen. Lucy Cranwell stated: 'considerable use was once made of *Typha* [reedmace] pollen ... bucketsful were beaten out gently from the spikes ... mixed up with water into cakes and baked.'[28] According to the famous English nineteenth-century botanist Sir Joseph Hooker, the natives of Scinde in India did exactly the same.[29]

Sea Buckthorn
A leaf hair of this spiny shrub was found in one of the gut samples. These hairs which cover the undersides of the leaves are so highly distinctive in their shape as to unmistakable. In Britain the shrub's native distribution is entirely coastal, but in Central Europe it occurs far from salt water. It is widespread in *Ötziland*. This leaf can be taken as an entirely involuntary ingestion with no medicinal or any other particular significance.

Pollen of Hop Hornbeam
This tall shrub or small tree gets its English name from its leaves resembling those of hornbeam and its fruits are like those of hop (see Plate 18). It can be grown in Britain, as in the Royal Botanic Garden in Edinburgh, but is not native nearer than south-eastern France. Around Meran it thrives in the small gorge-like valleys cut into limy rocks as at Obertalmühl, south of that town. In *Ötziland*, it reaches over 1000m and grows on warm, moist slopes. It is connected with calcareous soils there and elsewhere, as in the Insubrian Southern Alps.[30] Reputedly, it grows in southern Schnalstal as far north as Katharinaberg, which lies at about 1250m altitude, but I have not seen it there despite repeatedly searching around that village and lower down the valley. The catkins shed their pollen in late spring or early summer and the seed is ripened through the later summer. There have been several archaeobotanical finds from the Neolithic of northern Italy but none from north of the Alps which is no surprise because of the tree's geography.

Diatoms
These are a very distinctive group of microscopic algae which are mainly planktonic, both in the sea and in fresh water. Other habitats include rocks and large water plants in rivers and lakes and there are even some diatoms that live in soils. They have siliceous shells, called frustules, with highly diagnostic shapes and patterns which allow the recognition of genera and species. No prehistoric uses for these tiny plants are known but they are good indicators of past environments in their own right and they add to the usefulness of pollen and other plant remains in deducing past environmental changes. Their importance in the investigation

of Ötzi is that they were found in quantitative and qualitative abundance in the initial sample taken from Ötzi's colon. Eugen Rott of Innsbruck Univerity identified 24 different species, all but one with water as the habitat. Mostly they inhabit pristine mountain streams or springs but two species are common at lower altitudes and nutrient-richer streams. He states (*Innsbruck 4*, p. 119): 'The results indicate that the Iceman, during the last day of his life, had incorporated diatoms by drinking water originating from different places situated at lower (below 1500m) and higher altitudes and/or by using water for the preparation of his meal.'

Mosses

Alone among all major groups of plants, there is little evidence that humans eat or ever have eaten bryophytes (mosses and the related liverworts) in large quantities. This is a topic I have discussed elsewhere and it is true to say that there has never been any report or archaeological finding to suggest that anyone has ever eaten mosses as a staple part of diet. However, 5000 and more years ago there were no materials such as polythene and paper – nothing manufactured for wrapping, packing, stuffing and wiping. Mosses were highly convenient for all such uses, as many archaeological discoveries across Europe have made clear, and these uses have come right down to the modern era. Had Ötzi's provisions been wrapped in moss then that neatly explains, as accidental ingestions, the several leaves and leaf fragments of flat neckera recovered from the samples, representing no less than three meals, taken from the ileum, colon and rectum. Native groups in North America used 'mosses' (a term which they often use to mean both moss and lichen) for a variety of purposes, but I have not come across any reference precisely to wrapping food. (See Plates 12,13 and 14.)

In all the gut samples there are tiny fragments of flat neckera and there are five more species but each of these five was extracted from only one gut sample. These gut samples represent at least three meals, and so the flat neckera was ingested three times or more. When, in 1997, only one leaf of flat neckera was known from the first tiny colon sample that Klaus Oeggl had investigated, my tentative explanation then was that Ötzi had used this moss to wrap his provisions. Now this explanation seems all the more likely. As mosses go, flat neckera is quite large and is often several centimetres long, reaching 20cm long but rarely longer. It often grows in large amounts on shady rock faces, often limy rock, and on trunks of trees growing on the richer soils (*Innsbruck 4*, p. 77).

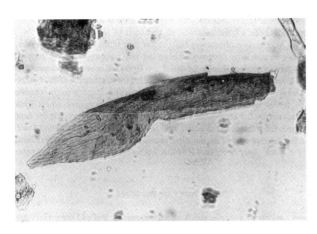

Fig. 4.2 Flat neckera leaf from a gut sample.

Charcoal and Anthracosis

There are minute charcoal fragments, many from coniferous wood, from a tree or trees such as pine and spruce, in every sample taken from Ötzi's gut and there is also charcoal in the gut samples from Kwäday Dän Ts'ìnchí Man (see Chapter 7). These new discoveries come as no surprise. More than 50 years ago, charcoal particles were recognised by the Dane Hans Haelbeck in the intestines of the famous Danish Iron Age bog bodies from Tollund and Grauballe, mentioned in Chapter 1, and there are such fragments in the gut of Lindow Man too. The eating of poorly washed or unwashed food is an immediate explanation, as is the inhalation of campfire smoke or the eating of meat removed from partly carbonised wooden spits.

Ötzi had anthracosis, that is to say there were blackened areas in his lungs; Konrad Spindler wrote (*Spindler* 2, p. 193): 'The lung tissue had a blackish colour. Evidently the Iceman had often sat by an open campfire and breathed in smoke and particles of soot, which had led to anthracotic changes in this organ.' This matter was taken further by Maria-Anna Pabst and Ferdinand Hofer, both of Graz, Austria. They thought that the soot particles most probably been inhaled from open fires in houses. The two Austrians also found and studied tiny mineral particles in the lungs and recognised mainly muscovite but also illite, quartz and plagioclase (see Chapter 5).[31] They also thought that the amorphous organic material they found derived from the threshing of cereals but they could see no cell wall structures that, perhaps, could have given confirmation. Konrad Spindler thought that Ötzi had consumed charcoal deliberately to get rid of the whipworms, as discussed later in this Chapter.

DRINK

As the sections immediately above make very clear, we know a lot about the food that Ötzi ate, especially the composition of some of his last meals. He drank water, of course, and also human milk, likely his mother's. Perhaps he drank milk from cattle or goats or sheep and also perhaps ate cheese, as Konrad Spindler speculated in his last scientific paper. Was anything else imbibed – alcohol? Humankind first produced an alcoholic drink a long time before Ötzi lived, indeed thousands of years before, perhaps not in Europe, but certainly in China. Patrick McGovern of the Pennsylvania University Museum has written a lot about this topic of the early history of alcoholic beverages. He even speculates that consumption of such drinks could have begun in Europe in Palaeolithic times but he admits there is no hard evidence from such an early period. With various colleagues, he analysed chemical residues found on fragments of pottery jars and jugs from the early Neolithic site in Henan Province, north-central China The very place is Jiahu, where a village flourished between 7000 and 5600 BC. He claims that they found hard evidence for 'the world's earliest known alcoholic beverage'.[32] The residues they found indicated that grapes and/or hawthorn and honey and rice had been fermented. That is really something to go on.[33]

How early was the first consumption of alcohol in Europe and in particular in *Ötziland*? Precisely for *Ötziland* the answer is unknown because we do not have there the quality of evidence found for China. However, for various far-flung parts of Neolithic and Bronze Age Europe we do have such evidence. Patrick McGovern's latest book is called *Uncorking the*

Past: The Quest for Wine, Beer and Other Alcoholic Beverages. His maps 1 and 2 show Europe, the Mediterranean region and the Black Sea and Caspian Sea areas. Shaded areas show zones of Upper Palaeolithic and Neolithic 'fermented-beverage experimentation, ca. 30,000 B.P. – 4000 B.C'. If we accept his claims as correct then alcohol consumption had spread westwards in north-eastern Italy by 5400 BC. So this is about 2000 years before Ötzi lived.[34]

If Ötzi had access to alcohol it is likely to have been ale or mead rather than wine. In her publication *Barley, Malt and Ale*, Merryn Dineley presents a case for ale production during the Neolithic in the Middle East and in widespread parts of Europe, where barley was cultivated throughout – Bulgaria, the Netherlands, southern Sweden and the Orkney Islands.[35] There are certainly good indications of alcohol consumption in the European Neolithic, and even better from the Bronze Age and later, and not just from the eastern Mediterranean area but in Germany (Baden-Württemberg, Bavaria, Hesse), Denmark and Scotland (several sites) and Wales (one site). Why not England or Ireland, one may ask? In these cases pollen analysis, especially the recognition of meadowsweet, has been crucial.

The use of sloes, the fruits of blackthorn, to flavour alcohol such as gin is well known in recent times but, perhaps much less common knowledge, is that in the Jura region of France the fruits were distilled to make a much appreciated *goutte* (drop). Sometimes the fruits were used to colour inferior quality wine.[36] However, there is nothing whatever that allows us to claim with any certainty at all that Ötzi or his tribe indulged in such a use of sloes. Though the stones have often been found in archaeological contexts in many parts of Europe there has yet to be any indication of blackthorn in connection with alcoholic drinks.

DRUGS AND DRESSINGS

We know that Ötzi had at least one intestinal parasite, various illnesses and wounds and so it is inevitable that thoughts turn to medical treatments. In Chapter 2 mention was made of his tattoos having been therapeutic rather than decorative, but there are other relevant matters to be considered here. The several topics discussed in this section are all, to some degree, speculative.

Blackthorn: Vitamins
Paraphrasing Konrad Spindler, Gudrun Sulzenbacher claims that Ötzi took medicine 'in a preventative manner through the discovery of therapeutic substances. Evidence for this lies in the sloeberry which was found beside him. Due to its high vitamin and mineral content, this fruit has long been cherished.' That Ötzi ate sloes is very likely but if he said to himself 'I must eat this because it is especially good for my health' is pure speculation. He had better have taken, if available, the fruits of wild roses which are famously rich in vitamin C.

Hop Hornbeam
Hop hornbeam does not appear in any of the old herbals such as that splendid one from the mid-sixteenth century by the German Lenhart Fuchs, which is both detailed and botanically accurate, although it should be stated that Fuchs mentioned only 6 of the 18 trees and tall shrubs we know to have been connected with Ötzi. Furthermore, from later herbals,

I know of no medicinal uses of the flowers or bark or any other part of the tree in Europe. By contrast, in eastern North America, medicinal infusions or decoctions of the bark of the closely related ironwood have been used by the Cherokee, Iroquois and Potawatomi for such ailments as blood, kidney and lung disorders. Willy Groenman-Van Waateringe was impressed by this. She has argued that Ötzi had taken such treatment using the bark of hop hornbeam and so swallowed the pollen of that tree which had been adhering to the bark.[37] Perhaps Ötzi had deliberately eaten male catkins? If either of these suggestions had indeed been the case there should be remains of the bark or catkins in the gut. None have been found.

Ferns

Some ferns have been used to expel intestinal worms for a very long time, indeed 2000 years and more. The point in discussing ferns in the context of Ötzi and other Neolithic people is that sporangia and spores of bracken have been found in the iceman's ingesta and sporangia of male fern and polypody have been found at Arbon Bleiche 3. In Europe there are several ferns closely related to the male fern, which is a very common, widespread plant, often growing in woodlands. When male fern was used as a vermifuge it was as an extract of the underground parts which, of course, do not produce the sporangia and spores are carried on the undersides of the fronds. From Arbon Bleiche 3 the sporangia were found in pollen samples of the sediments and not from faeces. So, as Mattieu Le Bailly and Françoise Bouchet themselves realise, it is very speculative indeed to claim that the villagers were deliberately using ferns as medicine. In the case of Ötzi, the spores of bracken are from the gut but how did they get into a preparation of subterranean parts? Klaus Oeggl is well aware of this difficulty but is strongly impressed by the strong positive correlation between the spores of bracken and the eggs of whipworm (and also of the pollen of wheat, presumably einkorn). He thinks the bracken had been deliberately ingested as a vermifuge.

Fungi: Birch Bracket Fungus

The young, short-lived fruiting bodies of the birch bracket fungus are edible, medicinal infusions can be made from them and another use is as a styptic. According to the Innsbruck University microbiologists Ulrike Peinter and Reinhold Pöder, it has both antimicrobial and anti-inflammatory activity (*Innsbruck* 4). As the name states, it grows on old birch trees, as in Pfossental just as it does over much of Europe, as in the woods on acid soils outside my native Glasgow and in woods on calcareous soils near my other home near Vesoul in Franche-Comté, France, where I have seen the roughly semi-circular brackets up to 22cm diameter. (See Plate 19.)

On fur strips, Ötzi had carried two shaped and pierced pieces of the birch bracket fungus and so he may have used them medicinally. The same two microbiologists argue strongly for its 'medical-spiritual' use by Ötzi. Luigi Capasso made interesting sweeping claims concerning this fungus, quoted here from a one-page article in *The Lancet*, the famous medical journal. On page 1864 there are the statements: '… contains toxic resins and an active compound, agaric acid, which are powerful purgatives and result in strong though short-lived bouts of diarrhoea.' The fungus 'also contains oils that are toxic to metazoans and antibiotic properties acting against mycobacteria'. The infection of whipworm 'more likely resulted in abdominal pain and cyclic anaemia; this cyclic anaemia would explain the low iron content of the mummy's striated muscles and the repeated ungual hypoplasia'. If the worms caused diarrhoea, one may wonder why Ötzi needed to take a purgative, unless these worms, which can be numerous, had caused a blockage. Be that as it may, Capasso's claims were immediately subject to devastating criticism both by the Innsbruck microbiologists and by Håkan Turón and Ingvar Svenberg of Uppsala, Sweden. Extraordinarily, Luigi Capasso's reply in *The Lancet* addresses none of the criticisms.[38]

True Tinder Fungus

Seemingly unaware of either Ursula Pietner and Reinhold Pöder or Luigi Capasso, four French mycologists (fungus scientists) from Montpellier discussed at length in scholarly fashion the many uses of the true tinder fungus. The medical uses they mention are many and various. Their list includes styptic dressing, bandages, cauterisation, dentistry, chiropody, treatment of rheumatism, anxiety, haemorrhoids, urinary problems and sciatica. Do we have a forgotten panacea? They also list, among other uses, the making of clothes such as hats, fishing floats, pin cushions and fuses for fireworks.[39] If Ötzi ever used this fungus for medicine or other purposes, we shall probably never know. (See Plate 20.)

Fly Agaric

However engaging and even plausible it may be that the prehistoric inhabitants of the southern Alps and elsewhere in Eurasia consumed the fly agaric (the famous red-capped and white-spotted toadstool) for its hallucinogenic effects, there is absolutely no hard evidence that they did. See Gordon Wason's intriguing account of the shamanic uses of this large toadstool.[40] The ORF (Austrian) television programme made by Kurt Mündl and then broadcast in whole or in part by other television companies which shows Ötzi and his fellow tribesmen mixing this fungus, as well as the equally famous and toxic deadly nightshade, into what looks like a witch's brew. Though the participants are all male, it is reminiscent of the famous witches scene in *Macbeth*. The book that Kurt Mündl wrote has photographs of this potion making, which may well never have happened.[41]

If only because different groups of people have had different taboos, such an assumption without any qualification is misleading. Though it is likely to have been millennia ago, we simply do not know when and where the use of fungi as food or as drugs started. Thus, it is misleading, also, to show any large toadstool in connection with Ötzi, as is done in the book by Gudrun Sulzenbacher. Brenda Fowler is another who simply takes it for granted that fungi were eaten as food: 'Mushrooms must have contributed to the diet or pharmacy of Neolithic people.' The use of fungi as medicine may seem likely, as Ötzi shows, but as food we simply cannot be sure as yet. We do know that prehistoric and later people used deadly nightshade and other members of the same family such as henbane because seeds have been found in archaeological layers at various places and from different periods. The claim that Ötzi's people used these toxic seeds as well as fly agaric can be regarded as either extrapolation or speculation but it is certainly not established scientific fact.

Charcoal

Konrad Spindler stated (*Spindler* 2, p. 94): 'The enormous infestation with the parasite *Trichuris trichuria*, which also irritated the intestinal mucous membranes, possibly led to impairment of the digestive tract, which caused diarrhoea. It may be cautiously conjectured that the man treated this complaint – as would be done today – with powered charcoal.' Other explanations for the charcoal have been discussed above in the section on unintentional ingestions.

Bog Mosses as Wound Dressings

Being highly absorbent and even antiseptic because of their strongly acidifying effects, bog mosses have been used as very efficient nappies. Until very recent times, they have also been used as wound dressings, a use that may go well back into prehistoric times, as a tantalising example from the Scottish Bronze Age perhaps shows. The late Terence Painter of the Norwegian University of Science and Technology in Trondheim investigated these favourable properties of bog mosses and found that such wound dressings were three to four times as absorbent as cotton equivalents. But even more cogently he found that they immobilised whole bacterial cells, as well as enzymes, exotoxins and lysins secreted by the most invasive pathogens. The active substance is essentially a kind of pectin called sphagnan.[42] Colleagues of Terence Painter now claim that the sphagnan theory is not correct. However, it should be stressed that they consider that bog moss holocellulose has indeed preservative properties. They end 'The remarkable properties of peat and *Sphagnum* [bog mosses] remain a challenging area'. (See Plate 14.)

Two species of bog moss were found with Ötzi; these are imbricate bog moss and the tentatively identified rigid bog moss. The latter was one tiny piece of branch with several leaves attached and it was found in sample 91/103 'string, grasses, hair'. This could well have been a purely accidental matter because there are boggy places that he could have traversed on his last or some previous journey. Much more difficult to explain is microscopic-sized piece of leaf of the imbricate bog moss. It consists of only about 30 cells and was found on a pollen slide made up from a colon sample; this quite unexpected discovery has been discussed at length recently by the author and several others. (See Fig. 4.3.)

So we have two species of bog moss represented by a mere single fragment of each, which is not much on which to build a hypothesis of medicinal use. There is nothing to make us certain that he was carrying bog moss but we know he had carried other mosses. Because bog mosses are well known as wound dressings and we know that Ötzi had at least two wounds, both probably inflicted in the last few days, even hours, of his life, it is very tempting to make the obvious connection.

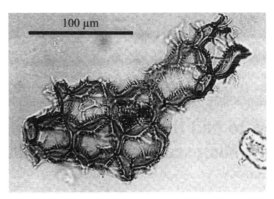

100 µm

Fig. 4.3 The tiny leaf fragment of bog moss from the colon.

Mosses other than Bog Mosses

As already mentioned, the moss flat neckera occurred in every gut sample studies so far. Could it have been internal medicine? There are only very sparse records from Europe, North America and elsewhere of mosses used in such a way but no species of *Neckera* has been listed for such a purpose. One example can be mentioned, taken from *Bryonet*, a web service for bryologists. When Dr Masanobu Higuchi of the National Science Museum in Japan visited Yunnan, China, he saw local people at the roadside selling herbal medicine, which included the moss *Rhodobryum giganteum*. He was told that it was traditional Tibetan medicine for heart trouble. So, though not totally discountable, this idea that flat neckera could have been medicine seems unlikely.

Notes

1 Hellrigl, K. 1996. *Die Tierwelt Südtirols.* Band 1, Veroffentlichungen des Naturmuseums Südtirol, 831 pages; p. 816. 'Capra ibex ibex (Linnaeus, 1758) Alpensteinbock D1; O3; O4; Stilfs, Texelgrse'. Chauvet, J.-M., Brunel Deschamps, E. and Hillaire, C. 1996. *Chauvet Cave The Discovery of the World's Oldest Paintings.* There are three radiocarbon dates from the cave drawings at Chauvet. However, Paul Bahn thinks the true age of the drawings is about 20,000 years old, not 30,000. Delluc, B., Delluc, G., Roussot, A. and Roussot-Larroque, J. 2001. *Discovering Périgord Prehistory.* Luçon, Éditions Sudouest. Roussot, A. 1979. *L'Art préhistorique.* Third edition. Luçon, Éditions Sudouest. Gamble, C. 1999. *The Palaeolithic Societies of Europe.* Cambridge University Press. Guthrie, D. 2005. *The Nature of Paleolithic Art.* Chicago University Press. Pailhugue, N. 1995. 'La faune de la Salle Monique, Grotte de La Vache (Alliat, Ariège)'. *Bulletin de la Société Préhistorique Ariège-Pyrénées* 50, pp. 225–89. Gailli, R. 2003. *La Grotte de La Vache.* Courbet, Éditions Lacour. Pigeaud, R. 2006. 'La Grotte du Lazaret. *Archéologia* 433, pp. 18–27. Dalmeri, G., Basetti, M., Cusinato, A., Kompatscher, M.H. and Kompatscher. K. 2006. 'Le site Épigravettien de l'Abri Dalmeri: aspects artistiques à la fin du Paléolithique supérieur en Italie du nord'. *L'Anthropologie* 110, pp. 510–29.
2 Ibid.
3 Ibid.
4 Ibid.
5 Bahn, P.G. 1997. *The Story of Archaeology.* London, Weidefield & Nicholson. Oegg, K. and Schoch, W. 'Neolithic plant remains discovered together with a mummified corpse ("Homo tyrolensis") in the Tyrolean Alps'. In Kroll, H. and Pasternak, R. (eds) *Res archaeobotanicae.* Kiel, Symposium IWGP, pp. 229–38. Dickson, C. & Dickson, J. 2000. *Plants and People in Ancient Scotland.* Stroud, Tempus.
6 Ibid.
7 Ibid.
8 Piperno, D.R., Weiss, E., Holst, I. and Nadel, D. 2004. 'Processing of wild cereal grains in the Upper Palaeolithic revealed by starch grain analysis'. *Nature* 430, pp. 670–3.
9 Zohary, D. and Hopf, M. 2000. *Domestication of Plants in the Old World.* Third edition. Oxford University Press, p. 83.
10 Ibid.
11 Holden, T.G. 1996. 'Detailed analysis of the macroscopic remains from the colon of the Tyrol Ice Body (ICE96)'. Unpublished report. Edinburgh, Headland Archaeology.
12 Zohary, D. and Hopf, M. 2000. *Domestication of Plants in the Old World.* Third edition. Oxford University Press, p. 83.
13 Heiss, A. and Oeggl, K. 2009. 'The plant macro-remains from the Iceman site (Tisenjoch, Italian-Austrian border, eastern Alps: new results on the glacier mummy's environment'. *Vegetation History and Archaeobotany* 18, pp. 23–36.
14 Zohary, D. and Hopf, M. 2000. *Domestication of Plants in the Old World.* Third edition. Oxford University Press, p. 83.
15 Ibid., p. 126.

16 Bell, B. and Dickson, C. 1989. 'Excavations at Warebeth (Stromness Cemetry) Broch, Orkney'. *Proceedings of the Society of Antiquaries of Scotland* 119, pp. 101–31. Davis, O.K. 2006. 'Feces in the Geological Record'. *Palaeo 3*, 237, pp. 1–3.

17 Ibid.

18 Holden, T.G. 1996. 'Detailed analysis of the macroscopic remains from the colon of the Tyrol Ice Body (ICE96)'. Unpublished report. Edinburgh, Headland Archaeology.

19 Oeggl, K., Kofler, K. and Schmidl, A. 2005. 'New Aspects of the Diet of the Neolithic Tyrolean Iceman "Ötzi"'. *Journal of Biological Research* 80, pp. 344–7.

20 Behre, K.-E. 2008. 'Collected seeds and fruits from herbs as prehistoric food'. *Vegetation History and Archaeobotany* 17, pp. 65–73.

21 Oeggl, K., Kofler, K. and Schmidl, A. 2005. 'New Aspects of the Diet of the Neolithic Tyrolean Iceman "Ötzi"'. *Journal of Biological Research* 80, p. 346.

22 Rollo, F. *et al*. 2002. 'Ötzi's last meals: DNA analysis of the intestinal content of the Neolithic glacier mummy from the Alps'. *Proceedings of the National Academy of Science* 99, pp. 12594–9.

23 Emsley, J. 2001. *Nature's Building Blocks An A–Z Guide to the Elements*. Oxford University Press.

24 Macko, S.A. *et al*. 1999a. 'The Ice Man's diet as reflected by stable nitrogen and carbon isotopic composition of his hair'. *Federation of American Societies for Experimental Biology Journal* 13, pp. 559–62. Macko, S.A. *et al*. 1999b. 'Documenting the diet in ancient human populations through stable isotope analysis of hair'. *Philosophical Transactions of the Royal Society of London* B 354, pp. 65–76.

25 Dickson, C. and Dickson, J. 2000. *Plants and People in Ancient Scotland*. Stroud, Tempus.

26 Macko, S.A. *et al*. 1999a. 'The Ice Man's diet as reflected by stable nitrogen and carbon isotopic composition of his hair'. *Federation of American Societies for Experimental Biology Journal* 13, pp. 559–62. Macko, S.A. *et al*. 1999b. 'Documenting the diet in ancient human populations through stable isotope analysis of hair'. *Philosophical Transactions of the Royal Society of London* B 354, pp. 65–76.

27 Knights, B.A. *et al*. 1983. *Journal of Archaeological Science* 10, pp. 139–52. Dickson, J.H. *et al*. 2000. 'The omnivorous Tyrolean Iceman: colon contents (meat, cereals, pollen, moss and whipworm) and stable isotope analyses'. *Philosophical Transactions of the Royal Society* 355, pp. 1843–51. Soon after the publication of the rebuttal paper, pages appeared on the web entitled 'The Iceman's Food Fight'. The website still exists. Some of the comments therein indicate that the particular reader had not properly understood the arguments in the rebuttal paper. What is more surprising is the section devoted to this topic in *The Molecule Hunt Archaeology and the Search for Ancient DNA*, by Martin Jones, Professor of Archaeological Science at Cambridge University; this accepts the claims by Stephen Macko. Jones, M. 2001. *The Molecule Hunt Archaeology and the Search for Ancient DNA*. London, Allen Lane.

28 Linskens, H.F. and Jorde, W. 1997. 'Pollen as food and medicine – a review'. *Economic Botany* 51, pp. 78–87. Balls, E.K. 1962. *Early Uses of California Plants*. Berkeley, University of California Press. Cranwell, L.M. 1953. 'New Zealand Pollen Studies. The Monocotyledons'. *Bulletin of the Auckland Museum* 3, pp. 1–91.

29 Ibid.

30 Oeggl, K. *et al*. 2007. 'The reconstruction of the last itinerary of "Ötzi", the Neolithic Iceman, by pollen analyses from sequentially sampled gut extracts'. *Quaternary Science Reviews* 26, pp. 853–61. Oeggl, K. In *Innsbruck* 4, pp. 89–116. Gobet, E. *et al*. 2000. 'Influence of human impact and bed-rock differences on the vegetational history of the Insubrian Southern Alps'. *Vegetation History and Archaeobotany* 9, pp. 175–87. Franz, W.R. 2002. *Die Hopfenbuche (Ostrya carpinifolia Scop.) in Österreich und Nord-Slowenien*. Klagenfurt, Naturwissenschaftlicher Verein für Kärten.

31 Pabst, M.A. and Hofer, F. 1998. 'Deposits of Different Origin in the Lungs of the 5,300-Year-Old Tyrolean Iceman'. *American Journal of Physical Anthropology* 107, pp. 1–12. Gaber, O. and Künzel, K.-H. 1998. 'Man from Hauslabjoch'. *Experimental Gerontology* 33, pp. 655–60.

32 McGovern, P.E. 2003. *The Origins and Ancient History of Wine*. Princeton University Press. McGovern, P.E. *et al*. 2004. 'Fermented beverages of pre- and proto-historic China'. *Proceedings of the National Academy of Sciences* 101, pp. 17593–8. McGovern, P.E. 2009. *Uncorking the Past The Quest for Wine, Beer and Other Alcoholic Beverages*. Berkeley, University of California Press. Rösch, M. 1999. 'Evaluation of honey residues from Iron Age hill-top sites in southwestern Germany: implications for local and regional land use and vegetation dynamics'. *Vegetation history and Archaeobotany* 8, pp. 105–12.

Rösch, M. 2005. 'Pollen analysis of the contents of excavated vessels – direct archaeological evidence of beverages'. *Vegetation History and Archaeobotany* 14, pp. 179–88. Rösch, M. 2006. 'Wein und Weinbau'. Real Lexicon der Germaninem Alterung Kunde. Dickson, C. and Dickson, J. 2000. *Plants and People in Ancient Scotland*. Stroud, Tempus. Dineley, M. 2004. Barley, Malt, and Ale in the Neolithic. *BAR International Series* 1213, Oxford.

33   Ibid.

34   Ibid.

35   Ibid.

36   André, M., Blanchard, O. and Le Pennec, C. 2002. *La Flore de la Montagne Jurassienne*. Besançon, NEO editions.

37   Groenman-Van Waateringe, W. 1997. 'Ostrya carpinifolia as medicine in the European Neolithic'. Abstract. In Gerachty, S. (ed.) *18th Annual Conference of the Association for Environmental Archaeology, held in Limerick, Ireland*, p. 6. Groenman-van Waateringe, W. 2011. 'The Iceman's last days – the testimony of *Ostrya carpinifolia*'. *Antiquity* 85, pp. 1–8.

38   Capasso, L. 1995. 'Ungueal morphology and pathology of the "Ice Man"'. In *Innsbruck* 2, pp. 231–9. Capasso, L. 1998. '5300 years ago, the Ice Man used natural laxatives and antibiotics'. *The Lancet* 352, p. 1864. Pöder, R. and Peintner, U. 1999. 'Laxatives and the Iceman'. *The Lancet* 353, p. 926. Turón, H. and I. 1999. 'Laxatives and the Iceman'. *The Lancet* 353, pp. 925–6. Capasso, L. 1999. Author's reply. *The Lancet* 353, p. 926. Roussel, B., Rapior, S., Masson, C.-L. and Boutie, P. 2002. '*Fomes fomentarius* (L.: Fr.) Fr.: un champignon aux multiples usages'. *Cryptogamie, Mycologie* 23, pp. 1–18.

39   Ibid.

40   Wasson, R.G. 1968. *Soma Divine Mushroom of Immortality*. Harcourt Brace Jovanovich Edition. This scholarly book ends with a thundering anti-climax. The author ate some of the mushroom to see what would happen. Nothing did! Mündl, K. 1999. *Der Ötztal-mann und seine welt*. Graz, Verlag Styria.

41   Ibid.

42   Dickson, J. H. *et al.* 2005. 'How to find the Bogmoss, *Sphagnum imbricatum* sensu lato, in South Tyrol, Italy: Microscopically examine the Iceman's Colon Contents'. *Vegetation History and Archaeobotany* 14, pp. 207–10. Dickson, J.H. *et al.* 2009. 'Six mosses from the Tyrolean Iceman's alimentary tract and their significance for the events of his last days and his ethnobotany'. *Vegetation History and Archaeobotany* 18, pp. 13–22. Painter, T.J. 2003. 'Concerning the wound-healing properties of *Sphagnum* holocellulose: the Maillard reaction in pharmacology'. *Journal of Ethnopharmacology* 88, pp. 145–8. 'Sphagnum moss, sphagnan and conservation properties'. *Web pages of the Norwegian University of Science and Technology July 2010*. Gottesfeld, L.M.J. and Vitt, D. 1996. 'The Selection of *Sphagnum* for Diapers by Indigenous North Americans'. *Evansia* 13, pp. 103–8.

5

Homeland, Social Role, Last Journey and Death

For no less than for any other strange person who has suddenly and unexpectedly arrived, Ötzi instantly provoked surprise and then quickly various questions followed, perhaps the first two being 'who are you?' and 'where did you come from?' Ötzi cannot immediately describe his experiences to us because none of us would understand a word he said if he could speak, but how dearly we would like to know what language was spoken in Central Europe over 5000 years ago.[1] However, slowly, we have ways of making him talk. From the application of traditional archaeology and many ever-increasing, powerful scientific techniques, mutely he has told us plenty already but, no doubt, with much more to follow in the coming years.

'And make it look as if he'd been run over by a glacier.'

Fig. 5.1 Cartoon from the *New Yorker*. (*New Yorker*)

HOMELAND

Traditional Archaeology

Konrad Spindler was disappointed that there was no pottery found with Ötzi because, had there been any, then his homeland, 'which corner of the Alps or pre-Alps had been his home', would have been easily deduced. He thought that other methods of finding this out would be very complex and produce only vague results (*Spindler* 2, p. 100). However, the science, particularly recognition of the plant remains and stable isotope analyses, described in the following two sections goes a long way to resolving this intriguing matter. Very soon after the discovery of the body, archaeologists, for example Lawrence Barfield, Ebba Koller and Andreas Lippert in their book and Konrad Spindler in his books, argued for southern rather than northern connections. Very few studies have argued the opposite.[2]

A very long time before Ötzi lived people occupied *Ötziland* even if only sparsely. In north Tyrol, in southernmost Ötztal, just where Rofental joins Niedertal at 1950m, there is a Mesolithic site, now preserved under a wooden shelter. There, Walter Leitner of Innsbruck University found not just small knapped flints but worked rock crystal too, and both rock types must have come from far off, the latter from Zillertal, nearly 100km to the north-east on the map and much further on the ground.[3]

To the south there are clear signs of Mesolithic occupation, as at Tisental and Finailtal, both very close to the Ötzi site, and Penaudtal and Saxalbergsee. These hunter-gatherers were widespread in all Tyrol far from the Ötzi site because flints have been found in north Tyrol too, as at Loas Sattel and at Pill, near Pitztal, as well as at Münster between Schwaz and Kufstein and at Texer Joch, near Kufstein. Much nearer in time to Ötzi, there are many indications of Neolithic occupation to the south in Südtirol and Trentino and even in the very nearby Vinschgau, as at Juval castle. Lorenzo Dal Ri describes the prehistoric site at this medieval castle on a rocky knoll, one of many such situated castles in Tyrol, as follows:

> Besides ample Neolithic and Bronze Age stratifications, the Chalcolithic is also in evidence. It has been argued that Castel Juvale could have been the place where the Iceman lived. An important factor to consider is the geographical proximity (unlikely to be more than a day's march for a fit man).[4]

By contrast, to the north, the nearest known late Stone Age settlements are many tens of kilometres away and, it should be stressed, no Neolithic settlements are known in Ventertal or elsewhere in Ötztal or even in the adjoining part of Inntal. There are very few prehis-

Fig. 5.2 Hohler Stein prehistoric site.

Fig. 5.3 Menhir from Latsch. (*Lorenzo Dal Ri*)

toric sites anywhere in Ötztal. However, one is spectacular. An enormous erratic block, the Hohler Stein (Hollow Rock) is at the north end of Niedertal, at 2050m, only a short way from Vent and close to the Mesolithic site just mentioned above.[5] There, Walter Leitner uncovered fireplaces, postholes and worked flints. He stated that the discoveries came from 'late Southern Alpine Mesolithic period of the 7th/6th century BC'. Because one flint is the same variety of flint stone as those of the Iceman, Konrad Spindler claims (*Spindler* 2, p. 250), 'The discovery of the Stone Age picnic area by the Hohler Stein proves that the Upper Ötztal was indeed known and traversed in the Iceman's day.'

The Neolithic inhabitants of Vinschgau erected large stones called statue menhirs, with incised and shallow relief carvings which are highly relevant concerning Ötzi, as the archaeologists just mentioned quickly realised. The carvings show axes and daggers; the former resemble Ötzi's, but the latter do not because they obviously show metal blades. One of these menhirs was found at Latsch in Vinschgau. About this stone Konrad Spindler stated (*Spindler* 2, p. 227): 'Thus it seems appropriate to seek the native village of the Iceman in the Val Venosta [Vinschgau]. I would go even further and say that perhaps the Iceman had taken up residence on the castle hill of Juval and had seen the sacred stone of Latsch with his own eyes.' Though not an altogether unreasonable notion, this is a great precision which contrasts strongly with his pessimism quoted in the first paragraph of this chapter. The menhir can be seen in the church Unsere Liebe Frau auf dem Bichl, now a museum, in Latsch. Evidently unknown to Konrad Spindler, that very stone shows a bowman seemingly about to fire an arrow into the back of another man. See the section 'Shot in the Back' later in this chapter.

Lorenzo Dal Ri briefly listed these anthropomorphic statues. Apart from the one just discussed, there are discoveries at Lagundo at the mouth of Vinschgau and at Corces in Vinschgau. In the Eisacktal (Val d'Isarco) there such stones, and also at Velturno-Tanzgasse,

Santa Verena, Tötschling, Fiè and Laion.[6] To be seen in the museum in Arco, at the northern tip of Lake Garda, there is a beautifully displayed group of menhirs excavated by Annaluisa Pedrotti of the University of Trento. It includes seemingly a whole family – a man, a woman and a child.

Soon after the discovery of Ötzi, archaeologists began to compare his equipment with the Remedello culture, which, according to Lawrence Barfield, is an unclear entity and, in the strict sense, applies only to cemeteries on the central Po Plain, well to the south of Ötziland. But that was nearly 20 years ago and things have moved on.[7] Following Annaluisa Pedrotti, Angelika Fleckinger states:

> Based on the meagre Copper Age finds discovered in what is today the South Tyrol, everything
> indicates that he should be classified as a member of the first independent Alpine cultural group
> Tamins-Carasso-Isera 5. Emerging during the last centuries of the fourth millenium BC, this
> group is characterized by simple ceramic vessels with edging, notches and rows of dots.[8]

Plant Geography

The arguments now presented take for granted that the broad geographical patterns shown by the especially crucial plants have not changed in any very substantial way over the last 5000 years. This may seem an unreasonable standpoint because 5000 years may be considered a long time for climatic variation and human alteration of the environment to have wreaked much change in where plants grow. However, this has not been the case. Fig. 5.4 shows the regional pattern of the moss flat neckera. Climatic change has simply not been great enough, nor human destructiveness of woodland complete enough, to have spoiled the deductions given here.

The botanical evidence, the remains of both flowering plants and mosses, clearly points to the south, as I and four others explained in a 1996 paper entitled 'Mosses and the Tyrolean Iceman's Southern Provenance'.[9] When Ötzi's clothes were conserved, the washing revealed many plant fragments including a mass of the large woodland moss flat neckera. This moss and others he had carried are to be found growing much closer to the site to the south than to the north. Crisped neckera grows in some abundance at and around Juval castle at the south end of Schnalstal, over 2000m lower than but only 16km away from the site, as the crow flies. Though only in moderate amount, flat neckera grows as close to the site as Vernagt; on the map, only 5km separates the site from Vernagt. Similarly, other mosses found with Ötzi, such as rambling tail moss, pendulous wing moss, creeping feather moss and many-fruited thyme moss, all grow in southern to mid-Schnalstal but not Ventertal, other than pendulous wing moss which occurs at Zwieselstein, only just in Ventertal at the northernmost end.

Hop hornbeam has already been discussed in Chapter 4. It is said to grow at the south end of Schnalstal and perhaps even as close to the site as Katharinaberg, but I have not seen it at these places where the very steep topography makes thorough searches very difficult. Many of the other woody plants found with Ötzi grow at the south end of Schnalstal: hazel, wych and small-leaved elms, ash, small-leaved lime, wayfaring tree, dogwood and juneberry (Klaus Oeggl and Walter Schoch *Innsbruck* 4, p. 29). A Chalcolithic site was discovered at Juval castle, as just mentioned. Juval is the nearest place to the site where many of the important plants, both flowering and mosses, are to be found now. There is no reason to suppose

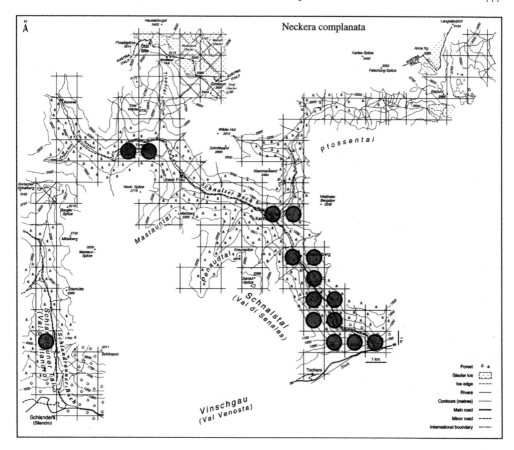

Fig. 5.4 Map of flat neckera.

that they did not grow there in prehistoric times, and so perhaps that is the very place where Ötzi lived, as we pointed out in the *Scientific American* articles. However, see the next section.

Mineralogy and Stable Isotopes

As discussed above in connection with Ötzi's blackened lungs, Maria Anna Pabst and Ferdinand Hofer of Graz University did not just find carbon therein but mineral particles too.[10] They used the minerals to try to deduce where Ötzi had lived. As outlined in Chapter 2, the geology of *Ötziland* is very complex. The most abundant mineral they found was muscovite. And this did not surprise them because they state that 'the Ötztal Alps are composed of muscovite-bearing rocks, including large amounts of paragneiss and schists with intercalated muscovite granite-gneiss and two-mica augen-gneiss … the smallest crystals easily become airborne and then inhaled … the illite could refer to a muscovite-rich area too'. Influenced by the archaeological findings, they suggest Vinschgau and even mention the Naturns region, but the area of muscovite containing rock stretches over a very large area. So this study does not get us very far, but the investigations of stable isotopes do.

Stable isotopes have already been discussed in relation to Ötzi's diet. Now we come to the second major importance of these isotopes: determination of the place of a person's origin.

A particularly striking case is the Amesbury Archer, from the Early Bronze Age, about 4300 years ago. He was buried near the famous Stonehenge in southern England. Among many exciting discoveries the archaeologists made were knives, the earliest copper implements known from Britain and the earliest gold ornament too. There was also a cushion stone for working and smoothing copper. However, perhaps the most dramatic finding is from stable isotopes in his tooth enamel. His origin was the western/central Alps.[11] So, his burial was some 1000 km or more from his provenance. Ötzi's provenance was probably only some 100km or less from his frigid resting place. Nonetheless, it is a fascinating story too and, like the Amesbury Archer, he spent many years away from his original homeland.

Wolfgang Müller *et al.* investigated the isotopes from the iceman's tooth enamel and dentine, bones and intestinal contents, clothing and gear, soils as well as river water. These numerous, varied analyses produce the result that Ötzi had grown up into early adulthood in one area but spent the later decades of his life in a different one. This was an exciting development.[12] The isotope evidence from teeth enamel indicates that his childhood area was not on limestone, basalts or Permian volcanics; this excludes most of region south of Bozen, even south and south-east of Meran (see Plate 6). But it could have been on gneisses and phyllites, which include the site and north to Inntal, Schnalstal, Vinschgau, Ulettal, the middle Eisack valley and lower Pustertal. Wolfgang Müller and co-authors chose Feldthurns, lower Pustertal and lowest Vinschgau near Meran (see Fig. 2.2). In later adulthood Ötzi lived in an area of gneiss, such as approximately 10 to 20km south-west to north-west of Meran.

How does this square with the botanical results? Clearly, the remains of plants found in, on and around the iceman's corpse can tell us nothing whatever about his early years, but they can tell us about where he was during his last few days. There is no fundamental disagreement. However, the isotope results indicate that Juval castle is unlikely to have been his home in later life, as had been suggested from the traditional archaeology and plant geography.

SOCIAL ROLE

If the equipment recovered from the hollow had all belonged to Ötzi then he had been carrying a lot of stuff, a matter which needs a full explanation. Why so much? What, if anything, can we learn from the gear (and the clothes too) about his occupation? Perhaps it is better to say occupations because is there anything improbable about him having been, say, both a chieftain and a hunter? A very early idea about Ötzi was that he was an outlaw. On what evidence, one may ask? Nothing cogent that I know of! Two others were a trader of flint (again on what evidence?) or a shaman. None of these has any solid basis, unless the two pieces of the birch bracket fungus mentioned in Chapter 4 had medical-spiritual use by a shaman and that is not very much to go on. Perhaps many people carried this fungus. These ideas merit no further discussion in my view but several other ideas certainly do and in detail.

Apart from deductions from the clothing and equipment, written about by many people, few investigators have tried to deduce Ötzi's occupation from the body itself. One such is Luigi Capasso, who has published (on at least three occasions) about the dirty, broken and scratched fingernail and on the worn front teeth.[13] In 1993 he wrote, 'The severe dental wear of the upper incisors … could be consistent with the use of dentition in the preparation of leather artifacts and of plant or animal fibers.' In 1994 he stated: 'the aspect of the Val Senales nail plate parallels that of nail plates from modern workers, such as peasants, stone masons, mechanics, etc., and indicates that this man made constant use of his nails as working tools.' He added that the nail had belonged to a 'coarse laborer'. In 1995, in a paper virtually identical to that from 1994, he changed 'peasants' to 'farmers'.

This does not get us to any firm conclusion. If Ötzi had been a shepherd or metal prospector/smelter or some other kind of manual worker would his nails not have been frequently or constantly dirty and broken? Had he been fleeing for his life and scrambling across difficult, high terrain and involved in a fatal fight, as discussed below, it is not hard to envisage nails in a dirty, poor state. In stark contrast, Eduard Egarter Vigl has told me that Ötzi's fingers are rather delicate without the appearance of those of a manual worker (see the section on appearance in Chapter 2).

Shepherd/Herdsman

If you visited the Iceman Museum in Bozen and Archeoparc at Unser Frau in Schnalstal in the last 10 years or so, as many people have done, you may well have gained the impression that there were substantial grounds for considering that Ötzi was a shepherd. This is because Konrad Spindler strongly espoused that notion in his books. He made statements such as 'The Iceman had with him everything that such an activity would require' and 'There is in fact no detail which does not fit this interpretation' and 'the main occupation of the Iceman was flock herding' (*Spindler* 1, p. 247).

In an article published in 2005, the year of his death, Konrad Spindler did not just cling to his idea but expanded it. He even suggested that the birch bark containers could have been used in the preparation of cheese.[14] He makes no mention of the statement he had made years before concerning the negative and totally unspecified examination for 'microtraces' (*Spindler* 2, p. 100). Perhaps the inside of the container should now be examined for fats, with well-established techniques as discussed by Richard Evershed of the University of Bristol and three others in the *Handbook of Archaeological Sciences*.[15] A good example concerns the recognition of animal fats in Roman cooking pots from Turkey.[16]

Various scientific articles have supported the shepherd hypothesis, such as those by Christopher Ruff *et al.* who think his sturdiness deduced from bone structure is consistent with a herding lifestyle.[17] However, surely it is consistent too with some other strenuous activities, such as hunting in the mountains or training and fighting? There is now very good evidence that the idea that Ötzi was a shepherd/herdsman is simply wrong and, indeed, some people, including an important English expert on the worldwide history of sheep and herding, have thought so from a very early stage.

To this day, in what may well be an old custom, sheep are taken in early summer (second week of June) on long treks from Schnalstal and Schlandraunertal up to high-level pastures in the Ötztal Alps and then brought back in early autumn (second week of September). Because the body was found near one of the traditional routes for this transhumance, it was an early thought that Ötzi had been a shepherd. On 9 June 2002, with some of the Innsbruck botanists, I had the engaging experience of watching the thousands of sheep including small lambs that had come from Schlandraunertal arrive at Vernagt to be penned for the night. They were then taken very early the next morning up Tisental past the Similaun Hut at 3019m and finally down to the high-level pastures in Ventertal. The shepherds, old and not so old, all sported the royal-blue aprons, so beloved by south Tyrolean farmers as to be almost a uniform. Before the narrow path was cut into the very steep cliff below the Similaun Hut the shepherds took their flocks over the Tisenjoch, about a kilometre or so to the north-west.

During these few hours, I could not know that only three months later, in mid-September on a visit to see the Ürümchi mummies, I would also be high up the Ürümchi River in the Tian Shan (Heavenly Mountains) of Xinjiang, north-westernmost China. There I watched sheep (Kazakh fat-rumps) and goats which were cute in their small size, pure whiteness and short upright tails. They were being brought down to lower pastures for the winter by Kazakh herdsmen on horseback, but without dogs as far as I saw during my observation. Such seasonal movement of animals is widespread in Eurasia and may well be a very ancient activity in all these places, not just in the Alps. Both the Alpine and central Asiatic herdsmen had very little gear. The Tyrolean shepherds had staffs but not crooks. The Kazakhs had neither, as far as I could see on my admittedly too brief observation.

This lack of equipment is characteristic of shepherds the world over, according to Michael Ryder, who wrote the definitive volume on this topic, *Sheep & Man*.[18] In a letter to *The Times*, 12 December 1994, he wrote of Ötzi: '... among all the elaborate (mostly hunting) equipment he carried, the man did not have a single piece of shepherding equipment' – the very opposite of Konrad Spindler's claim. And that was a point Michael Ryder had made already in 1992 in a learned society newsletter. Seemingly, Konrad Spindler was unaware of Michael Ryder's works or, if he was conversant with them, then he chose to ignore them in the 1990s and even into the 2000s.

In the *Scientific American* articles I wrote with two others we stated, and I have said it repeatedly in lectures, that 'No wool was on or about his person, no dead collie by his feet, no crook in his hand'. However, it is only fair to make the qualification that Michael Ryder states:

> My own findings from microscopic studies have shown the lack of wool clothing till the Bronze Age. This accords with evidence from surviving sheep of the earlier New Stone Age that, although sheep had already been domesticated, they had not yet developed a fleece. They were still like wild sheep with a coat similar to that of deer.

So, despite Konrad Spindler's polemical certainty, there was no evidence of any direct connection between Ötzi and sheep. Some support for the shepherd hypothesis came from the grass/bast cape which has modern parallels worn by shepherds in the Balkans. However, that alone is not conclusive and, for all we know, it was standard dress for travellers in the mountains, or in the lowlands for that matter, at that time. If indeed he was closely connected with animal husbandry, perhaps the term shepherd is inappropriate in any case, and it would be better to say goatherd or the less specific herdsman. We know he had contact with goats because his clothes were made in part of that animal. However, since sheep and goats are often run together, as in the Tian Shan already mentioned, in Greece and elsewhere, then it is hardly a very crucial point and, to be fair to Konrad Spindler, he did use the term 'flock herding', meaning both sheep and goats.

At an early stage of the investigations of Ötzi, the pollen analyst Sigmar Bortenschlager published pollen profiles from peat high in the Ötztal Alps and not too far from the Ötzi site (see Fig. 2.7). These indicated that the land above the tree line before Ötzi's time supported pastures. This was based on the recognition of pollen types such as parsley, chenopod and dock families, nettles and others, already listed in Chapter 2. However, Klaus Oeggl considers that these pollen types can be interpreted in other ways and certainly are not unequivocal indications of pastures.[19]

Now there is another hard-hitting blow to the flock-herding hypothesis based on pollen analyses. Alexandra Schmidl, Werner Kofler and Klaus Oeggl found that grasslands in *Ötziland* at low altitude and those at high altitude have distinctive pollen signatures. These pollen analysts found that dung of sheep travelling near the Ötzi site on their journey from Schnalstal to Ötztal in June 2002 had the pollen content of the low-altitude pastures they had very recently left. Furthermore, crucially, none of the prehistoric droppings extracted from the sediments at the Ötzi site, probably expelled by Alpine ibex or chamois rather than domestic sheep or goats, had the characteristic low-altitude pasture signature. Therefore these animals had not recently arrived during transhumance. Finally, in any case, radio-carbon dating showed that none of the ancient droppings produced by the herbivores had been produced at precisely Ötzi's time. To quote the words of Alexandra Schmidl and her colleagues:

> Recently coprolite analysis was conducted on a hundred caprine dung pellets found at the Iceman's find spot and dated from 5400 to 2000 BC. The lack of caprine faeces from valley bottoms as well as the absence of dung pellets at the find spot between 3700 and 2900 BC questions the practice of transhumance in the area during the Iceman's lifetime and for this reason also his social status as a shepherd.[20]

Copper Prospector/Smelter

That Ötzi might have been a prospector was a very early suggestion by Konrad Spindler. Had he been a searcher of copper ores (or less likely native copper – this means actual pure copper sticking out of the bedrock) then he inhabited a rich territory, as Fig. 3.3 shows. Somewhat raised levels of both arsenic and copper have been found in Ötzi's hair by Walter Gössler of Karl-Franzens University in Graz, Austria, with several others (*Innsbruck 2*, p. 269). Geoffrey Grime, then at Oxford University, in a television programme, also revealed raised values, as he did subsequently in a paper with Don Brothwell of the University of York.[21] These several investigators claimed that an obvious explanation is that he took part in smelting copper – arsenic being present to some degree in copper ores. They gave little or no consideration to other possible explanations. There are four in all that need consideration in my opinion:

1. *Breathing in fumes from smelting of copper ores:* If copper ore is heated to high temperatures arsenic sticks to soot particles and is gaseous too and so can be inhaled. The particles and gas circulate through the blood reaching the hair. Copper is less volatile and so less likely to be

inhaled. However, perhaps tiny particles of the ore stuck to Ötzi's hair or small fragments produced by working copper items adhered to his hair.

2. *Diagenesis:* This means contamination of his hair from the immediate environment of the corpse. That the keratin of hair has a marked affinity for arsenic is very easily demonstrated by placing hair in a solution of arsenic and that element is readily absorbed. Had Ötzi washed his hair in arsenic-rich water shortly before his demise then arsenic would be there.

3. *Unintentional drinking of arsenic-rich water:* Here and there this is a worldwide problem, both present and past.

4. *Arsenicophagy (arsenic eating):* This is the deliberate ingestion of arsenic trioxide crystals. Unlikely as it may seem because of the infamous toxicity of arsenic, such behaviour did happen in Styria, Austria, not too far east of *Ötziland*, and some claim in Tyrol and Switzerland too.

Arsenic has had many uses, not least in medicines and in pesticides. All that, and much more, as is obvious from the title, is covered by the book *Is Arsenic an Aphrodisiac?* by William Cullen of the University of British Columbia in Vancouver.[22] It is a fascinating, authoritative account of the chemistry of this element. Bill gives details of arsenic levels in human hair as follows:

Normal: Less than 1mg/kg, i.e. micrograms per kilogram, (but can get up to 8mg/kg in polluted areas).
Chronic poisoning: Greater than 10mg/kg.
External contamination: Up to 800mg/kg.

Walter Gössler *et al.* found approximately 5mg/kg of arsenic in Ötzi's hair. So, this is high but not greatly so and is no indication of chronic poisoning.

As perhaps not being very likely, explanations 3 and 4 can be dealt with first:

Explanation 3: Arsenic is dissolved in drinking water sometimes in high enough amounts to be dangerous. Such water is consumed in many parts of the world and can be locally a serious problem such as in Bangladesh at present and in Chile, not just at present but in the distant past too. Apart from run off from pesticides or industrial sources, arsenic-rich water comes from thermal and mineral springs and wells issuing from the bedrock. Such places have been found in Austria, Italy and Switzerland. Italian Professor Andrea Fuganti of the University of Trento and three others published a map of potentially arsenic-rich water in south Tyrol. Interestingly it shows the area south of Brixen and middle and western Vinschgau as places where the probability of drinking arsenic-rich water is highest. These are two very areas where there is botanical and/or stable isotope evidence for considering that Ötzi had lived as a youngster and then as an adult.

Explanation 4: With a long history of use as medicine, arsenic is one of the most toxic elements, like lead, mercury and cadmium. To this day at Lake Levico in Trentino to the south of Bozen, there is reputedly therapeutic water, noted for its arsenic, copper and iron content. The 1970 edition of the *Encyclopedia Britannica* gives: 'Some inhabitants of Styria, Tyrol and other regions believe that arsenic compounds exert a tonic effect and the habit of arsenic eating is prevalent in these regions.' These reports did not come just from the nineteenth century. Ronald Bentley of the University of Pennsylvania and Thomas Chasteen of Sam Houston State University in Texas say that there is a report that in the mid-twentieth century arsenic was eaten by Swiss and Austrian mountaineers.

In his book, Bill Cullen discusses why the inhabitants of Styria are known to have deliberately eaten arsenic because it: 1. Produces a bloom on the cheeks of women and hence is beautifying; 2. Improves the wind and so increases the ability to undertake strenuous tasks such as hiking up mountains; 3. Prevents infectious diseases; 4. Aids digestion; 5. Increases courage; 6. Increases sexual potency; and 7. Is contraceptive.

With Bill Cullen and Jörg Feldman, Gudrun Przygoda of the University of British Columbia published on this topic and stated that the habit of arsenic-eating was known in Styria from as early as the twelfth century AD. Ötzi was an inhabitant of Tyrol, just west of Styria; his corpse was found at very high altitudes and it is more than likely that he had been repeatedly in the mountains, as discussed in Chapters 2 and 5. This leads directly to the speculative thought: was this beneficial arsenic eating a habit so ancient that the then people of these rugged regions indulged in such a practice?

Intriguing as they may seem, I am assured by the analytical chemist Joerg Feldman of Aberdeen University that there is no way of proving either explanation 3 or 4, both speculative.

Explanations 1 & 2: Walter Gössler and colleagues cautiously thought that exposure to fumes from smelting was the cause. However, arsenic in Ötzi's axe head was present merely as a trace but the arsenic content of copper ores varies considerably from place to place and so Ötzi, had he been a copper worker, might have smelted ores much richer in the poisonous element.

After considering environmental reasons for the presence of the copper, Don Brothwell and Geoffrey Grime state: 'Diagenetic changes should clearly make us very cautious in interpretation'; these are changes brought about over the years by the influence of the particular preserving environment. Hair of red deer found at the site was also measured for arsenic and other elements. The deer hair showed much lower values of copper and no arsenic at all. So if the copper and arsenic in the iceman's hair were due to the environment, why was the red deer hair not the same? Therefore they believe that: 'the copper enrichment near the hair surface, together with arsenic in the keratin cells of the interior of the hair shaft, strongly argues for the long term and direct involvement of the Iceman with copper working.' This inference has gained wide, unreserved acceptance and appears in many books.

Geoffrey Grime had second thoughts about the copper being *on* Ötzi's hair rather than *in* it. In this context, therefore, that elongate copper moss has been found growing at the site independently by Ronald Porley and I is intriguing. As the name indicates, this small moss grows preferentially on heavy metal-bearing rocks. It is found at several places at Vent southwards up to the site. As I wrote in the 2005 *Scientific American* article, can this be an indication that the hair sample was contaminated post-mortem? I am not aware that any geologist has looked for any copper ores around the site. However, very recently I asked Joerg Feldman to examine these mosses and adhering soil and he found both copper and arsenic; this needs to be considered thoroughly and then published in detail. The whole matter of Ötzi the copper ore prospector/smelter needs re-evaluation based on further chemical investigation.

Chieftain/Warrior

In the Neolithic, well before Ötzi's time, societies were so organised as to have warriors and chieftains. That Ötzi was a person of high status has been claimed by various people, including Angelika Fleckinger who stated: 'copper axes belonged to men of the highest echelons of society, and were also used as weapons.' She continues: 'proof that copper axes and daggers were status symbols is provided by the human-like stone statues of that time. The Iceman and his family probably had considerable status within their community and may well have been cattle owners, chiefs or villages representatives.' There is Paul Gleirscher, an archaeologist from Klagenfurt, Austria. He wrote, 'By Copper Age standards, the Iceman was spendidly armed', that 'he was a warrior of some nobility' and also 'The Iceman should not be thought of as a shepherd in the common sense but much more a leader comparable to the figures depicted on the Southern Alpine menhirs'. The basis of this status argument is Ötzi's possession of the axe head which was made not of stone but copper; such an object is assumed to have been rare and precious at that early stage in the use of metal. Another who accepts this idea is Christian Strahm of Freiburg University. He states: 'The Similaun glacier man carries also a very well crafted copper axe which without doubt makes him an outstanding person in his community.'[23]

However, in his book Konrad Spindler (*Spindler* 1, p. 237) had cautioned against such reasoning. He claimed that Ötzi could have been a 'perfectly ordinary person' and stated that metal objects in the graves of the Remedello culture are 'not particularly rare'. In reviewing Konrad Spindler's book, Lawrence Barfield agreed that Ötzi need not have belonged to an elite and stated: 'The axe was a working tool: hafted as it was, only 2.6cm of the metal blade would have been visible anyway, and in this way could hardly have functioned as a display item.' In 1999 Konrad Spindler published photographs of experimental archaeologist Harm Paulsen cutting down a small yew tree and wrote: 'the Iceman's copper axe represents a fully functional work tool.' However, that was nearly 20 years ago and now Konrad Spindler and Lawrence Barfield are certainly in the minority.

Considering the large number of graves and small number of copper axe blades, Raffaele De Marinis in his long article about the large cemetery at Remdello, a site much quoted with regard to Ötzi, says, 'It is therefore clear that throughout the Copper Age metal objects were particularly precious, a sure sign of high social status.'[24] Marcus Egg agrees with that but sidesteps the issue with regard to Ötzi because he told me in a recent email that '... we cannot define his real status ... because we have to ask was he the original owner of the axe or had he taken it away or stolen from some other person. We are not able to answer this question.'

As the discovery of Ötzi is totally without parallel from such a remote period, how can anyone know with certainty what about his clothing and gear was usual at the time, what was uncommon then, or perhaps even peculiar to him as a person of high rank, if that is what he was? Such thoughts always give me pause. As suggested above, perhaps everyone had a grass/bast cape. There was certainly no difficulty about obtaining the raw materials in that case, tall grasses and lime trees being not just commonplace but readily recognisable in *Ötziland*, and perhaps many of the women knew how to plait such clothing, just as the women of the Pacific Northwest coastal tribes twined bark clothing and basketry including very fine hats from Sitka spruce roots that are discussed in Chapter 7. Whereas knowing how to acquire copper ores and then smelting them were altogether more complex matters, demanding the abilities and knowledge of perhaps only a few specialists.

Hunter

Another early thought of Konrad Spindler's is that Ötzi had been a hunter and, because of the DNA work of Franco Rollo and colleagues, we now know that meat of both alpine ibex and red deer were part of his last meals and so he may have obtained the meat by his own efforts during his last days. But perhaps he had acquired the meat, fresh or dried, from someone else or took it from a store at his base, if there was such a thing.

The longbow and quiver of arrows may support this notion that he was a hunter. If, however, he had been actively engaged in hunting at the time of his death (or, for that matter, fighting and fleeing), why is the bow unfinished and unstrung and all but two of the arrows without heads and feathers and those two both broken? Gudrun Sulzenbacher accepts that he was a hunter but wonders why he was on a glacier without serviceable weapons. That he was very high up in the mountains is not a problem in itself because he could have been on a lengthy pursuit following game animals and descending to some favoured grassy spot where he knew from previous experience that chamois or alpine ibex congregated. Hunters of Dall's sheep, such as Bill Hanlon who appears in Chapter 7, do just that very thing in the mountains of the Pacific Northwest.

With great bearing on the hunter hypothesis, there are claims for traces of blood on the bow and arrow shafts (over a length of 30cm). These claims have not been properly published by Tom Loy of the University of Queensland and now six years after his death (in October 2005) probably never can be. Eduard Egarter Vigl told Geneviève Lécrivain and I that Loy had no special microscope (as related by Konrad Spindler in *Spindler* 2) but Loy claimed at the Iceman Museum that he could see red blood cells. However, Eduard could not do so, despite examining such cells daily as a part of his particular medical profession. Tom Loy said he could tell human from other mammalian red cells.[25] See also the death in battle section below.

LAST ROUTE

When Ötzi's body was first found there were some surprised reactions that he had been in such a remote place so very high in the mountains. The growing evidence for ancient people travelling in very high terrain, even across glaciers, banishes such surprise, if it was ever justified. An outstanding European example, as discussed in Chapter 6, concerns the numerous artefacts discovered in very recent years from the disappearing Chilchi glacier at Schnidejoch, Switzerland. That ancient people ventured very high in the mountains was no surprise to the late Professor Bernardino Bagolini of the University of Trento (*Innsbruck* 1).

Whatever Ötzi may have been doing at 3210m there is growing evidence that other people had been in and around the hollow at periods before and after Ötzi's time. From the hollow the 1992 excavation produced a piece of pine wood from nearly 7000 years ago and too large to have got there by any natural means (see Fig. 2.9). There is also a metal-cut piece of binding material made of green alder dating from about 2500 years ago. In 1998, the oak shaft of an axe was found at Hauslabjoch. It had been lost for several hundred years after Ötzi's time.[26] Finally and notably, another object that must have got there by human means is a tiny Mesolithic flint blade (eighth to sixth millennia BC). Lorenzo Dal Ri states: 'This is the highest altitude mesolithic find recovered in the whole of the Alps.' Sadly, this artifact has been lost since its recovery.[27]

There are remains of plants that grow only at low to moderate altitudes and never in the nival zone that have been extracted from the coarse mineral sediments that accumulated in the hollow. An astonishing number of species of mosses and liverworts have been recovered from the sediments or were washed from Ötzi's clothes or taken from his innards – about 80 species in all. This compares with about 20 species growing around the hollow now as found by myself and my helpers. A good case is the large species pendulous wing moss. It is common and locally abundant in Schnalstal, mostly on shaded rocks in woodland to an altitude of about 1700m. How did the fragments of this moss found in several sediment samples reach the hollow? The species could never have grown around the hollow and its habitats make dispersal uphill by winds unlikely though perhaps not impossible. Did the fragments come on the hoofs or hair of herbivores, or on the feet and clothes of people, perhaps even deliberately carried? This scatter in the hollow of moss fragments of species that never grew in the nival zone may well be evidence of humans passing through, perhaps en route to summer pastures.

I have examined the moss fragments extracted from the caprine (sheep or goats) droppings investigated by Alexandra Schmidl et al. and made one important finding. There is a leaf of the moss called, by the English name, dimorphous tamarisk moss. This species has never been recorded from the zone of perennial snow and ice in the Alps, though it does grow above the timber line. In all of Austria the altitudinal limit is 2800m but it has not been recorded in Ötziland above 2600m. So, the animal that produced the dropping may have carried the moss internally up some 400 to 500m.

The layout of the towering Tyrolean mountains and the valleys is such that Ötzi's last journey cannot have been east to west (or vice versa) but from north to south (or vice versa). Ventertal and Schnalstal may readily be thought of as the most obvious routes for Ötzi to have taken but it is difficult to rule out completely a southward passage along Rofental, rather than Niedertal, and then over the Hochjoch glacier. Nor can it be excluded that he took a northwards passage up Schlandraunertal down into Schnalstal and then up Tisental or even up Finailtal. But the question still resolves itself to north/south and not east/west.

I have no quarrel with the general tone of Konrad Spindler's statement (*Spindler* 1, pp. 212 and 213) that, bearing in mind the location of the site, from Vinschgau and up Schnalstal to the site could have been reached 'quite comfortably in a few hours, or at the most in a short day's ascent. From the Inn valley it would take at least three, if not four, strenuous days over difficult, at times pathless, terrain.' To go to the site from Vinschgau in a '*few* hours' would demand good fitness, in my opinion. All this assumes, of course, that Ötzi was indeed in a fit state, which in the light of some of the medical information might make one wonder.

Had Ötzi been taking part in transhumance then the reason for being so high in the mountains is clear, so too if he had been hunting or metal prospecting. Such explanations presuppose, of course, that Ötzi arrived at Hauslabjoch on his own two feet. The cartoon from the *New Yorker* at the head of this chapter is very apposite because it makes the point strongly in its humour that Ötzi may have been killed and then dumped by malevolent people. In the 2005 issue of the *Scientific American*, we wrote, '… we cannot completely exclude the possibility that perhaps Ötzi died somewhere else and was carried at some point to the hollow where the hikers found him 5,000 years later'. If the claim that Ötzi had been sacrificed, made by Johan Reinhard and discussed in detail below, is true then he may well not have reached the hollow on his own. However, had he been put where the body was found by his murderer or murderers, why was a valuable copper-headed axe (if it was valuable) and other equipment left and not taken away?

From the microscopic analyses of the intestinal contents comes important evidence that Ötzi's last journey was a complex one.[28] A sample from the colon was taken at an early stage but then later five samples were taken from the intestines; one from terminal ileum, two samples from the transverse colon, one from descending colon and one from rectum. These samples were given to Klaus Oeggl and his team who also took 45 samples from the surface vegetation north and south of the Ötzi site. These pollen samples removed from altitudes between 400 and 2600m and so these come from the zones colline, submontane, montane and from well into the alpine, as shown in Fig. 2.5. The crucial point is that the different zones have different pollen signatures.

The five gut samples were compared to the 45 surface vegetation samples by a variety of statistical methods. The conclusion is that during the brief period represented, perhaps his last 36 hours or so Ötzi was first in the alpine zone (about 2500m, rectal sample), then in the submontane to montane zones (1200m or less, colon sample) and then in the alpine zone again (terminal ileum sample). Lastly, of course, he was well into the nival zone, the body having been found at 3210m. So in a short period he had travelled from very high up to low down to finally even higher up. This elegant use of pollen analysis by Klaus Oeggl and his colleagues demonstrates such a journey for the first time in archaeology.

DEATH

Season

For whatever reason, such as fleeing from enemies, Ötzi was at one of the passes between Schnalstal and Ötztal at the great height of over 3200m. He was caught by bad weather, took shelter in the hollow but nonetheless froze to death. This is the explanation of Ötzi's death outlined in Konrad Spindler's books and it seemed not unreasonable. Such an explanation assumes that Ötzi reached the site on his own two feet and that he had died where the body was found. Additionally, Spindler thought that the tragedy had happened in the autumn. The time of year when Ötzi died is an important but contentious matter. The argument for an autumnal demise was based on the finding of the sloe, the fruit of the blackthorn, beside the body, on the sparse cereal remains in crevices of his clothing and on the pollen in the ice at the site. The case was always weak and certainly not conclusive. Structurally exactly like small plums, sloes ripen in late summer or autumn but, so bitter are they that they are only palatable when dried. Had Ötzi been carrying such food the drying could have taken place long before his journey and so the autumnal argument falls. Similarly, cereals keep indefinitely if dry and a few scraps could have been carried unnoticed in the seams of his clothes for a long time.

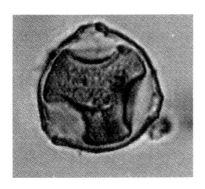

Fig. 5.5 Hop hornbeam pollen grain with cell contents from a colon sample.

A pollen analysis from ice at the site and taken close to where the quiver lay led Konrad Spindler to state (*Spindler* 2, p. 239): ' the ice in which the Iceman rested was formed between late summer and early autumn.' This is very feeble indeed simply because there is no certainty whatever that that particular ice sample was exactly contemporaneous with the iceman's death and indeed the likelihood must be that it was not. It is an assertion, not a scientifically proven matter.

If these particular plant remains are inconclusive, is there some other botanical evidence for the season of death? There are now indications for Ötzi's demise in late spring or early summer based on microscopic analyses of his intestinal contents. The pollen count of the first tiny sample of food residue taken from Ötzi's colon revealed the presence of the pollen of hop hornbeam. Strikingly, much of that pollen has retained its cellular contents. Klaus Oeggl stated that the cell contents remained in 'approximately 80% of the Hop Hornbeam' and also in some pollen grains of birch (*Innsbruck* 4). Klaus Oeggl reports that (*Innsbruck* 4, p. 93): 'It is well-known empirical knowledge that the cell content of pollen grains is decomposed after several weeks in oxidizing conditions in water or soil.' However, Klaus cited no references. Hop hornbeam is a small tree that flowers in spring/early summer and Ötzi must have ingested the pollen at that time. He might then have drunk water containing freshly shed pollen shortly before he died. The study of the diatoms from the colon sample showed that he had drunk water or prepared his meals with water originating from a wide range of altitudes, including below 1500m. In *Ötziland* today hop hornbeam reaches to less than 1500m.

Willy Groenmann-van Waateringe thinks that the hop hornbeam pollen got into Ötzi's gut from his consumption of that bark as medicine or an infusion of the bark. She gets round the difficulty of the cell contents by claiming that the pollen had retained the contents for months, not merely for a very short period. She collected bark from a hop hornbeam tree in Amsterdam in December and saw cell contents in the pollen she extracted.[29] Her case is weakened by the lack of any evidence from the oldest medicinal literature of the use of hop hornbeam in Europe. Klaus Oeggl's arguments do not solely depend on the hop hornbeam cell contents but the suite of other pollen types he found in the gut suggest an earlier rather than a later part of summer and in addition there are the still green leaves lacking stalks of the Norway maple (see Fig. 3.4).

Konrad Spindler (*Spindler* 2, p. 194) denies the importance of the hop hornbeam pollen but on no good grounds that I see. Either ignoring or offering no denial of the evidence for the spring or early summertime death, there are still people such as Elisabeth Zissernig and Andreas Lippert *et al.* who accept the autumnal death.[30]

Hypothermia

Soon after the discovery of Ötzi in 1992, Andreas Lippert and Konrad Spindler speculated that 'The bad weather must have come on suddenly and he must have therefore tried to find refuge in a sheltered cavity. He then probably died of hypothermia or of something completely different'.[31] Well, he certainly died of something, one might add! In another 1992 article, this one in the famous journal *Science*, Horst Siedler and seven others proposed that an exhausted Ötzi died of hypothermia.[32] They say: 'allowing for the necessary caution with regard to broad assumptions, we propose that the Similaun man was in a state of exhaustion perhaps as consequence of adverse weather condtions. He therefore may have lain down in a small depression, fallen asleep, and froze to death.' In view of what transpired later, it is just as well they hedged their bets in the cautionary clause.

The weather in the zone of perennial snow and ice, and also at much lower altitudes, is treacherous even during the summer months in *Ötziland*. This I can vouch for from personal experience, having been forced to turn back on various occasions in June, July, August and September. As an example, on 8 June 2005 with Geneviève Lécrivain, I have retreated from halfway up Tisental because of a very chilling north wind blowing strongly down the valley, where streamside alpine flowers in full bloom had become totally encased in ice during the previous bitter night. Cold snaps in June are familiar to the local people in Schnalstal who call them the 'sheep cold' because often there is cold weather at the time of the transhumance of the sheep. On 10 July 1997, close to the Ötzi site, with my geologist friend, Jim MacDonald, I was worried lest we would shortly be icemen by the sudden arrival of a blizzard, which luckily, however, proved very brief. It is easy to believe that hypothermia could have contributed to Ötzi's death during the summer months, even if he was warmly dressed and in vigorous good health. Of course, as we now know, it was certainly not the sole cause and in all likelihood had little or nothing to do with the matter.

However, for the many unfortunates who die each year in the Alps there is no doubt that hypothermia or some violent accident such as an avalanche or a fall into a crevasse caused death. In the case of Ötzi, his death occurred thousands of years ago and the precise circumstances are not known and it is hard to see how they can ever be known with total confidence. There was no thick ice in the hollow, if any at all, and so he could not have fallen down a crevasse, and even a jarring, possibly stunning, fall, though certainly far from impossible, is unlikely to have happened. At that time of year, say May or June, the hollow would have been thick with snow, to such an extent perhaps even to have been unrecognisable as a hollow at all.

Fleeing from Enemies

The occupations considered above can account for Ötzi's presence at high altitude but his being there need not, of course, have had anything whatever to do with his social role or roles. It could have been that he had been fleeing from an enemy or enemies, as, indeed, was an early idea. Part 10 of Chapter V of Konrad Spindler's book is called 'The Disaster'. He wrote that at Ötzi's home village:

> There was certainly a violent conflict, perhaps more than one, as a result of which the Iceman had to flee. In the process he lost some of his equipment and other items were damaged. He himself suffered a serial rib fracture … Until death caught up with him at the Hauslabjoch.

Followed by: 'So the man set out in the direction of the Hauslabjoch, hoping that beyond the main ridge of the Alps, he might escape his pursuers.'

In 1994 the Innsbruck University medical doctor, Dieter zur Nedden, with Konrad Spindler and no less than eight others, most of them medical men, wrote their conclusion:

> The following scenario is suggested for his journey over the high Alps shortly before winter. He had had a 'violent discussion' which caused the costal fractures on his right side. He was poorly equipped with many broken or damaged belongings because he had insufficient time to repair or replace them. The fact that the man went to such an inhospitable region, though suffering from extreme physical handicap caused by pain from the evident injuries, with such inadequate equipment, may be taken as circumstantial evidence for an escape born of desperation. This interpretation is also supported by our observations of the position of the body of the dead man, who was lying on his left side, which would have been a relatively comfortable, and least painful position, especially in comparison with lying on his back.[33]

The rib fractures, the assumed traumatic event before death, the peculiarities of the equipment, clothing and lack of supplies suggest that the hypothesis of 'a personal disaster before his death' is plausible enough to be put forward for further discussion. In 1996, Konrad Spindler repeated this theory in even greater detail (*Innsbruck* 3).

Serious issue can be taken with some of the points in these extensive quotations. Firstly and cogently, as we now know, the right ribs were broken after and not before death. Secondly, the position of the body when first found. Not one of the 10 authors saw the body until after it was pulled from the ice. So what do they mean by 'our observations'? Consult the photographs in Konrad Spindler's book. The famous photograph taken by Helmut Simon on 19 September 1999 shows only the head, face-down, and the upper back, and the one taken on the 20th, when more of the body was exposed, shows right down to the base of the spine. Clearly both, especially the latter, show that Ötzi was not lying on his left side but fully prone. Konrad Spindler realised that there had been slight movement.

Thirdly, there is no good evidence for a lack of supplies, which was a tendentious assumption on Konrad Spindler's part, as already criticised at the beginning of Chapter 4. A few Alpine ibex bones were found by the corpse, as well as the sloe. He assumes that everything that was found was all there ever had been in or near the hollow. It could well have been that other provisions were scattered at the time, soon afterwards or long afterwards. Additionally, we now know very convincingly indeed that he certainly did not die with an empty alimentary tract.

Shot in the Back

That the Neolithic period was a violent one of fighting and massacres has been stressed by many archaeologists, including Konrad Spindler himself, who discussed in detail the killing of 16 children and 18 adults, known from their skeletons at a mass grave at Talheim in south-west Germany. The French archaeologists Jean Guilaine and Jean Zammit devoted their book called *Le Sentier de la Guerre Visages de la Violence Préhistorique* to the topic of the development through prehistoric time of fighting and warfare. They emphasised that the Neolithic had been a particularly significant time.[34]

The Reading University professor, Steven Mithen, believes that 'war is mainly a product of sedentary, farming societies', which, of course, were first set up in the Neolithic.

A recent example of the evidence for much violence concerns the work of Rick Schulting of Queen's University, Belfast, and Mick Wysocki of the University of Central Lancashire in Preston. They studied about 350 skulls from early Neolithic Britain (about 6000 to 5200 years ago). They discovered healed depressed fractures of the skull in 4 to 5 per cent and unhealed head injuries that had presumably been fatal in about 2 per cent. So an inhabitant of Neolithic Britain had a 1 in 14 chance of being hit violently on the head, often on the left side, which is an indication of right-handed people fighting. In another example pertaining to early Neolithic Britain, the skulls from the Boles Barrow in Wiltshire, southern England, show traumatic damage to the left side, as reported by Martin Smith and Megan Brickley of Birmingham University.[35] The *Independent* of 12 March 2007 reported the massacre of 14 Neolithic people buried at Wayland's Smithy, Oxfordshire: 'The position of the wounds found on the remains have led scientists to believe the people were killed in a violent way.'

In late July 2001, shortly before the symposium held to commemorate the tenth anniversary of the discovery and before any scientific publication, it was announced to the media that an arrowhead had been found in Ötzi's back under the left shoulder. This caused numerous statements by the media that Ötzi was murdered. Obviously, Ötzi did not shoot himself in the back but what was at issue is did the arrow kill him and, if so, was it a slow or quick death. The scientific publications by Paul Gostner and Eduard Egarter Vigl came later.[36] There were calls for the object to be removed to provide the proof and to dispose of any thought that it is something else, such as a calcified lymph gland. Furthermore, the object had to be removed in such a way that it is clear what fatal damage, if any, it may have done. Assuming it was an arrowhead, it need not have caused the death, at any rate an immediate death. Many people stay alive long after large foreign objects such as bullets have violently entered their bodies. Konrad Spindler mentions (*Spindler* 2, p. 261) without citations that there are Neolithic graves with human bones in which flint arrowheads are embedded ('not particularly rare') and there are a few instances in which the arrowhead is enveloped in callous tissue. There are numerous illustrations of flints embedded in human bones in the book *Le Sentier de la Guerre*, mentioned above. To add a notable archaeological example from another continent and period, the cascade spear point in the right pelvis of the famous ancient Kennewick Man (see Chapter 1) had been there long enough for the bone to begin healing around it.

It is natural for forensic scientists to seek a full autopsy to confirm the cause of death but such a grossly invasive action is impossible for this unique corpse. However, despite the lack of surgical extraction of the arrowhead, there is no doubt that is exactly what it is. Its density is correct for that of flint and the size and shape are just right too. This is made obvious by the fine illustrations reproduced here from Lorenzo Dal Ri's 2006 article (see Fig. 2.12).

Illustrated in 2006 by Lorenzo Dal Ri, the menhir from Latsch in Vinschgau is highly intriguing. Like the others from the region, including the one from Algund already discussed, it is heavily decorated (see Fig. 5.3). It shows various objects and what is of great interest are the matchstick figures of two men. One is an archer with his bow ready for firing. Seemingly standing in front of the archer is another man about to be shot in the back. He says:

> among their rich figurative repertory, there is a scene in which an archer is firing an arrow
> directly into the back of another personage (of slightly smaller dimensions). And the victim is

clearly represented in profile with outstretched arms. That such a subject was chosen for repro-duction on an object of cult adoration could not have been accidental and probably responds to very precise motivations, linked to religion or the mythical world. The coincidence with the Iceman's death is undoubtedly remarkable.

But we do not know that the very menhir coincides with Ötzi or not. Do we even know if the scene was carved at the same time as all the other carvings or not?

In the *National Geographic France*, the journalist Geneviève de Latour states (translated from the French): 'The two superimposed figurines show an archer and a man who seems to be running away in front of the first one. Is it a hunting scene or a murder? Difficult to say. The only sure thing is the two figures are posterior to the stele.'[37] One can readily agree that it is difficult to be sure if it is a murder scene or a hunting one. However, in Neolithic rock art, violence cannot be said to be a particularly rare or unexpected subject, as many of the illustrations in the book *Le Sentier de La Guerre* clearly show. The thought occurs to me, could the 'victim' not be another bowman unfinished by the sculptor?

Lorenzo Dal Ri stated in 2006:

> The fatal arrow wound is entirely consistent with our knowledge of armaments, conflicts and the general level of violence prevalent in the Chalcolithic.[38] The bow (and arrows) are weapons that date from a very distant period (at least from the end of the Paleolithic), but it is only in the fourth and third millenia (i.e. the Chalcolithic) that we find a huge increase in arrowheads recovered amongst archaeological deposits. Research at the red jasper quarries at Valle Lagorara in Liguria confirm the manufacture of an enormous quantity (millions of specimens) of arrow-heads during this period. Futhermore, there is a clear increase in archaeologically confirmed signs (on human skeletons) of arrow injuries between 3500 and 2000 BC.

Then there was another statement to the media that there was a deep wound in Ötzi's right hand and then publication in July 2003 by Andreas Nerlich of the Academic Hospital München-Bogenhausen, with four others.[39] They state: 'This finding [the arrowhead] indi-cates that Ötzi died from a lethal assault.' They found 'an irregularly shaped 3.7cm long, deep stab wound on Ötzi's right hand, extending from the palm to the back of the hand between the thumb and index finger', but by visual inspection alone they could not 'ascer-tain whether this wound arose during life'. They examined a small sample of the damaged palm by histochemistry to find haemosederin. They also used 'high resolution scanning force microscopy', laser-based micro-dissection and found no intact erythrocytes, but the guaiacum-based test revealed a blood clot. Their interesting conclusion is:

> Since forensic medical practice suggests that macrophages that contain haemosederin develop between 3 and 8 days after injury, we believe that the wound was inflicted a few days before his death. We do not yet know if the skin wound happened simultaneously or shortly after Ötzi was hit by the arrow, but if so this finding would suggest that he survived the attack for a few days.

In August 2005 Eduard Egarter Vigl told me and Geneviève Lécrivain that the wound between the thumb and index finger was so deep, reaching the metacarpal bone, that Ötzi

Fig. 5.6 Badly cut right hand. (*Nerlich et al., 2003*)

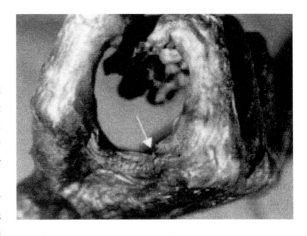

could not have flexed his fingers and thumb and therefore could not have carried anything in that hand and he now thought that the arrow wound led to death within a matter of minutes.

In 2007 came the paper by Patrizia Pernter with four others 'Radiologic proof for the Iceman's cause of death'. Special scanning had revealed a torn artery. They stated: 'In summary, the Iceman's cause of death by an arrowhead lacerating among others a great thoracic artery – the left subclavian artery – and leading to a deadly hemorragic shock can now be postulated with almost complete certainty.' Such damage to the subclavian artery causes massive active bleeding, expanding haematoma and shock-related cardiac arrest.

In 2009 Andreas Nerlich and two others produced 'New evidence for Ötzi's final trauma'. They confirm that 'the Iceman suffered from chronologically different wounds with an "older" intavital stab wound of the right hand and a fresh laceration at the arrow injury site as well as a very fresh contusion at Ötzi's back'. They consider that the contusion shows that a blunt object hit the Iceman's back shortly before his death. So now we have the badly cut right hand, the arrow shot into the back and the blow of a blunt instrument to the back.[40]

Regarding the full stomach, in an email of 12 January 2011 Patrizia Pertner told me:

> We radiologists (Dr Gostner and I) believe that Ötzi was not on the run when he was shot from behind. The murder must have occurred right after having taken his meal and just some metres from where he had stopped for a rest. Could he perhaps have been murdered by a companion?

Death in Battle

Some years ago the death in battle idea came to the fore, though in a far from satisfactory way. This claim stems from the work of Tom Loy, which has never been published in any major, peer-reviewed journal (or even any minor journal, as far as I know) but, from 2003 onwards, it was announced at press conferences and discussed on television as though it was an established, widely accepted scientific fact but, categorically, this is not so.[41]

Place

Konrad Spindler simply assumed that Ötzi died in the hollow. More than that, he thought that, apart from very slight post-mortem turning from lying on the left side to lying prone, the body lay precisely where death had occurred. Even until now, there is no scientific proof of precisely where death occurred and probably there never can be. In the light of the distribution patterns of the plant remains in the sediments removed from the hollow, Klaus Oeggl thinks that the death took place at the hollow or in its immediate vicinity.

Considering the nature of the fatal injury and position of the corpse, the medical investigators think along similar lines. Even if death happened in the hollow, that it happened exactly
where the corpse was found is unlikely to have been the case. See the last section of this
chapter on movement by water.

Sacrifice and Burial

The first suggestion known to me that Ötzi had been buried was made by Paul Bahn
and Katherine Everett. Perhaps over-impressed by the fine preservation of the corpse, they
argued that Ötzi might have been deliberately mummified and then buried.[42] The first
person to mention sacrifice was one of the *National Geographic* explorers in residence, Johan
Reinhard, who is an expert on the very high-altitude burials of children in the Andes (see
Chapter 1). He has claimed that Ötzi had been sacrificed and ritually buried and so this
explains the great height of his former resting place. Why would it have to have been a sacrifice rather than burial after death in fighting? Also I wonder why that precise spot would
have been chosen. It is on a col, not on a summit or even very close to a summit. There are
extensive, fine long views to the north and east but not to the south or west. The Andean
sacrificed children were often buried very close to summits and put into specially made
platforms of more or less elaborate construction dug into the fine-grained volcanic deposits
on slopes.

In the 2003 *Scientific American* article the last sentence is '… we cannot completely exclude
the possibility that perhaps Ötzi died elsewhere and was carried to the hollow …' It is
simply not possible to dig a grave where Ötzi was found and so, if he was placed there, then
it must have been under a covering of stones. Eduard Egarter Vigl has written in 2006 about
the covering of the body 'with debris and stones like a type of sepulcre'.[43] However, the
excavators found nothing that even hinted at such a burial, though they had no particular
reason at the time to consider such a thing. There is, as Angelika Fleckinger has pointed out,
no previous evidence from the Alps, or even, one might add, from Eurasia, as far as I know,
for such burials – that is to say internments of sacrificed people very high in mountains.

Discarding the sacrifice idea, Franco Rollo *et al.* wrote:

> Almost 30 years ago, Nanna Noe-Nygaard showed that Mesolithic deer and wild boar hunters
> used to aim their arrows and spears at the left shoulder blade as this gave them the best chance
> of killing the prey at the first shot. As the arrow that struck Ötzi actually pierced the left shoul-
> der blade, it seems to us much more reasonable to assume that, rather than of a ritual sacrifice,
> he had been the victim of some rivalry among big game hunters.[44]

This seems to me to have some force but why specify only 'rivalry among big game hunters'
rather some other reason for the murder?

With no mention whatever of any of the previous claims just listed that Ötzi may have
been deliberately buried, even sacrificed, now there is a very detailed claim in 2010 by
Alessandro Vanzetti of the Sapienza University of Rome with four others in *Antiquity*. In
this article the reader finds no indication that the authors visited the site. If true, I find that
utterly stunning. So the claim is armchair archaeology and the approach explains the lack
of any photograph or a properly detailed plan that might have helped the reader to make

up his or her own mind that there had indeed been a 'platform' bounded by boulders.[45] A press release by the Iceman Museum in late August 2010 refuted this claim with a detailed rebuttal to follow. As this book goes to press, the full rebuttal has been sent to *Antiquity*. It was written by a group of Iceman scientists and archaeologists led by Albert Zink and including Klaus Oeggl and myself. Alessandro Vanzetti and his co-authors misunderstand the important archaeobotany, especially the pollen analyses by Klaus Oeggl. But they are wrong about more than that. They misunderstand how the mummification came about and how to explain the precise position in which the body was found. Furthermore, they misquote me. There was only one medicinal moss, the bog moss, and not the other five found in the gut. The burial hypothesis being rejected means that the comments on the matter by Carancini and Mattioli, and also Fasolo, published by *Antiquity* in 2011, have no significance.[46]

WHAT HAPPENED AFTERWARDS?

As recounted by Brenda Fowler, Klaus Oeggl realised the serious implications of his deduction of a death much earlier in the year than early autumn. Accepting that Ötzi's journey to his death took place some time in late spring or early summer, that is to say in late May or in June, then much of what Konrad Spindler and others had written about the circumstances of the death and subsequent preservation of the body cannot be correct. We do not and cannot know what the weather had been like during his very last hours (is it really too much wishful thinking to say perhaps some day we will?). Perhaps it was inclement being snowy and windy or perhaps it was benign being sunny and still. It does not matter because at that time of year and at that great altitude the ground would have been thick with snow. The very hollow in which his body was found may well have been so deeply snow covered as not to be recognisable as a hollow at all. Ötzi could not have entered the hollow to take shelter from poor weather, or to rest having been seriously wounded and possibly exhausted or to take his very last meal (because we now know his stomach was full). His body must have got into the hollow in some other way. The spread of the body, clothes and gear in the hollow is a crucial matter concerning what had happened in the hollow not just when Ötzi arrived there, by whatever means, but also what happened afterwards, and not just immediately after but long after too.

Though qualifying his account in German as fictive (meaning 'fictitious', surely an extraordinary adjective to use in a scientific work, if indeed it can be regarded as such), Konrad Spindler argued that Ötzi arrived totally exhausted at Hauslabjoch (*Spindler* 2, p. 175). He took shelter in the hollow where he carefully placed his axe, bow and backpack on a rock ledge, and then, dropping other pieces of gear, expired where he had lain down on his left side because that would have eased the pain from his very recently broken right ribs. After very slight disturbance by ice movements, his corpse remained frozen in place until the discovery more than 5000 years later in 1991. Even though he mentions the peculiar position of the left arm, he claims that the body was 'more or less in line with a natural dying posture'. This is accepted by Angelika Fleckinger with no qualification. If it ever was, this not now a plausible explanation.

Were there ever good grounds for thinking that the body was lying in position of death? The posture was strange, face-down and draped over a boulder with the left arm sticking out to the right under the chin and the right arm down to the right. Ötzi's feet were 50cm lower than his head. This posture can be perhaps best explained by the corpse having floated into that position. Is there any evidence of such a contention?

In order to understand the mummification and loss of the epidermis Thomas Bereuter *et al.* considered that the iceman's corpse was first submerged in water for at least one to three months and then desiccated.[47] They make points from many disciplines to support their case and are critical of the earlier work on the skin by three University of Bradford scientists. Then, they postulate:

> Shortly after his death at the site of discovery in that prehistoric early autumn, the Iceman's corpse was covered by snow and ice. At some later stage, perhaps during Roman times, his sheltered corpse thawed and became immersed in the water collecting within the depression where it lay. During this brief warm period, most of the physical changes incurred by the corpse, as well as the formation of adipocere and loss of epidermis took place. In light of its excellent preservation, it would seem likely that desiccation of the corpse occurred shortly after its immersion in water.

At no stage do Thomas Bereuter and colleagues say that the corpse had floated, though such a happening may be regarded as an obvious implication of their claims. The first to use the verb 'floated' was Klaus Oeggl in his article 'Wurde die Mumie bewegt?' (Has the Mummy moved?).[48] I think it very improbable that at the great altitude of the site ensuring very low temperatures there could have been enough water for the corpse to have floated for three months, one month perhaps but not three. An argument in favour of the hollow frequently containing water comes from the numerous moss fragments recovered from it. One of the commonest mosses found in the sediments removed from the hollow is water grimmia, which is a moss of high to very high altitudes where it grows in a very precise habitat – on rock faces but only where very cold water from melted snow or ice flows through it. It has been extracted from many of the samples I studied. This shows that through much or perhaps even all of the period of deposition of the sediments, water in summer flowed into the hollow which could not therefore have been totally filled, far less overtopped by ice.

Klaus Oeggl carried out a very neat and satisfyingly revealing bit of work concerning three pieces of round wood that neatly fitted together. He realised that short, narrow pieces of round wood were part of a broken arrow shaft. He says: 'Three splinters of the wayfaring tree (*Viburnum lantana*) excavated at different locations in the gully at least four metres away from the quiver, indicated that the find [Ötzi and gear] drifted in meltwater.' The three splinters fit together and seem to belong to a broken arrow shaft from the quiver.[49] Fig. 5.7 shows the eastern corner of the hollow. The axe is obvious and the remnants of the backpack are at the top right. Diagonally across in the foreground, the longbow is stuck in the ice. One wonders just how it floated or was pushed by water into such a position.

There is also the broken quiver stiffener. In his book Konrad Spindler wrote no less than 11 pages on the quiver and its contents, because he felt sure that these items were crucial in understanding the last hours of Ötzi's life – why so is not too clear to me. He says (*Spindler 2*, p. 124): '… it was immediately obvious that the stiffening strut had broken in three – a long lower piece, short middle piece and an even shorter upper piece.' However, 'The middle

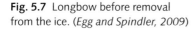
Fig. 5.7 Longbow before removal from the ice. (*Egg and Spindler, 2009*)

piece was not found with the quiver, which was recovered by the archaeologists with meticulous care. Instead it was found at the spot where the corpse lay.' He claims that Ötzi had been 'carrying it separately on his person, presumably intending to repair the quiver when a suitable opportunity arose'. If pieces of an arrow shaft drifted out of the quiver when there was sufficient water in the hollow for the corpse to float could not the broken piece of the stiffener have floated away too?

Thomas Berreuter and colleagues mention only one period of warmer climate which may have led to the corpse being freed from ice and surrounded by water. However, as discussed in Chapter 2, we know about many climatic fluctuations through the years since the end of the last ice age but, crucially, what is known about warm periods in the last 5500 years? Klaus Oeggl discusses two further warm periods, one between 3000 and 2500 BC and the other between 2416 and 2158 BC.[50] So there are at least three warm spells to consider. Klaus Oeggl argues that the complete find assemblage was submerged and parts had floated at least once before the discovery in 1991. He continues that this must have happened before 800 BC, because the ice layer with the artefacts was superposed by a sterile one which was removed before the real excavation started in 1992. That reasoning eliminates the Roman period as having seen the floating of the body and some of the artefacts.

Now further consideration is needed of the 'Rough Recovery' mentioned in Chapter 2 – an appropriate phrase first used by the National Geographic magazine. During the rapid removal of the body from the ice, it was inevitable that information was lost but how much that was lost was trivial and how much was important we shall never know for sure. The use of a cordless electric drill very badly damaged the left buttock and damaged the rectum, which caused problems for those of us who later have studied the contents of that organ. Breakages of some bones took place during the removal and transport of the body to Innsbruck University. Concerning the author directly is not just the possibly contaminated rectal sample but the inevitably vague description of what had been the exact position of the important large mass of the flat neckera, discussed in earlier chapters. 'Sample 91/124 Grass, pieces of leather or hide (upper body clothing and leggings)' is all there will ever be from which to make deductions. So was the mass of that moss from his leggings, from the upper body clothing or from neither?

There is a matter concerning the small dagger that has been given prominence in the last several years but was not mentioned at the time of the recovery of the body. This is the so-called 'Grotesque Grip'. The Austrian hotelier and mountain guide, Aloïs Pirpamer, who helped to remove the corpse from the ice in 1991, stated on the Discovery Channel in the 2003 broadcast that Ötzi had been holding the dagger in his right hand. In her little book Ötzi, the Iceman: The Full Facts at a Glance, Angelika Fleckinger put Aloïs Pirpamer's claim as follows: 'At first Franz Gurschler and I were unable to remove the right hand from the ice, as it seemed to be trapped between two rocks. By twisting the forearm, we finally managed to free the hand and noticed that the dead man was holding something. Later it turned out to be a dagger.' This quotation has a crisp, convincing ring that is not the case when, face to face, one hears Aloïs Pirpamer talking of the recovery. Sitting in the bar of his hotel in Vent, I have heard him state that the water from the melted ice was very murky, being full of silt and clay, and so it was difficult to discern anything. There is neither a photograph nor any other confirmation of his claim, made long after the recovery of the body.

Probably many thousands of people have read Angelika Fleckinger's little book. Furthermore, it is certain that many more thousands have read the November 2006 issue of National Geographic France in which journalist Geneviève De Latour has repeated the Grotesque Grip story without the slightest hint of caution. She states: 'Aloïs Pirpamer, one of the first to be present at the crime scene, remembers having seen a dagger in the left [sic] hand.'[51] So the left hand this time!

It is worth repeating what Konrad Spindler wrote about the rough recovery (Spindler 1, p. 104):

The resulting trough then kept filling with meltwater … during that time Weigele kept probing the gully with his ice-pick and salvaged various remains of clothing and equipment, which he dropped on a little heap next to the ice trough. These finds were photographed three times … and the pictures show the pencil-shaped object [i.e. the retouching tool] and the dagger lying on the snow, on the edge of the heap.

So no mention of the dagger clutched in a fist.

The right fist would need to have been very tightly clenched to have been gripping the small, thin dagger. However, the hand was badly cut and Ötzi could not have clenched his fist. The iceman's left hand is also semi-clenched and so does that mean there had been a dagger in that hand too but it was never found? As related above, the corpse was not in the position of death; it had floated and so the dagger must have stayed in the hand during that movement whenever it took place during the last 5200 years; all this is very unlikely. The semi-clenched fists could be the result of post-mortem contraction. A most important observation is this, as told to me by the British Columbian Government archaeologist Al Mackie, who helped remove the corpse of Kwäday Dän Ts'ìnchí Man. The left hand contracted to a semi-clenched position after the body was removed from the ice. Ötzi's Grotesque Grip holding the dagger is certainly not established fact. It is merely a dubious claim which can never be corroborated.

AN ECONOMICAL SUMMARY

If not before, definitely starting with Konrad Spindler's confessed fiction in 1993, there have been various accounts of the events leading to Ötzi's arrival at the hollow, his death and mummification and later happenings. Written mainly by journalists and archaeologists, all are very speculative – not to say, even if somewhat harshly perhaps, flights of fancy. I find the putting forward of an all-encompassing, factually based explanation with the very minimum of speculation exceedingly troublesome. It all happened well over 5000 years ago. The task is very difficult – perhaps it is better to say an impossible one – made all the more difficult by the unsatisfactory initial recovery of the corpse, clothing and gear.

What can indeed be regarded as firmly established about the arrival of Ötzi at the site? What happened around that moment and at the precise spot and then afterwards? What events led to the final spread of Ötzi's body, the clothing and the gear as found in the hollow in 1991 and 1992?

What the cautious scientist demands is the most parsimonious explanation from what can be called the palaeoforensic results.

The analyses of the contents of Ötzi's innards reveal a complex last journey from high up to low down and then the final climb to even higher. The lie of the land and the plant remains from the ingesta and also from on and around the corpse make Vinschgau and Schnalstal the very probable route of the fatal journey. But what made Ötzi go to high altitude in the first place cannot be known. That is so even if it could be established with confidence that he had been a chieftain, warrior, hunter, copper prospector or whatever. That he was a herdsman is now an unlikely idea. Similarly unknowable is what made him go down and then very shortly thereafter ascend again during his very last hours.

Ötzi's right palm was badly cut down to the bone between thumb and index finger shortly before his death. This rendered that hand useless, which brings an unsolvable puzzle.

How did he manage to carry all the gear, if all the gear was indeed his, with one hand so painful that he could not clench it?

The death took place at or in the very immediate vicinity of the hollow. Only two people were certainly involved in Ötzi's death. They were Ötzi himself and that person who shot the arrow leading to a swift demise from shock and great loss of blood. Ötzi's stomach was full. Therefore, the fatal attack took place either during his last meal or very soon after because the ingesta quickly start leaving the stomach. There is no scientific evidence that other people were involved in the death.

The season of death is disputed but the pollen and other botanical evidence is compelling. Accepting the demise in spring/early summer, then it is highly unlikely that the hollow was anything other than very full of snow and so Ötzi and all his stuff lay on the snow at first and then, with the snow melting, sank down into the hollow where water movement put them in their final positions.

Notes

1   See Renfrew, C. 1987. *Archaeology & Language The Puzzle of Indo-European Origins.* London, Jonathan Cape; Dalby, A. 2004. *Dictionary of Languages.* London, Bloomsbury Publishing; and Cunliffe, B. 2008. *Europe between the Oceans Themes and Variations: 9000 BC – AD 1000.* Ötzi perhaps spoke that version of proto-Indo-European which became Germanic. Barry Cunliffe states (p. 138): 'there is a growing consensus, at least among a significant group of archaeologists, that the most appropriate context for the introduction of the Indo-European language into Europe is the spread of the Neolithic way of life … the language originated among the early food producers of south-west Asia and thereafter spread through Europe.'

2   Prinroth-Fornwagner, R. and Niklaus, T.R. 1994. 'The man in the ice: results from radiocarbon dating'. *Nuclear Instruments & Methods in Physics Research Section B* 92, pp. 282–90. Hoogewerff, J. *et al.* 2001. 'The last domicile of the Iceman from Hauslabjoch: A geochemical approach using Sr, C and O isotopes and trace element signatures'. *Journal of Archaeological Science* 28, pp. 983–9.

3   Leitner, W. 1999a. 'Archäologische Forshungen im Ötztal'. *Schriften des Südtiroler Archäologiemuseums* 1, pp. 69–79. Leitner, W. 1999b. *Ötzi – der Mann im Eis und die Steinzeitjäger von Vent.* Imst, Alpendruck. Booklet of 12 pages.

4   Dal Ri, L. 2006. 'The Archaeology of the Iceman'. *Schriften des Südtirorler Archäologiemuseums* 3, pp. 17–44.

5   Leitner, W. 1999a. 'Archäologische Forshungen im Ötztal'. *Schriften des Südtiroler Archäologiemuseums* 1, pp. 69–79. Leitner, W. 1999b. *Ötzi – der Mann im Eis und die Steinzeitjäger von Vent.* Imst, Alpendruck. Booklet of 12 pages.

6   Dal Ri, L. 2006. 'The Archaeology of the Iceman'. *Schriften des Südtirorler Archäologiemuseums* 3, pp. 17–44.

7   De Marinis, R. 1998. 'The eneolithic cemetery of Remedello Sotto (BS) and the relative and absolute chronology of the Copper Age in Northern Italy'. *Notiziario Archeologico Bergomenese* 5, pp. 41–59.

8   Pedrotti, A. 2000. 'L'età del rame'. In Lanzinger, M., Marzinger, F. and Pedrotti, A. (Eds) *Storia del Trentino I. La preistoria e la protostoria.* Bologna, Il Mulino, pp. 183–253.

9   Dickson, J.H. *et al.* 1996. 'Mosses and the Tyrolean Iceman's Southern Provenance'. *Proceedings of the Royal Society B* 263, pp. 567–71.

10   Pabst, M. and Hofer, F. 1998. 'Deposits of Different Origin in the Lungs of the Tyrolean Iceman'. *American Journal of Physical Anthropology* 107, pp. 1–12.

11   Wessex Archaeology web pages.

12   Müller, W. *et al.* 2003. 'Origin and Migration of the Alpine Iceman'. *Science* 302, pp. 862–6. Müller, W. *et al.* 2003. 'Origin and Migration of the Alpine Iceman: Constraints from Isotope Geochemistry'. *Schriften des Südtiroler Archäologiemuseums* 3, pp. 75–90.

13 Capasso, L. 1994. 'Ungueal Morphology and pathology of the human mummy fround in the Val Senales (Eastern Alps. Tyrol, Bronze Age)'. *MUNIBE* 94, pp. 123–32. Capasso, L. *et al.* 1997. 'The Health of the Tyrolean Ice Man: Evidences from Nail, Skin and Hair'. *Journal of Paleopathology* 9, pp. 153–8. Capasso, L, La Verghetta and D'Anasasio. 1999. 'L'Homme du Similaun: Une Synthèse Anthropologique et Palethologique'. *L'Anthropologie* 103, pp. 447–70.

14 Spindler, K. 2005. 'Der Mann in Eis und das Wanderhirtentum'. In Holzner, J. and Walde, E. (eds) *Brüche und Brücken*. Wien, Folio Verlag, pp. 22–41. Evershed, R.P., Dudd, S.N., Lockheart, M.J. and Jim, S. 2001. 'Lipids in Archaeology'. In Brothwell, D. and Pollard, A.M. *Handbook of Archaeological Sciences*. Chichester, John Wiley & Sons, pp. 331–49. Kimpe, K., Jacobs, P.A. and Waelkens, M. 2005. 'Identification of animal fats in late Roman cooking pots of Sagalassos (southwestern Turkey)'. In Mulville, J. and Outram, A. (eds) *The Zooarchaeology of Fats, Oils, Milk and Dairying*. Chippenham, Oxbow Books, pp. 183–92.

15 Ibid.

16 Ibid.

17 Rubb, C. *et al.* 2006. 'Body size, body proportions, and mobility in the Tyrolean Iceman'. *Journal of Human Evolution* 51, pp. 91–101.

18 Ryder, M. L. 1983. *Sheep & Man*. Norwich, Duckworth.

19 Oeggl, K. 2009. 'The significance of the Tyrolean Iceman for the archaeobotany of Central Europe'. *Vegetation History and Archaeobotany* 18, pp. 1–11.

20 Schmidl, A., Kofler, W. and Oeggl, K. 2005. 'Was the Neolithic Tyrolean Iceman "Ötzi" a shepherd?' *Journal of Biological Research* 80, pp. 316–9. Oeggl, K., Kofler, W. and Schmidl, A. 2005. 'War Ötzi wirklich ein Hirte?' *Berichte der Reinhold-Tüxen-Gesellschaft*. 17, pp. 137–49.

21 Brothwell, D. and Grime, G. 2003. 'The analysis of hair of the Neolithic Iceman'. In Lynderup, N., Andreasen, C. and Berglund J. (eds). *Mummies in a New Millenium*. Copenhagen, Greenland National Museum and Danish Polar Centre, pp. 66–9. Cassallas, R. *et al.* 2003. 'Trace Element Analysis of Ancient Hair: a Word of Caution'. In Lynderup, N., Andreasen, C. and Berglund J. (eds) *Mummies in a New Millenium*. Copenhagen, Greenland National Museum and Danish Polar Centre, pp. 72–5.

22 Cullen, W.R. 2008. *Is Arsenic an Aphrodisiac? The Sociochemistry of an Element*. Cambridge, RSC Publishing. Przygoda, G., Feldmann, J. and Cullen, W.R. 2001. 'The arsenic eaters of Styria: a different picture of people who were chronically exposed to arsenic'. *Applied Organometallic Chemistry* 15, pp. 457–62. Raab, A. and Feldman, J. 2005. 'Arsenic speciation in hair extracts'. *Annals of Bioanalyitc Chemistry* 381, pp. 332–8. Pfeifer, H-R. *et al.* 2002. 'Natural arsenic-contamination of surface and ground waters in Southern Switzerland (Ticino)'. *Bulletin of Applied Geology* 7, pp. 81–103. Fuganti, A. *et al.* 2004. 'Arsenic in drinking water: legal, toxicological, hydrogeological, hydrochemical aspects and evaluation of dearsenification processes'. *Journal of technical and environmental geology* 1, pp. 45–53. Fuganti, A. *et al.* 2005. 'L'arsenico nelle rocce, nelle acque superficiali e nelle acque sotterranee della Valle dell'Adige fra Mezzolombardo e mattarello presso Roveré della luna (Trento)'. *Atti dell'Academia Rovereto degli Agiati* ser VIII, VB, pp. 59–94. Boston, C.E. and Arriaza, B. 2009. 'Arseniasis and terstogenic anomalies in the Atacama desert coast of ancient Chile'. *Interciencia* 34, pp. 1–13. Arriaza, B. *et al.* 2010. 'Exploring chronic arsenic poisoning in pre-Columbian Chilean mummies'. *Journal of Archaeological Science* 37, pp. 1274–8. Byrne, S. *et al.* 2010. 'Were Chinchorros exposed to arsenic? Arsenic determination in Chinchorro mummies' hair by laser ablation inductively coupled plasma-mass'. *Microchemical Journal* 94, pp. 28–35. Pfeifer, H.-R. and Zobrist, J. *EAWAG news* 53, pp. 15–7. Cevey, C. *et al.* 2006. 'Neue archäometullurgische Untersuchungen zum Beginn cder Kupferverarbeitung in der Schweiz'. *Archeolgie Suisse* 29, pp. 24–33. Bentley, R. and Chasteen, T.G. 2001. 'Arsenic Curiosa and Humanity'. *The Chemical Educator* 7.

23 Gleirscher, P. 2003. 'Ausstattungselemente des mannes aus dem Eis mit Blick auf Rangzeichen im kupferzeitlichen Mitteleuropa'. *Schriften des Südtirorler Archäologiemuseums* 3, pp. 41–56. Strahm, C. 1997. 'Les groupes culturels de l'espace circumalpin contemporains de l'homme de Similaun'. *Dossiers d'Archeologie* 224, pp. 40–3.

24 De Marinis, R. 1998. The eneolithic cemetery of Remedello Sotto (BS) and the relative and absolute chronology of the Copper Age in Northern Italy. *Notiziario Archeologico Bergomenese* 5.

25 Loy, T. 1998. 'Blood on the axe. What the Iceman's tools tell us'. *New Scientist* 2151, pp. 40–3.
    Tom Loy's claims are in this article in the *New Scientist* which, though famous, is a news
    magazine, not a peer-reviewed journal suitable for conveying highly detailed results that need
    scrutiny by appropriately qualified people. The opportunity that was presented to Tom Loy
    to investigate Ötzi was unique – a subject of enormous worldwide interest. Given proper
    scientific writing with full presentation of his data, there were any number of reputable
    journals which would have been pleased to publish his work after peer review. Tom Loy makes
    claim after detailed claim in his *New Scientist* article. His claims should be treated with caution
    until others repeat the work, if indeed it can be repeated. Loy stated, p. 43, that the 'DNA tests
    to determine which animals the blood spots come from have still to be completed.' Were they
    ever completed? Konrad Spindler's book has the following questionable statement concerning
    blood on the two fletched arrow shafts (*Spindler* 2, p. 131): 'The man (or the previous
    owners of one of the arrows) had therefore shot at and hit game (or even human beings?).
    Subsequently he pulled the arrows out of his victims with blood-smeared hands. That explains
    the traces of blood on the shafts, *because actual fingerprints could be identified on them.*' (My italics.)
    Both positive and negative handprints are well known as rock art from Palaeolithic times
    onwards, as are fingerprints on fired clay, from as early as Palaeolithic times, but, it should be
    stressed, very rarely on any other materials. Colin Renfrew and Paul Bahn in their well-known
    archaeology textbook state, p. 447: 'Fingerprints have survived on fired loess from the Upper
    Palaeolithic site of Dolni Vestonice, the Czech Republic, and on artifacts from many other
    periods such as Babylonian clay disks and cuneiform tablets from Nineveh (3000 BC) and on
    ancient Greek vases and sherds, helping to identify different potters.' There is a fingerprint
    on 5000-year-old pot from the River Thames. Old fingerprints are not just on pottery from
    Eurasia but from the Americas too, as pot shreds from the Canadian Plains of several hundred
    or more years ago. Renfrew, C. and Bahn, P. 2004. *Archaeology: Theories, Methods and Practice.*
    Fourth edition. Miroslav, K. 2005. 'Dermatoglyphics of ancient ceramics'. In Svoboda, J.A. (ed.)
    Pavlov I A Window into Gravettian Lifestyles. Brno, Academy of Sciences of the Czech Republic,
    pp. 449–97. Parker Pearson, M. and Chamberlain, A. 2001. *Earthly Remains.* OUP, pp. 159–62.
    Smith, P.R. and Wilson, M.T. 'Blood Residues in Archaeology', pp. 313–29. Bryan, L. 2005.
    The Buffalo People Pre-contact Archaeology on the Canadian Plains. Surrey, Heritage House. If
    indeed these prints *in blood* on the arrow shafts are genuine, anciently prehistoric fingerprints,
    perhaps even Ötzi's, then the discovery is unique. As is often said, extraordinary claims need
    extraordinary proof. Who saw them other than Tom Loy? Were photographs taken and, if so,
    have they been published or at least kept safe somewhere? If not, then this claim by Tom Loy,
    given credence by Konrad Spindler, is an example of both slack scientific practice and poor
    scholarship.
26 Spindler, K. and Oeggl, K. 2000. 'Ein weiterer Beilholm vom Hauslabjoch'. *Archäologisches
    Korrespondenzblatt* 30, pp. 53–60.
27 Dal Ri, L. 2006. 'The Archaeology of the Iceman'. *Schriften des Südtiroler Archäologiemuseums* 3, p. 35.
28 Oeggl, K. *et al.* 2007. 'The reconstruction of the last itinerary of "Ötzi", the Neolithic Iceman by
    pollen analyses from sequentially sampled gut extracts'. *Quaternary Science Reviews* 26, pp. 853–61.
29 Groenman van-Waateringe, W. 2011. 'The Iceman's last days – the testimony of *Ostrya carpinifolia*'.
    Antiquity 85, pp. 1–8.
30 Lippert, A. and Spindler, K. 1992. 'The Discovery of a Late Neolithic Glacier Mummy at the
    Hauslabjoch in the Ötztal Alps'. *Proceedings of the 1st World Congress on Mummy Studies.* Museo
    Arqueologico y Etnographico de Tenerife.
31 Ibid.
32 Siedler, H. *et al.* 1992. 'Some Anthropological Aspects of the Prehistoric Tyrolean Iceman'. *Science,*
    pp. 455–7.
33 Zur Nedden, D. *et al.* 1994. 'New findings on the Tyrolean "Ice Man": Archaeological and CT-Body
    Analysis Suggest Personal Disaster before Death'. *Journal of Archaeological Science* 21, pp. 809–18.
34 Guilaine, J. and Zammit, J. 2001. *Le Sentier de la Guerre Visages de la Violence Préhistorique.* Paris,
    Éditions de Seuil. Mithen, S. 2006. 'On the Origins of Warfare'. *New Scientist* 22, July, pp. 53–4. Young,

E. 2006. 'Muggings were rife in New Stone Age'. *New Scientist*, 13 May, p. 16. Smith, M. and Brickley, M. 2007. 'Boles Barrow Witness to Ancient Violence'. *Archaeology* 93, pp. 23–6.

35   Ibid.

36   Gostner, P. and Egarter Vigl, E. 2002. 'INSIGHT: Report of Radiological-Forensic Findings on the Iceman'. *Journal of Archaeological Science* 29, pp. 323–6. Gostner, P. and Egarter Vigl, E. 2003. 'Beitrag zur abklärung der todesursache de Mannes aus dem Eis'. *Schriften des Südtiroler Archäologiemuseums* 3, pp. 57–64. Nerlich, A., Bachmeier, B., Zink, A., Thalhammer, S and Egarter Vigl, E. 2003. 'Ötzi had a wound on his right hand'. *The Lancet* 362, p. 334. Pernter, P., Gostner, P., Egarter Vigl, E. and Rühli, F.J. 2007. 'Radiologic Proof for the Iceman's cause of death (ca. 5,300 BP)'. *Journal of Archaeological Science* 34, pp. 1–3. Nerlich, A.C., Peschel, O. and Egarter Vigl, E. 'New evidence for Ötzi's final trauma'. *Intensive Care Medicine* 35, pp. 1138–9.

37   De Latour, G. 2006. 'Ötzi Quinze Ans Apres'. *National Geographic France* 15, pp. 4–13.

38   Dal Ri, L. 2006. 'The Archaeology of the Iceman'. *Schriften des Südtirorler Archäologiemuseums* 3, p. 33.

39   Gostner, P. and Egarter Vigl, E. 2002. 'INSIGHT: Report of Radiological-Forensic Findings on the Iceman'. *Journal of Archaeological Science* 29, pp. 323–6. Gostner, P. and Egarter Vigl, E. 2003. 'Beitrag zur abklärung der todesursache de Mannes aus dem Eis'. *Schriften des Südtiroler Archäologiemuseums* 3, pp. 57–64. Nerlich, A., Bachmeier, B., Zink, A., Thalhammer, S and Egarter Vigl, E. 2003. 'Ötzi had a wound on his right hand'. *The Lancet* 362, p. 334. Pernter, P., Gostner, P., Egarter Vigl, E. and Rühli, F.J. 2007. 'Radiologic Proof for the Iceman's cause of death (ca. 5,300 BP)'. *Journal of Archaeological Science* 34, pp. 1–3. Nerlich, A.C., Peschel, O. and Egarter Vigl, E. 'New evidence for Ötzi's final trauma'. *Intensive Care Medicine* 35, pp. 1138–9.

40   Ibid.

41   In May 2005, with the backing of my co-authors, Klaus Oeggl and Linda Handley, I published in *Scientific American*, pp. 12–3: 'In 2003 a claim that Ötzi had been involved in battle because of the other people's blood on his clothing was made by Tom Loy of the University of Queensland. So far it has been promulgated only at a press conference and on television. Until this work is reputably published, it cannot be assessed.' If Tom Loy was aware of what we wrote he chose not to respond to us. Nor did he respond to what had appeared in a box written by one of the editors in the North American edition of *Readers Digest*, p. 186: 'But Dickson and Oeggl, coauthors of the accompanying article, question the DNA results' validity …'. Dickson, J.H., Oeggl, K. and Handley, L. 2004. 'A Really Cold Case'. *Reader's Digest American Edition*. February, pp. 181–281.

42   Bahn, P.G. and Everett, K. 1993. 'Iceman in the cold light of day'. *Nature* 362, pp. 11–2.

43   Egarter Vigl, E. 2006. 'The Preservation of the Iceman Mummy'. *Schriften des Südtiroler Archäologiemuseums* 4, pp. 45–70. Rollo, F.U. 2003. 'Vita, morte e mummificazione nella preistoria; lo studio del DNA batterico nel cadabere dell'Uomo venuto dal ghiaccio'. *Schriften des Südtiroler Archäologiemuseums* 3, pp. 101–10.

44   Ibid.

45   Vanzetti, A. *et al.* 2010. 'The Iceman as a burial'. *Antiquity* 84, pp. 1–12. Carancini, G.L. and Mattioli, T. ' "The Iceman is a burial": new remarks'. *Antiquity* 85, 2 pages. Fasolo, R. 'The death and ritual deposition of the "Iceman": a hypothetical scenario'. *Antiquity* 85, 3 pages. Zink. A. *et al.* 2011. 'The Iceman is not a burial: reply to Vanzetti *et al*'. *Antiquity* 85, 3 pages.

46   Ibid.

47   Bereuter, T.L. *et al.* 1996. 'Post-mortem alterations of human lipids – part I evaluation of adipocere formation and mummification by dessication'. Bereuter, T.L. *et al.* 1996. 'Post-mortem alterations of human lipids – part II: lipid composition of a skin sample from the Iceman'. *Innsbruck* 3. Bereuter, T.L., Kikenda, W. and Reiter, C. 1997. 'Iceman's Mummification – Implications from Infrared Spectroscopical and Histological Studies'. *Chemistry – A European Journal* 3, pp. 1033–8. Bereuter, T. 1999. 'Dead, drowned and dehydrated'. *Chemistry in Britain*, April, pp. 25–8. Bereuter, T.L., Reiter, C. and Mikenda, W. 1999. 'Ice cold in the Alps'. *Chemistry in Britain*, November, p. 23. Oeggl, K. 2003. 'Wurde die Mumie bewegt?' *Schriften des Südtiroler Archäologiemuseums* 3, pp. 91–100. Oeggl, K., Schmidl, A. and Kofler, W. 2009. 'Origin and seasonality of subfossil caprine dung from the discovery

site of the Iceman (Eastern Alps)'. *Vegetation History and Archaeobotany* 18, pp. 37–46. Egarter Vigl, E. 2003. 'The Iceman Mummy in the Archaeology Museum of South Tyrol: Development of a New Method of Conservation'. In Niels, N., Andreasen, C. and Berglund. (eds) Copenhagen. Danish Polar Centre, pp. 82–5.

48 Oeggl, K. 2003. 'Wurde die Mumie bewegt?' *Schriften des Sudtiroler Archaologiemuseums.*

49 Ibid.

50 Ibid.

51 De Latour, G. 2006. 'Ötzi Quinze Ans Apres'. *National Geographic France* 15, pp. 4–13.

6

Ancient People and their Belongings from Other European Glaciers and Ice Patches

Human remains melting out of Alpine glaciers were recorded long before the discovery of Ötzi; in fact no less than 250 years before him. Lorenzo Dal Ri drew attention to this in 2006 in his article on 'The Archaeology of the Iceman', p.18–19. In 1738, at the height of the Little Ice Age, Anton Roschmann published *Regnum Animale Vegetabile, et Minerale Medicum Tyrolense*. In journeying through the very territory where Ötzi was found, he encountered an enormous glacier (*Der Grosst Verner*) with voluminous crevasses, expelling things along its edges that it had swallowed up, such as grass, stones and even human and animal bones. This may be one of the first reports of a glacier mummy but if a prehistoric one or not we shall never know.

NORBERT MATTERSBERGER, POACHER

Born in 1796 and dying in 1839 out hunting chamois, Norbert (Bertil) Mattersberger was a poacher and otherwise known as Spiegelburger.[1] He met his end in the glacier at above 2700m at Gradetzkees, Grossglockner, east Tyrol. Found on 9 August 1929 by a local man Aloïs Hanser, his mummified body lacked the head and the right leg had been broken off below the knee. Parts of the chest and back were well preserved, with skin and hair still adhering. A leather brace still lay over the corpse's shoulder. There were teeth, scattered hair, shreds of clothing, buttons, lead shots, a rifle with a leather sling, a clasp knife, parts of a telescope, a silver watch and other artefacts.

There was no forensic examination of the bones, soft tissues or alimentary contents. As already stated in the very first paragraph of this book, he is the only ancient glacier mummy with a real name, which was easy for the authorities to find. His last occupation was that of farm labourer and so the question arises how did such a man acquired a rather special rifle, a muzzle-loader but a state-of-the-art weapon with an under-hammer percussion lock (the lock was usually positioned above and so the flash could sometimes impair vision). However, under-hammer rifles were often owned by poachers. The rifle had been roughly repaired and was perhaps second hand or stolen. (See Fig. 1.1.)

THEODULPASS MERCENARY

Based on an article by Peter Lehner and Annemarie Julen, the two Swiss who made the discovery, and on another article by Werner Mayer of Basel University (*Innsbruck* 1, p. 321), Konrad Spindler briefly recounted the discoveries from the Upper Theodul glacier.[2] Between 1985 and 1990, scattered human remains and many artefacts were found overlooked by the nearby dramatic peak of the Matterhorn, reaching 4478m. The site lies at about 3000m, some 300m below the pass, in the Wallis Canton near Zermatt in southern Switzerland. For many years this pass was important, if dangerous, certainly after the onset of the Little Ice Age, between southern Switzerland and northern Italy. Though there were no soft tissues surviving and so the remains cannot strictly be called a mummy, the discovery certainly deserves discussion. The remains are unique in that the dating of the unfortunate man's fatal accident, about 1595, comes from coins and the deduction that he was a soldier, comes from the weapons. A full set of arms was found at the site (sword, pistol, dagger in a sheath that also held a small knife and a wooden container possibly for gunpowder). That he was a mercenary is deduced from the sheer quantity of coins he carried. Konrad Spindler says (*Spindler* 2, p. 44) there were 'more than two hundred pieces of silver altogether'.

Concerning the clothing, Peter Lehner and Annemarie Julen state that 'Shredded pieces of cloth, most not larger than a few square centimetres, were the most common objects. Several large and more or less intact pieces of silk may have come from a shirt. The remaining material consists of very coarse tissue of bluish or reddish tints, some decorated with "gold braid".' About footwear they say that 'leather pieces appear to belong to one pair of boots, made of multiple layers of thin leather. The soles show slight signs of wear but were probably fairly new.' Concerning adornment, they say that there were two small silver objects (which Konrad Spindler calls 'pendants'). One has a coat of arms with the letters 'H.N., corrected at a later date to H.A.' The reverse side shows a bird resembling an eagle as depicted on the medieval banner of the city of Brig, which lies some 40km away to the north.

Fig. 6.1 Theodulpass glacier.

Fig. 6.2 Skull cap and long bones of Theodulpass Mercenary (*Werner Meyer, University of Basel*)

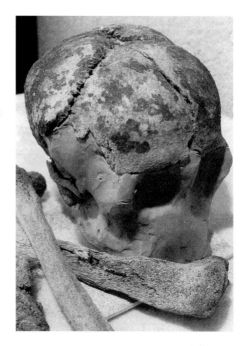

With regard to beasts of burden, they state: 'About 100m below the site numerous bones and teeth of horses, mules and donkeys lay scattered on the ice and on the discovery site only a single horse-shoe and some horse teeth were found.' However, Konrad Spindler claims (*Spindler* 2, p. 44): 'some [bones] from two mules complete with horseshoes' were found at the site.

Only the skull cap and some long bones were found of the mercenary.[3] The decalcified bones, including the skull cap, had the consistency of sponge rubber before they dried out. A photograph in the Peter Lehner and Annemarie Julen article clearly shows only the skull cap and no other parts of the skull, though the English version of Konrad Spindler's book misleadingly translates '*Schädelkalotte*' as 'skull'. Konrad Spindler says that when found the skull cap had 'matted hair'; this is a puzzle because the Peter Lehner and Annemarie Julen article makes no mention of hair. The skull cap, weapons and coins are on display in the recently opened Matterhorn Museum in Zermatt. The museum also has Roman coins found at the Theodul glacier, a clear indication that the Theodul Pass was used for a very long time.

PORCHABELLA SHEPHERDESS

In August 1988 some human remains were found melted from the rapidly receding Porchabella glacier, near Bergün in the Grisons Canton of eastern Switzerland (see Plate 22). The police report stated: '… it can be assumed that the remains are very old and come from a male person.'[4] The first claim was correct but the second was wrong. This mummy turned out to be a woman. The report continued that more remains might be found and in due course this proved correct. In August 1992 there were more discoveries. So, in addition to most of her skeleton, some of the soft tissues still existed and therefore the human remains can be called 'mummified'. The list includes hair, pieces of muscle and of intestines, a skull with pieces of brain, a hat, a necklace, two buttons, a spoon, a comb and a bowl, all of wood, parts of a pair of shoes and large pieces of cloth. However, no remains of plants, seeds, leaves and so on, were found with the mummy.

Fading from auburn to light brown during conservation in alcohol, her hair, under the microscope, had some tiny remnants of scalp and also dandruff and 'rare' nits. So, like the

Beauty of Loulan (see Plate 1) but unlike Ötzi and Kwäday Dän Ts'ìnchí Man, she had lice. The Swiss anthropologist, Bruno Kaufmann, deduced that the Porchabella Woman, dying at the age of 'nearly 22', had lived some time in the sixteenth or seventeenth century; her shoes, of Austrian type, indicated the earlier part of that period. It has been shown that the order of eruption of teeth, molars and incisors, has changed over the centuries in Switzerland and middle Europe. The woman's teeth have the sequence typical of the late Middle Ages or early modern period. A radiocarbon date, mentioned without any details by Konrad Spindler as mid-nineteenth century, is thought to be incorrect due to contamination, as told to me by Bruno Kaufman. However, Jürg Rageth published the dates (calibrated AD) in 1995 as follows: 'Wooden bowl: 1728–1906 Textile fragment: 1719–1904 Hair: 1714–1903.'

Again contamination is mentioned and Jürg Rageth gives his preference for the true date as about 1700 AD. That all three samples of differing natures could all have been contaminated and by what is a puzzle.

The corpse of the shepherdess took about 200 to 300 years to travel about 1800m along the glacier and to 400m lower than the assumed point of the fatality and became very fragmentary in the process, some pieces of bone and soft tissue being only a few centimetres long.[5] In his book Konrad Spindler refers baldly to the Porchabella Woman as a 'shepherdess'. He gives no reason for this conclusion. However, Jürg Rageth in his 1995 article discusses the matter and tells that her long coat, a wooden bowl and spoon (for milk and bread) indicate such an occupation. But surely there cannot be great confidence in that. Harold Stadler of Innsbruck University calls her a 'dairymaid', just as reasonably in my opinion.

Bruno Kaufman could not tell if the woman had been travelling from Bergün to the Engadin or the Engadin to Bergün. However, there was very little to go on and, unfortunately, there were no plant remains such as those which have been so helpful in the cases of both Ötzi and Long Ago Person Found. Though Bruno Kaumann's publication was in 1996 there have been no further scientific studies of the human tissues, other than the radiocarbon dates mentioned above. The contents of her intact stomach, which are as yet unexamined, could add substantially to the story. Jürg Rageth told me by email that 'Also today shepherd people in our alpine regions are coming frequently from Southern Tirol'.

At the end of his publication (*Innsbruck* 3, p. 245), Bruno Kaufmann states, concerning the name Porchabella: 'It is first mentioned in 1540; the language is late Romansch and means

Fig. 6.3 Shoe of the Porchabella Shepherdess. (*Jürg Rageth*)

nice pig. In everyday use this designates a prostitute. This is surely an unusual name for a mountain and a glacier.' This is a statement that gets ready acceptance.

On examining topographic maps and standing on the ground below the Kersch Hut and looking up, one thinks that the woman could perhaps have used the Porta d'Es-cha, which is the modern route, or the gap between Pix Porchabella and Pix Val Mura, which is strongly reminiscent of the Schnidejoch Pass. However, one is forced to wonder why, whichever direction she was taking, she chose such a route at all because the Albulapass is only a few kilometres to the south, reaches only 2312m and there is no glacier to cross. With all that in mind, Jürg Rageth tells me that he does not think she had been on a journey at all but was following her occupation in tending livestock and went on to the glacier for some reason such as to rescue a sheep or goat or merely out of curiosity and fell down a crevasse.

These two examples of ancient human remains from Swiss glaciers can be thought of as typical of glacier bodies in their very fragmented state with most or all of the flesh and innards lost. There is no harm in stressing again that in his intactness including all the intestines and the very much older date, Ötzi stands in very great contrast, as Konrad Spindler has already sensibly pointed out.

ARTEFACTS FROM SCHNIDEJOCH, SWITZERLAND

In the last several years an extraordinary assortment of prehistoric and historic artefacts has been found at Schnidejoch, in the Bernese Oberland.[6] The suffix *joch* means pass and is found in many Alpine place names, not just in Switzerland but *Ötziland* too. For instance, there are Hauslabjoch, Niederjoch and Timmelsjoch.

Found around 2740m above sea level, these newly discovered Swiss artefacts had been uncovered by the melting ice of an almost vanished lobe of the Chilchli glacier. They range in age from about 5000 (Late Neolithic) to about 1200 years ago (medieval) and so for about 4000 years ancient people used this pass, Schnidejoch, as hikers still do today. It is so narrow as to be almost a defile and to avoid climbing higher up steep slopes the ancient travellers were forced to cross the ice, sometimes losing their belongings or with even sadder consequences. (See Plate 23.)

There are fragments of late Neolithic leather shoes, one being so well preserved as to allow a reconstruction. Also from that period there is a large part of a pair of patched trousers, arrow shafts and a Birch bark quiver containing two arrowheads but no shafts, as well as a very small piece of woven bast clothing. The last listed is tantalising because, if it is a remnant of an item of dress entirely made of bark, it would be the

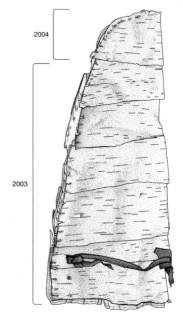

Fig. 6.4 Quiver from Schnidejoch.

only one from prehistoric Europe. For Ötzi's cape (or mat or hood) bast had been used only for tying up the bundles of grass which composed the bulk of the garment. From the Early Bronze Age came an arrow shaft, a shoe fragment and binding materials, but the outstanding object is a 23cm-long bronze pin, the flat head being decorated with a cross. From Roman/ Iron Age times came iron shoe studs, a small part of a woollen tunic and a well-crafted fibula. There are two shoe fragments from medieval times. Full details of these fine discoveries, with radiocarbon dates, are given by Swiss archaeologist Peter Suter and two colleagues in their very well-illustrated article.[7]

ARTEFACTS FROM NORWEGIAN ICE PATCHES

Especially on mountain slopes getting little sun (on northern and eastern aspects), snow can accumulate to a depth of metres and slowly turn to ice without necessarily in the long run becoming glaciers. Such ice patches, as they are often called (but sometimes snow patches), can have formed over thousands of years. In summer reindeer go on to the ice patches, which are cooler than the surroundings, to avoid biting and egg-laying insects. Reindeer (or caribou in North America) are good to eat and the skins are very useful too. Hunters would get as close as possible to shoot arrows or throw projectiles with the aid of atlatls. Such throwing sticks, or *propulseurs* in French, are powerful extensions of the hunter's arm. Inevitably, some of the implements were lost and along with layers of reindeer dung became stratified into the ice patches. Atlatls have a very ancient history, certainly in Europe, being well known from the Palaeolithic of France, including two splendidly and similarly decorated ones, real works of art, from Mas-D'Azil and Bédeilhac in Ariège. There is a fascinating account of the use of atlatls by Dale Guthrie in *The Nature of Paleolithic Art*.[8]

The now melting ice patches are revealing these artefacts and consequently fascinating long-term histories of hunting are developing in both Northern Europe and North America. Such archaeological sites were first noticed in the mountains of central Norway nearly 100 years ago. There at Oppdal, the artefacts come from as early as *c.* AD 400 to *c.* 1700, as related by Oddmunn Farbregd and Martin Callanan, both based in Trondheim, though the first is Norwegian and the second Irish.[9] However, in Oppland there has been the discovery of a 2000-year-old shoe and at Finnmark, northernmost Norway, and of a decorated bone arrowhead from 2000 to 3000 years ago. The North American history of hunting derived from ice-patch archaeology is very much older than that, as outlined in the beginning of the next chapter.

Fig. 6.5 Proximal end of arrow of AD 400–600 date, ice patch, Kringsollfonna, Norway. (*Martin Callanan, University of Trondheim, Norway*)

Notes

1   Stadler, H. 2005. '"Untertan kontra Obrigkeit". Die Gletscherleiche des Wilderers Norbert Mattersberger vom Gradetzkees in Ostirol'. In Holzner, J. and Walde, E. (eds) *Brüche und Brücken*. Folio, Bozen, pp. 236–49.

2   Lehner, P. and Julien, A. 1991. 'A man's bones with 16th-century weapons and coins in a glacier near Zermatt, Switzerland'. *Antiquity* 65, pp. 269–73.

3   Ibid.

4   The account of the Porchabella woman is taken largely from Rageth, J. 1995. 'Ein Gletscherleichenfund im Piz Kesch-Gebiet'. *Bünder Monatsblatt* 5, pp. 365–91 and from Kaufmann, B. 1996. 'The corpse from the Porchabella-glacier in the Grisons, Switzerland, Community of Bergün'. *Innsbruck* 3. I also had the benefit of direct contact with both these authors. Page 45 of the paperback English edition of Spindler's book lists the following: 'Bits of skeleton, hair and shreds of private parts of the mummified body itself …' 'Private parts' is a mistranslation of *Weichteilfetzen*, which means merely soft tissues.

5   Ibid.

6   Suter, P., Hafner, A. and Glauser, G. 2005. 'Lenk – Schnidejoch. Funde aus dem Eis – ein vor- und frügeschichlicher Passüberergang'. *Archäologie im Kanton Bern* 6B, pp. 499–522. Suter, P.J., Hafner, A. and Glauser, K. 2005. 'Prähistorische und frügeschichtliche Funde aus dem Eis – der wiederentdeckte pass über das Schnidejoch'. *Archéologie Suisse* 28, pp. 16–2. Grosjean, M., Suter, P.J., Trachsel, M. and Wanner, H. 2007. 'Ice-borne prehistoric finds in the Swiss Alps reflect Holocene glacier fluctuations'. *Journal of Quaternary Science* 22, pp. 203–7.

7   Ibid.

8   Guthrie, R.D. 2005. *The Nature of Palaeolithic Art*. The University of Chicago Press.

9   Farbregd, O. 1972. 'Finds from the Mountains of Oppdal, Sør-Trøndelag, Norway'. *Det Konglike Norsk Vidensabers Selskab Museet Miscellanea* 5, pp. 105–7. English summary. Farbregd, O. 2009. 'Archery History from Ancient Snow and Ice'. *Vitak* 7, pp. 158–70. Callanan, M. 2010. 'Northern Snow Patch Archaeology'. *BAR International Series* 2154, pp. 43–54.

Ancient People and their Belongings from North American Glaciers and Ice Patches

ARTEFACTS FROM ICE PATCHES

Very few human remains have emerged from the melting glaciers of North America, either in Canada or the United States. However, in the last 10 years and more, the vanishing ice patches have produced lots of artefacts which had been used for the hunting of caribou and not just projectiles such as darts and arrows, but also other objects such as an old shoe (moccasin) from about 1500 years ago. The most productive places have been the south-west Yukon, Alaska and the greater Yellowstone area (Montana and Wyoming) (see Plate 24). In Colorado remains of bison, from about 2300 years ago until about 250 years ago, as well as bighorn sheep, mule deer and elk have been recovered from ice patches but no artefacts as yet, though Craig Lee of the University of Colorado and two others think it likely that they will be found in due course.

What is so very remarkable is that these findings of hunting artefacts cover thousands of years back to more than 10,000 years ago. A complete wooden dart foreshaft was found at about 3000m melted from an ice patch in the Rocky Mountains near the Yellowstone National Park. Dated to about 10,400 years ago, it is the oldest artefact melted from ancient ice. Craig Lee thinks that the prey had been bighorn sheep.

Another dramatic discovery is that there was a long period of the use of atlatls (throwing darts) and then quite abruptly archery begins. This was shown from the Yukon ice patches where atlatls began to be used at least as early as about 8500 years ago, but then at about 1300 years ago they were replaced by bows and arrows. A similar story of change in hunting technique has emerged from ice patches in the Mackenzie and Selwyn Mountains of the Northwest Territories. Carla Dove of the Smithsonian Institution and two others identified by microscopy feathers of at least six different birds from the Yukon ice patches. The three feather samples that had certainly been used for fletching proved to be from eagle, duck and northern flicker. Yet another revealing aspect of ice patch studies is that pollen and macroscopic fossil analyses of caribou dung have revealed vegetation changes over the thousands of years.[1]

KWÄDAY DÄN TS'ÌNCHÍ MAN (LONG AGO PERSON FOUND)²

Human Bodies from Glaciers

The American and Canadian Alpine Clubs were founded almost 50 years later than that in Britain and, so, organised, recreational alpinism came much later and this may account, at least partly, for the fewer human bodies in North American glaciers than in the Alps. In 2005, a man's body 80 per cent encased in ice was found on the Mount Mendel in Kings Canyon National Park, California, at 4179m (13,710 feet). It was that of a Second World War airman. A mummified human arm has recently been recovered from the Mount Sandford glacier in Alaska. It belonged to one of the passengers on an aircraft crashed in 1948. DNA and fingerprint analyses identified to whom it had belonged.³

Accounts of unfortunate mountaineers who fell to their deaths in crevasses can be found in back numbers of the *New York Times*, but many of the bodies resulting from these sad accidents were recovered very quickly and so can hardly be called mummies, or else the bodies were found frozen up but not in or even on glacier ice. From the scientific standpoint, by far the most interesting recovery has been that of the Kwäday Dän Ts'ìnchí Man. Though the carbon dates are far from simple to interpret, the young man had certainly lived well before AD 1900, which is an appropriate date to suggest for the boundary separating modern from ancient glacier mummies in North America, the foundation of the Alpine Club of America having been in 1902.

Place, Discovery and Body

The Province of British Columbia in Canada is enormous by the standards of Western European countries. It covers 944,734 square km – a figure not easy to comprehend. That is an area almost the combined sizes of France, Germany and the Netherlands. It is virtually

Fig. 7.1 Map of south-east Alaska and British Columbia.

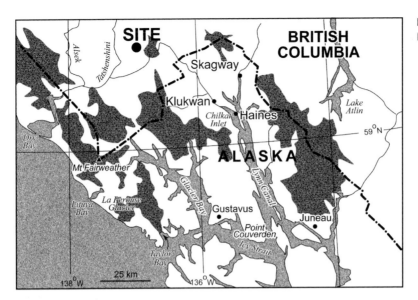

Fig. 7.2 Map of Icy Strait area.

four times the size of the United Kingdom. The place of the discovery is in the far north-west of the province at 59° N, some 4° south of the Arctic Circle. It is in an area often called the Haines Triangle because of the triangular shape of the boundary between British Columbia, the Yukon and Alaska. The narrow angle of the triangle points southward to the west of Haines, Alaska.

Preceded by a note in the newsletter of the Canadian Archaeological Association in 1999, the first full scientific paper was by the Canadian forensic anthropologist Owen Beattie of University of Alberta with 10 co-authors and they described the place as follows, p. 129,

> The human remains and artefacts were discovered in and around the margin of a glacier in the Tatshenshini River watershed, at an elevation of approximately 1600 metres. The setting is in the Tatshenini-Alsek Park, which includes the southern end of the St. Elias Mountains, Canada's highest range. The park is known for its wilderness qualities, including massive glaciers, wild rivers, precipitous canyons, forested valley bottoms, grizzly bears, Dall's sheep, eagles and spawning salmon.[4]

There are neither metalled roads nor settlements in the park and Owen Beattie and co-authors continued: 'The find area is about equidistant between the two closest aboriginal settlements, Kluwan, a Chilkat Tlingit community near Haines, Alaska, and Klukshu, a Champagne and Aishihik First Nations' settlement in the Yukon, south of Haines Junction.'

The discoverers of the remains of Kwäday Dän Ts'ìnchí Man were William (Bill) Hanlon and his friends Michael Roche and Warren Ward, all school teachers from south-eastern British Columbia. They were out hunting Dall's sheep on the morning of Saturday 14 August 1999 and they were seeking suitably rich, grassy vegetation where the Dall's sheep prefer to graze. In passing along the edge of a glacier, they saw a dark mass protruding from the ice. It proved to be part of the remains of Kwäday Dän Ts'ìnchí Man overlain by his robe. Owen Beattie *et al.* state:

The human remains are represented by two major body parts from a young male: an upper segment consisting of the fleshed torso with attached left arm, and a lower segment consisting of a lower segment of the fleshed pelvis with attached thighs. While in the glacier the body had been transversely bisected ca. 10cm inferior to the umbilicus.[5]

Adipocere formation was significant on the back. The bones were all soft and pliable.

The head was not found in 1999 but, 'While only small fragments of skin from the head were found, hair masses were recovered within 3m of the upper body segment. The hair appears black and is relatively long, with some sections just over 20cm.' Using X-ray photoelectron spectroscopy and scanning electron microscopy, Ronald Martin of the University of Western Ontario with two others found that the hair surface was degraded and 'extensively altered by oxidation'.[6]

On 14 August 2003, Bill Hanlon and Mike Roche visited the site of their earlier discovery and found pieces of the skull, with no remaining soft tissues, and other missing parts of the body. Yet more missing fragments were found in August 2004. The discoveries made in 2003 and 2004 were left at the site. Apart from various artefacts, only two items of clothing and were ever found with the body or close to it. These were a hat and a robe. No details of the precise location have been published and no archaeological plan of the site has been published as yet and may well never be. Moreover, the glacier ice in which the human remains and artefacts had been frozen has entirely melted away.

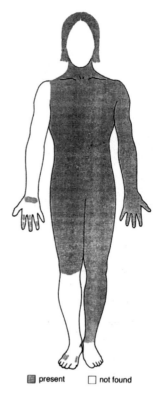

☒ present ☐ not found

Fig. 7.3 Body outline. (*Canadian Journal of Archaeology*)

Radiocarbon Dating

In stark contrast with the totally convincing series of radiocarbon dates concerning Ötzi, the dates concerning Kwäday Dän Ts'inchí Man are problematical and controversial. Nine dates were published in the 2000 paper, two of them seemingly indicating when Kwäday Dän Ts'inchí Man was alive.

The 'plant fibre' of the hat has an uncalibrated age of 500 ±30 and calibrated age of AD 1405–45. Hide of the fur garment has an uncalibrated age of 450 ±40 and calibrated age of AD 1415–90. Therefore Kwäday Dän Ts'inchí Man lived about 500 to 600 years ago.[7]

However, the 2007 paper by Michael Richards of the Max Planck Institute of Evolutionary Anthropology in Germany (with several others) discussed more carbon dates, including two directly from the body (bone collagen).[8] They are the same: 952 ±28 and 935 ±75 (uncalibrated). So the body appears about to be about 500 years older than the clothing.

At first thought this is totally crazy! How can it be? However, there is what is called the marine reservoir effect. In the sea there is 'old' C14 which is eaten or photosynthesised by

Lab #	Description	Material Analyzed	Conventional Radiocarbon Age (BP)	C¹³/C¹² ratio	Calibrated Date - 2 sigma	
Beta – 133765	Hat	Plant fibre	500±30	-20.0 o/oo	AD 1405 – 1445	BP 545 - 505
Beta – 133766	Fur garment	Hide	450±40	-23.9 o/oo	AD 1415 – 1490	BP 535 - 460
Beta – 133767	Faunal (moose)	Bone collagen	174.1±0.6% (modern)	-21.2 o/oo	AD 1962 – 1964 or AD 1967	Not available
Beta – 140633	Throwing board or snaring implement	Wood	230±40	-20.9 o/oo	AD 1530 – 1545 and AD 1635 – 1680 and AD 1740 – 1805 and AD 1930 - 1950	BP 420 - 405 and BP 315 - 270 and BP 210 - 145 and BP 20 - 0
Beta – 140634	Dart	Wood	360±40	-27.0 o/oo	AD 1445 – 1645	BP 505 - 305
Beta – 140635	Walking or bear stick	Wood	140±40	-25.5 o/oo	AD 1660 – 1955	BP 290 - 5
Beta – 140636	Projectile foreshaft	Wood	290±40	-24.9 o/oo	AD 1490 – 1665	BP 460 - 285
Beta – 140637	Arrow/dart shaft	Wood	120±40	-25.5 o/oo	AD 1665 – 1955	BP 285 - 5
Beta – 140638	Projectile fore/midshaft	Wood	500±40	-24.0 o/oo	AD 1400 – 1450	BP 550 - 500

Fig. 7.4 Radiocarbon dates. (*Canadian Journal of Archaeology*)

marine organisms so that an organism alive today gives a radiocarbon age of some hundreds of years. As well established below, Kwäday Dän Ts'ìnchí Man ate a lot of seafood and consequently these two dates are too old. They have to be calibrated to estimate the true age. What is controversial is just how many hundreds of years should be deducted. After detailed consideration, Mike Richards and co-authors state: '… we conclude that the individual likely dates to between cal A.D. 1670 to 1850, which is in the pre- (or early) European contact for this region.' So if that is correct then the clothing is much older than the body. How, therefore, to explain that? Perhaps the original two dates are both simply wrong or somehow the samples analysed had contained 'old' C14. See the note for further information on the radiocarbon dates.[9]

Genetic Affinities, Age and Health

The first published DNA study of Kwäday Dän Ts'ìnchí Man was that by Victoria Monsalve *et al.* of the University of British Columbia in 2002. These authors showed that he was a native, which was already obvious from the traditional clothing and equipment. He belonged to haplogroup A, one of the five haplogroups which characterise Native Americans. This haplogroup is the commonest in North America but is also found in Central and South America. His mtDNA was compared to those of Native American, East Siberian, Greenlandic and North-east Asian populations. His mtDNA lineage is that designated as A2-16189C and has been found throughout the Americas.[10]

The outline drawing of the body in the 2000 paper and reproduced here (see Fig. 7.3) was not made to show his stature and physique but merely to indicate which parts of the body had been found to date and which had not.11 Nothing has yet been published about his weight when alive, but he was about 169cm tall and of average build. His hair appears to have been cut, though with no signs of braiding or knotting. We cannot reveal his physiognomy because there has been no attempt at facial approximation and there never will be. No photographs of the body parts have been published, nor will they be.

With regard to age at death, Owen Beattie *et al.* state: 'late teens to early twenties.'[11] The brief examination in the field, by Daniel Straathof, of the pieces of the skull found in 2003 confirmed a young age. In 2000 there were several medical examinations of the remains. Dan Straathof of Vancouver General Hospital was the forensic pathologist and he carried out the autopsies; he found no evidence of foul play or even of ill health. Nor did he note any clear signs in the skull and other remains found in 2003. It has to be borne in mind, however, that some parts of the body were never found and so could not be examined.

However, Kwäday Dän Ts'ìnchí Man had a fish tapeworm. This internal parasite, which can be several metres long, attaches itself by its hooked head to the small intestine of humans and many other mammals which are the final host in a complex lifecycle including small crustaceans and fish as hosts. The infection happens after eating raw or partially cooked fish or hard roe, according to von Bonsdorff, who reports few ill effects on human hosts.[12] Infections can still occur in Alaska and elsewhere in North America by eating uncooked salmon. The worms can make their hosts anaemic and cause a range of other troubles, such as diarrhoea, abdominal cramp, weight loss and vomiting. However, the anaemia results from a particular species (*Diphyllobothrium latum*) and seemingly not from several other species known in North America such as *D. pacificum*. In the Americas, infection of humans is known as far back as 4500 years ago among the Chinchorro people of Chile by *D. pacificum* and has been found among the Chiribaya people of Peru about 1000 to 1 350 years ago.[13] The readily recognisable microscopic eggs occur in vast profusion in the lower gut of the mammalian hosts and such was the case with Kwäday Dän Ts'ìnchí Man.

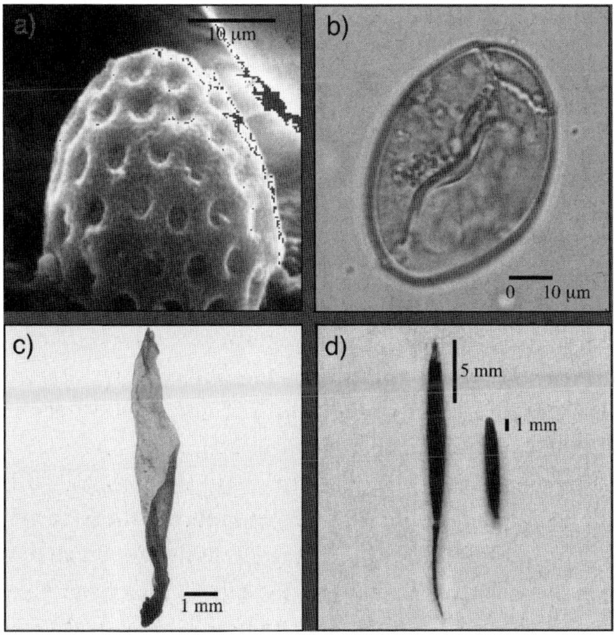

Fig. 7.5
a). Pollen grain of beach asparagus from stomach.
b). Egg of fish tapeworm from gut.
c). Endophragmal skeleton of marine crustacean from stomach.
d). Left: fruit of mountain sweet cicely. Right: needle leaf of mountain hemlock. Both from robe.

The unconcern until recent times with which at least one Tlingit has regarded intestinal worms as food is well shown by this statement by the German explorer Arthur Krause, writing a letter in 1882 from Chilkoot, near Chilkat. He had watched a young man 'cut open the intestine [of an American Porcupine] and in the half-digested mash of inner bark of spruce he fished for the enormous number of a kind of short broad tapeworm and gulped them down with signs of well-being at such speed, that I could barely save a handful for our collection.'[14]

Aboriginal Peoples and Environment

In accordance with the wishes of the First Nations, the remains of Kwäday Dän Ts'ìnchí Man were cremated in 2001 and returned to the mountain where the fatality happened.[15]

As the remains had been found in Tatshenshini-Alsek Park in northernmost British Columbia, close to the southern border of the Yukon Territory, they had been recovered from the traditional land of the Champagne and Aishihik First Nations. Accordingly, they took a leadership role in the management of this important discovery. As made clear by the archaeology and science now to be described, Kwäday Dän Ts'ìnchí Man had strong coastal connections and the nearby coast was the land of the Eyat and Tlingit Native Americans. Other aboriginal territories that Kwäday Dän Ts'ìnchí Man would have known about, and possibly even visited in some cases, are those of the Kluane, Kwanlin Dun, Ta'an Kwach'an, Teslin Tlingit, the Tagish and, well to the south, the Haida, a warrior people, as were the Tlingit.[16]

With few roads, the area that would have been familiar to Kwäday Dän Ts'ìnchí Man is even today wild, inhospitable country. There are massive mountains, some of the highest in North America. Mount Fairweather, on the border of Canada and the United States, reaches 4663m (15,300ft) and Mount St Elias is 5400m (18,008ft). Frances Barkley, the first European woman to visit Alaska, recorded in 1792 the arrival of her husband's ship, the *Halcyon*, at Yakutat Bay in laconic fashion merely stating, 'They are both very high mountains, with their Heads covered in Snow'.[17] Seen from Yakutat, when not obscured by clouds as very often happens, Mount St Elias is a glistening, snowy, white pyramid (see Plate 25). At about 50km from the open Pacific Ocean or some 30km from the nearest part of Icy Bay, it is the highest mountain in the world so close to the sea. It is easy to understand why the celebrated anthropologist, Frederica de Laguna, who studied the Yakutat Tlingit, called her large volumes *Under Mount St. Elias*. Mount Logan (6100m, 19,850ft) is the highest peak in Canada, and Mount McKinley (Denali, 6250m, 20,320ft) is the highest mountain in all North America. The former is not too far to the north-east of Mount St Elias and so Kwäday Dän Ts'ìnchí Man may perhaps have seen it, but Mount McKinley is much too far away to the north-west.

There are enormous ice fields and glaciers some of which are 50km plus long. Some of these rivers of ice reach the sea and are called tide-water glaciers. The La Perouse glacier is the only such example to debouch directly into the open Pacific Ocean. All the many others end in fjords or do not now quite reach the open sea.

Kwäday Dän Ts'ìnchí Man could well have been familiar with both the seas of the turbulent Gulf of Alaska and of the much quieter Lynn Canal. The fearsome difficulties for boatmen dealing with the Gulf of Alaska are eloquently recounted by Francis Caldwell in his well-illustrated book *Land of Ocean Mists: The Wild Ocean Coast West of Glacier Bay*.[18] Coastal natives such as the Tlingit and Haida had very large seagoing canoes. Jacinto Caamaño at Lángara Island, near Haida Gwaii (Queen Charlotte Islands), in 1792 described one such Haida canoe arriving with the most important chief and 45 people including women and children. There were with eight oarsmen on each side. All were seated or kneeling except the captain, who was standing and singing while all the others joined in.[19]

If Kwäday Dän Ts'ìnchí Man lived on the coast of Alaska then he lived in a very unstable land. Also tellingly told by Francis Caldwell is the colossal wave which swept seawards down the fjord that is called Lituya Bay on 9 July 1958.[20] A large chunk of a mountain at the head of the fjord fell down producing a wave that reached a height of no less than 524m (1720ft), sweeping everything before it, tearing up forests right down to the bedrock. Such reverse tsunamis had happened in Lituya Bay on various previous occasions.

If Kwäday Dän Ts'ìnchí Man lived in or near or merely visited what is now the south-west Yukon then he knew a country of much gentler topography, with many of the hills round-topped. Had he occasion to go into these hills hunting caribou then he may have stood on the very ancient ice patches which have recently yielded a marvellous array of ancient hunting implements and even footwear, as related earlier in this chapter.

Geology

As the Pacific crustal (tectonic) plate slowly slides under the North American plate by a few centimetres a year there are frequent earthquakes. As the ice has melted since the end of the last ice age so the land is still rising, this being particularly marked in the Glacier Bay/Haines area. At Dyea, just north-west of Skagway, the remains of a wooden harbour, built for the hopefuls arriving to be part of the Klondike gold rush in the late 1890s, now stand proud of the water. The two figures taken from Greg Streveler's book, *The Natural History of Gustavus*,

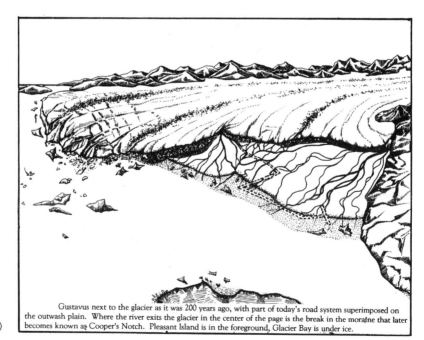

Fig. 7.6
Gustavus 200 years ago.
(*Greg Streveler*)

Gustavus next to the glacier as it was 200 years ago, with part of today's road system superimposed on the outwash plain. Where the river exits the glacier in the center of the page is the break in the moraine that later becomes known as Cooper's Notch. Pleasant Island is in the foreground, Glacier Bay is under ice.

Fig. 7.7
Gustavus
today.
(*Greg
Streveler*)

To the north of present-day Gustavus, notice the Beardslee Islands in Glacier Bay and the moraine at Bartlett Cove (including Cooper's Notch). Rivers now follow major channels created by glacial drainage patterns, and the beach front has been extended southward because of glacial rebound.

show how dramatically things have changed in the deservedly famous Glacier Bay National Park as the glaciers have melted greatly and the land has risen.[21] As the famous Captain James Cook sailed through Icy Strait in the late eighteenth century, past what is now the little settlement of Gustavus, there were icebergs, hence the name Icy Strait, and the whole of Glacier Bay was filled with a glacier. Now cruise ships can sail right to the head of the bay – more than 80km.

The great geological complexity of the region is well shown in the online maps.[22] In the general vicinity of the site there are limy rocks of about 400 million years ago. From about 150 to 50 million years ago, there are much younger volcanic rocks.

Climate

The climate changes enormously from the coast to the interior. West of the high mountain chains, the coast is exceedingly cloudy, mild and very wet with a large number of rain days. The day before I flew into Yakutat on my second visit there had been a rainfall of about 255mm or about 10in (Wednesday 25 August 2005). The mean annual temperature at Yakutat (sea level) is 3.9°C and the mean annual precipitation is 3843mm. The interior east of the mountains is much more continental: sunnier, warmer and drier in summer but very much colder in winter, with temperatures often tens of degrees centigrade below zero. At Haines Junction, Yukon, the mean annual temperature is -2.9°C and the mean annual precipitation is 306mm.

Even if Kwäday Dän Ts'ìnchí Man lived 200 or 500 years ago he lived during in the Little Ice Age, when as Julie Cruikshank of the University of British Columbia put it cogently, it meant living 'with uncertain glacier behaviour – unexpected advances, violent surges, catastrophic floods, and accompanying weather variations'.[23]

Vegetation

Just as in the case of Ötzi, the zones of vegetation are important in the investigation of Kwäday Dän Ts'ìnchí Man. The intertidal zone of the coasts of south-east Alaska and British Columbia is renowned for its richness of seaweeds in terms both of luxuriance of the plants and numbers of species. Two of the largest seaweeds found anywhere are giant kelp and bull kelp growing in large beds away from heavy surf.[24] At the upper end of the tides are salt marshes here and there, a vegetation type very important in the investigation of Kwäday Dän Ts'ìnchí Man because one of the component plants is beach asparagus; precisely where this plant grows is crucial to the story.

When the eighteenth-century European explorers and traders sailed along the coast they saw extensive forests with coniferous trees dominant and magnificent in stature. Their artists drew people, activities and landscapes but with no particular emphasis on vegetation. However, perhaps the first detailed illustration of the interior of a Pacific Northwest forest is that by Alexander F. Postels, an artist on the Russian ship *Seniavin*, which visited Sitka, then the main Russian base, as part of a round-the-world exploration cruise in 1826–28. It is so carefully an observed representation that many of the trees and lesser plants are readily recognisable. The trees are Sitka spruce and lodgepole pine, the shrubs are devil's club, red elder, a bramble (probably thimbleberry), skunk cabbage, a blueberry or huckleberry such as Alaskan blueberry, a large fern, probably lady or male fern, and, finally, on a fallen tree trunk the small, creeping liquorice fern, mosses and lichens. This fine drawing shows the temperate rainforest of the Coastal Western Hemlock Zone which stretches from the Oregon in the south to Yakutat in the north. With increasing altitude, from about 400m, this zone is replaced by that of mountain hemlock which peters out at about 1000m. Above is the Alpine zone in which the Kwäday Dän Ts'ìnchí Man was found.

The humid, mild conditions of this temperate rainforest are very favourable to the growth of ferns, mosses, including bog mosses, liverworts and lichens. There are hundreds of species. From Yakutat to Glacier Bay, especially at low altitudes, the trees are festooned with these types of plants. Great mounds of mosses such as pendulous wing moss can be profuse on the boughs. Lichens are dual organisms combining algae and fungi in a unique symbiosis. Some of them are extremely hardy creatures and very conspicuous in the vegetation of cold climates at both low and high altitudes. However, lichens are most luxuriant and occur in the greatest numbers of species in areas of wet, mild climates, such as the Pacific Northwest coast. According to Linda Geiser and three colleagues, there are 454 species of lichens in south-east Alaska and they think that several hundred more may well exist. In British Columbia there are approximately 1100 species but according to the lichenologist Trevor Goward and two others, 'it seems likely that hundreds of additional lichens await discovery in this province'.[25] Both these claims are likely to be correct.

The very wet climate is conducive to the growth of peat and there are many bogs, mostly below the tree line, in which various species of bog moss are prominent and a Bog moss is part of the story of Kwäday Dän Ts'ìnchí Man's last journey. There have been pollen analyses of some of these bogs and lake sediments too but there is nothing that is directly relevant in any great detail to Kwäday Dän Ts'ìnchí Man.

Fauna

At the end of the last ice age at least at the north end of area we are considering there were large numbers of spectacular mammals such as woolly mammoth, giant sloth, cave bear and giant beaver (which was no less than twice the length of the surviving American beaver) but all were soon thereafter to vanish from the face of the Earth, even if mammoths, having become very small, lingered on Wrangel Island, in the Arctic Ocean north of north-eastern-most Siberia, until only a few thousand years ago. Of course, that was a very long time before Kwäday Dän Ts'ìnchí Man lived. Nonetheless, he would still have been very familiar with large creatures, some much to be feared: two types of bear, black and brown (the latter being the famous grizzlies, the largest bears alive today) and moose (the largest deer alive today).

There were also caribou (reindeer), Dall's sheep, mountain goat, lynx, American beaver and wolf. On the coast he would have seen whales (of various kinds, large and small), dolphins and porpoises, as well as Stellar's sea lions, harbour seals, northern elephant seals, and both sea and river otters. Smaller mammals included Arctic ground squirrel, hoary marmot, collared pika, snowshoe hare and porcupine. In the sea there were many kinds of fish and readily found in the intertidal zone were many kinds of crustaceans, molluscs and other invertebrates. In the rivers to spawn there were several kinds of salmon, much appreciated by people, grizzly bears and bald eagles alike.[26] In the skies were birds such as ravens and various raptors including golden eagles. Blue herons and belted kingfishers fed on the beaches and perhaps Rufous hummingbirds searched for nectar from flowers and sap from trees wounded by sapsuckers. Some of these mammals and birds, and others such as frogs and salmon, figure prominently in the art of the Native Americans, as on totem poles and on painted house interiors as well as clan badges.[27] The First Nations in southern Yukon too had animals on clothing, as made clear by Catherine McClellan: '… the designs of the shirts and blankets showed the emblems of the different clans who claimed crest animals such as the beaver, frog, crow or killer whale.'

Fig. 7.8
Sockeye
salmon by
Delef Buettner.
(*Detlef
Buettner*)

Clothing, Equipment and Use of Resources

The hat and the robe described next were the total clothing found with the body. Both are fine items made by very skilful hands. So the question arises was that all that Kwäday Dän Ts'ìnchí Man had been wearing; clearly, he was on a journey, very possibly already many kilometres from home, wherever home was, through difficult country, reaching high in the snowy, icy mountains and had been crossing a glacier or at least skirting the edge of one. Had he really been wearing nothing warmer than a thin robe and a hat, walking unshod? At first thought this seems highly unlikely.

Hat

The book by Sharon Busby of the University of Washington has beautiful colour photos of the baskets, hats and other objects twined by hand and made from Sitka spruce roots.[28] Such containers could be so tightly twined as to be used for holding liquids. On page 29 Sharon Busby states: 'In traditional Tlingit basketry, the stems of a variety of grasses and of maidenhair fern are used for decoration. Grasses such as Fowl Mannagrass, Northern Mannagrass and Reedgrass are harvested in early summer while the stalks are thin and tender.' Continuing on page 31: 'The Tlingit, Haida and their neighbours use twining weaving techniques as opposed to coiling methods. The size of the spruce roots and the twining techniques are chosen to produce a basket or a hat with desired characteristics', such as strength, flexibility and beauty. On page 24 there is a reconstruction of a 'nearly six-thousand-year-old basket from Thorne River, Prince of Wales Island' – this represents the oldest extant specimen of north-west coast basketry. On page 73 there is a splendid photograph from 1895 of the Whale House at Klukwan, with males wearing at least six different styles of hat. The wearing of beautiful hats is a flourishing tradition.[29]

The broadly conical hat found with Kwäday Dän Ts'ìnchí Man is 'Tlingit in both style and construction method'.[30] The coastal peoples were not alone in making twined containers. The peoples who lived along the Columbia River between Washington and Oregon were also skilled in that craft.[31] The inland peoples did not wear hats like the Tlingit wore. So there were already good grounds for making a coastal connection before much of the laboratory-based science discussed in this book had even started and now such science has put the strong coastal connection beyond all reasonable doubt.

Spruces

There are over 30 species of spruce on Earth, north of the Tropic of Cancer. But the only two spruces that are relevant in relation to Kwäday Dän Ts'ìnchí Man and they are white spruce and Sitka spruce. The former reaches about 22 to 25m in height but the latter, reaching about 85 to 90m is the largest of all the spruces. Sitka Spruce makes an impressive, handsome tree even when young with its bluish, glaucous needles. Sitka spruce is only along the coast where there are extensive forests and white spruce is only in the interior. However, the two species can hybridise.[32] Neither Sitka spruce nor white spruce were in short supply but the roots were easiest to collect from trees growing on sandy soil.

Robe

This neatly stitched item was made primarily from the skins of arctic ground squirrel. Up to about 100 pelts were needed for such a robe which was a type of apparel highly appreciated by the coastal peoples and the interior people also. Catherine McClellan states: '... almost every older Indian woman in southern Yukon owns a gopher-skin robe.'[33] Incomplete and torn when excavated, the robe was cleaned, reassembled as much as possible and studied in great detail by Kjerstin Mackie of the Royal British Columbia Museum.[34] With overall dimensions of about 204 x 110cm, it had been made very skilfully of some 95 pelts of arctic ground squirrel in 5 rows of 19 skins. It was found around the torso in such a position that it was clear that the robe must have been worn fur-side out. The animals had been slit vertically along the belly and the pelts stitched side by side neatly at about 3mm intervals with the use of sinew of an as yet unidentified animal. The irregular side edges of the pelts were left on the fur side and later sliced into 10cm-long fringes. Draped over the shoulders and tied round the neck, the robe would have reached the ankle at the back but was open at the front. The ties were leather thongs attached to two reinforcement patches on the upper edge, which consisted of a 5cm-wide strip of moose or caribou or some other species of deer.

The inside horizontal seams were sealed with about 4 to 5cm-wide stripes of ochre and grease, as were the top and bottom edges and the centre vertical seam; the animal from which the grease was obtained, again, is as yet unknown, as is the source of the mineral. There are also several narrow vertical stripes of ochre not associated with the seams. The exterior fringes also provided waterproofing by carrying away rainwater.

Arctic Ground Squirrel

The males of this mammal reach to less than 40cm long, with the tail making about a quarter or more of the length, and so the bodies are small with the females being even smaller. They hibernate for most of the year and this is the only species of ground squirrel to inhabit the area considered here.[35] It occurs widely across northernmost North America, south to northern British Columbia, and lives colonially in shallow burrows dug into well-drained soils which are not permafrozen. The diet is mainly plant material, but fungi and animals such as young birds are also eaten. It is not to be found in the wet, coastal parts but is easily encountered in the south-western Yukon on sandy ground and also occurs at high altitude, in the upper parts of the Tatshenshini/Alsek drainage, as in the alpine zone of Fault Creek at 1425m, near the site. Elsewhere in British Columbia it lives at 2000m. In the Whitehorse

Fig. 7.9 Ground squirrel pelt.

region it inhabits the wet saline/alkaline flats where it burrows into the slightly raised and so drier parts. It is dug out and eaten by grizzly bears and is always referred to as gophers by the local people who eat it as well as making the thin, soft pelts into clothing. The skin is about a mere 1mm thick and the pelage to about 20mm long.

Were the hat and the robe all that Kwäday Dän Ts'ìnchí Man had worn on his last journey? That may well have been the case. The accounts and drawings of the late eighteenth-century seafaring explorers and traders are helpful in reaching such a conclusion because at that time the native coastal people wore very little other than traditional dress. There was the Englishman, Captain James Cook, Royal Naval sailor, the Englishman George Dixon of the British merchant marine, the French aristocrat Jean-Francois de Galoup, Comte de La Pérouse, of the French navy and lastly, but very importantly, there was the Sicilian Admiral Alejandro Malaspina of the Spanish navy. Of these four, only the observations of Cook do not pertain directly to the coast near where Kwäday Dän Ts'ìnchí Man's body was discovered.

When La Pérouse visited Lituya Bay (Port des Français) in 1786, he found that the Tlingit men there had 'their shoulders … covered with a simple skin; the rest of the body absolutely naked, except the head which is generally covered with a little straw hat, very skilfully plaited'.[36] In the atlas published with the account of La Pérouse's voyage there is a plate entitled '*Costume des habitants du Port des Français, sur la côte du nord-ouest de l'Amérique*'. This detailed drawing by the artist Gaspard Duché de Vancy shows a young man with a knee-length fur garment and nothing else, unless there were undergarments which cannot be seen, and a young woman similarly attired. There are five others with more elaborate costumes. All seven people show their feet bare, except one man well shod and, importantly, differently dressed from all the others. According to Julie Cruikshank, he is dressed in Athabascan style with a suit of tailored, tanned hide clothing strongly resembling drawings made six decades later in the Yukon.[37]

Two of the drawings from the Malaspina expedition of 1791 show young Tlingit men from the Yakutat area wearing just such minimal dress (fur robe and hat) and nothing more.

Fig. 7.10 Drawing from La Pérouse atlas.

Another artist on Malaspina's voyage was José Cardero who drew a view of Port Mulgrave, on Khantaak Island which is a few kilometres north-west of Yakutat. It shows two canoes in the foreground full of men who are wearing conical hats, fur robes and, as far as can be seen, nothing else. This sparse attire is even more evident in de Suría's aquatint of a confrontation at Port Mulgrave in which there are 10 or more native men opposing the Spanish sailors. His sketch of another disagreement with the Spaniards shows totally naked native men. Deriving from the same visit, is an anonymous drawing showing, in a canoe, five men wearing merely hats and robes. In his journal Tomás de Suría wrote of an old chief at Port Mulgrave that his cape, probably a brown bear pelt, was gathered in at the waist but left bare his 'breast, arms, thighs and endowments, all very muscular and strong'.[38]

Finally concerning Port Mulgrave, there are three Tomás de Suría drawings of the burial grounds. They show, among mixed groups of Spaniards and natives, a man with a hat and fur robe and, at his loins, what has the appearance of a square sporran and other men with only hats and robes.[39] That the coastal natives obtained their cloaks of small mammal pelts from inland people was already realised in the late eighteenth century, as this statement by George Dixon about residents of Yakutat in 1787 strongly suggests: 'Besides the skins I have already mentioned, we purchased some bears and some land beaver, but I rather think, that the marmot cloaks were procured by these people from some neighbouring tribe.'[40]

When Aurel Krause visited the Tlingit, in 1881, he found that 'The aboriginal costume can no longer be found anywhere'. However, in Krause, there is a drawing of a 'Chilkat [Tlingit] Indian on a trading expedition'; though otherwise fully clothed with European-style trousers and jacket, he is not wearing shoes. In Krause's, Emmons and De Laguna's books it noted that in winter the Tlingit wore snowshoes for travel, except where very steep climbing was required, when they were temporarily removed.[41] A photograph from 1890 shows a Chilkat Tlingit at Klukwan 'ready to pack into the interior'. He is well clad with a blanket, conical hat, with a jacket and trousers of European style pushed into long-legged, thin-soled boots. He carries snowshoes of Athabaskan make and holds a staff much like the long sticks

Fig. 7.11 Drawing from Malaspina.

found at the discovery site.[42] The father of Elaine Abraham of the Yakutat Tlingit was a young man in the late nineteenth century and that kindly, helpful lady assured me in 2005 that he never wore any kind of footwear outdoors, no matter what the season, weather or terrain, but did wear slippers of 'seagrass' indoors. None of the eighteenth-century images or words give any evidence for the wearing of the magnificent Chilkat blankets which are now famous and valuable; there are, however, fragments of a blanket from a shaman's grave from Knight Island near Yakutat which could date from the 1780s.[43] The eighteenth-century Tlingits had elaborate ceremonial clothing, as indeed they still do now, and could be well clothed, including armour of wooden slats for fighting, an activity for which they were renowned.

So, while it is clear that there was more than minimal clothing for some native men in the eighteenth century, nonetheless, with both written and pictorial evidence from four widespread parts of the north-west coast, perhaps indeed it was that Kwäday Dän Ts'ìnchí Man had been wearing merely a robe, a hat and no footwear on his final journey. There can be no absolute certainty about this, of course. However, as argued elsewhere, Kwäday Dän Ts'ìnchí's journey was in late summer, when clothing against extreme cold may have been thought unnecessary, and not in winter, when to be high in the mountains would not only have been especially unpleasant but foolhardy, even if warmly clad.

Moose, Caribou and Other Deer
As pointed out in *The Mammals of Canada*, there is confusion for both North Americans and British over the common names. In Britain moose is called elk and, in North America, elk is red deer. Moose, the 'eater of twigs', a word derived from Algonkian, stands up to 1.87m high at the shoulder, with widely spread antlers. They are frequent in the relevant area and one had wandered as far up as the Kwäday Dän Ts'ìnchí Man site, as the antlers found there show.

American Beaver
Kwäday Dän Ts'ìnchí Man had a small beaver-skin bag containing plants as well as a little 'medicine bag' which, being a very personal item, was unopened and cremated with the body. This aquatic animal, familiar because of its fine pelts, tree-felling and constructional powers, is the largest rodent native to North America. It occurs across a very large area of Canada and the USA. Its body can be about 100cm long with the flat tail almost half the total length. Bark of various trees such as trembling aspen and balsam poplar and the tissues of non-woody plants such as water lilies. Found throughout British Columbia, it occurs in the Haines Triangle and the rest of the territory that Kwäday Dän Ts'ìnchí Man traversed.

Tools
A variety of wooden tools were found around the site but only two were certainly associated with Kwäday Dän Ts'ìnchí Man. There was a hand tool or 'man's knife' with a metal blade and associated with a hide/fur sheath. There was also a carved and painted stick.

Scientific Visits to the Kwäday Dän Ts'ìnchí Site
In order to interpret best the numerous plant remains found in, on and around Ötzi it was necessary for all the botanists involved to visit the place of discovery. Consequently, I have been at the site or its near vicinity on six occasions, always with very congenial companions,

usually scientific experts, and in doing so I have walked up from both the Italian and Austrian sides. Due to the rough terrain, the great height of the site and the changeable weather, the appropriate clothing and other safety precautions are required. However, any sensible, reasonably fit person can do it and help, shelter, food and drink in mountain huts are not so very far away. In great contrast, the Kwäday Dän Ts'ìnchí site is a long way from anywhere and with no congenial hostelries nearby. Without a helicopter in constant attendance everything needed – sustenance, tents and all other requisite paraphernalia – has to be on the participants' backs. In addition there is the possibility of encountering grizzly bears, though you have to be either unlucky or imprudent to be attacked. With other scientifically or otherwise expert colleagues I have been there twice: on 9 August 2002 for less than a day and in and out by helicopter with poor weather and then again on 12–14 August 2005, that time with splendid weather and in by helicopter and then a few days later out by foot to the Haines Highway. The second visit was the more productive. Apart from gaining some familiarity with the territory that Kwäday Dän Ts'ìnchí Man had crossed, I collected vascular plants, bryophytes and lichens and Petra Mudie of the Geological Survey of Canada Atlantic collected water samples for microscopic algae and mineral particles. We were accompanied by Bill Hanlon, the discoverer of Kwäday Dän Ts'ìnchí Man, the photographer Al Harvey and also Frances Oles and Greg Eikland of the Champagne and Aishikik First Nations. (See Plate 26.)

Diet and Use of Resources
Archaeological deposits and ethnographic observations provide a good record from 6500 BP to the present for the consumption of intertidal shellfish, near-shore fish, salmonids, sea mammals and sea birds by coastal peoples.[44] Aurel Krause stated of the Tlingit that 'The principal dish of the day is always fish, boiled, roasted, dried, but never raw. Next in importance is the meat of land and sea mammals, fowl, crabs, squid, shellfish, sea urchins and finally from the vegetable kingdom, berries, roots, bulbs and other things.'[45]

At the autopsies several intestinal content samples were removed and made available for microscopic investigations. The samples were very small and came from the stomach, small intestine, colon and rectum. Kwäday Dän Ts'ìnchí Man had carried salmon because two pieces were found on the robe as were many scales and also near the body. The salmon was identified at first as a 4-year-old chum salmon, probably the remains coming from a single fish. However, with DNA analysis, the identification was changed to sockeye salmon. In the lower intestines there were bones which could well be from salmon.

Pacific Northwest Salmon
In contrast to the North Atlantic, which harbours only one species of salmon, there are several species in the sea and rivers of this large area and all five are good to eat. They are Chinook (king), chum (dog), Coho (silver), pink (humpback) and sockeye (red). Due to its high oil content chum salmon smokes the best of all the five. Sockeye is the most commercially important.[46] The salmon were an indispensable part of the diet of the coastal people but also very important to some groups who lived far from the sea as, for instance, the First Nations at Klukshu, some 100km from the northernmost Lynn Canal. It has often been claimed that this reliability and ease of catching salmon and other fish, such as eulachon and halibut, and gathering of other nutritious seafood from the intertidal zone gave the coastal

peoples the leisure time to pursue their highly distinctive, much admired art. 'When the tide is out the table is laid', is an old Tlingit saying.

All these salmon are anadromous, that is to say they live in the sea as well as in rivers and lakes where they spawn. Salmon are not just a very important part of the marine ecosystems but terrestrial ones too, because they are eaten by bears, as vividly related by Scott Gende of the National Park Service in Juneau and Thomas Quinn of the University of Washington.[47] They say: 'Bears actually fertilize the forests, nourishing them by discarding partially eaten salmon carcasses.' Other mammals too and many birds, such as bald eagles, eat the salmon. Sockeye kelt, the term for males in spawning state, develop a hooked lower jaw and bright red sides.

Salmon have been exploited by the native inhabitants of the Pacific Northwest for a very long time. It could well be that the earliest people to arrive along the Pacific Northwest coast, whenever that was exactly, ate fish such as salmon and other seafood. In Europe, the Upper Palaeolithic inhabitants of Périgord, France, made representations of fish including trout as well as salmon, including a sculpted one, 1.05m long, which could have been its natural size.[48] At about 25,000 years old, this is the 'earliest depiction of a fish known anywhere in the world'.

Marine Crustacean

I stated with several others in 2004: 'Five pieces of cartilaginous, internal (endophragmal) skeleton (ten to twelve millimetres long) and similar sized segments of abdominal outer shell (exoskeleton) of a decapod crustacean were found in the stomach and lower intestines. The large size of these pieces shows that the crustacean must have been marine, as no terrestrial crustaceans this big are found in the region … The crustacean pieces are quite similar to that of a crab.'[49]

As already mentioned, that marine crustaceans (crabs, shrimps and the like) were a component of the diet of the coastal peoples is well documented. Here is another example from the early nineteenth century: 'Among shellfish, there are large crabs here, shrimp, and various sorts of mollusks … All these types of shellfish are used as food.'[50]

Fat and Meat

The stomach contained numerous pieces of fat, pale in colour with darker stripes, which have not yet been closely identified as to species, but we thought they might be seal blubber. In the other gut samples (from the duodenum and small bowel) were very small pieces of meat fibres which we thought very tentatively might be caribou and bison.[51]

Beach Asparagus

Kwäday Dän Ts'ìnchí Man had carried and eaten beach asparagus as part of his very last meals; there was pollen of that seashore plant in his stomach and also lower down the gut too. See the next section on last journey and death for a full discussion of this important discovery.

Seaweeds

While examining the gut samples microscopically I was on the lookout for seaweed but found none. This does not mean conclusively that Kwäday Dän Ts'ìnchí Man had not eaten seaweed during the last few days of his life. Microscopically small scraps of seaweed could be difficult to recognise and so be overlooked. The coastal peoples most definitely consumed seaweed and, indeed, in quantity. Among the seaweeds that were eaten were giant kelp and red laver.[52] It is well known that seaweed was traded from coast to interior; square black cakes were made by pressing the seaweed into wooden boxes. In her book, *Part of the Land, Part of the Water*, which is a history of the Yukon Indians, Catherine McClellan states on p.159:

> By late June or July, when salmon reached Neskatahin [Old Dalton Post] and Klukshu, every-
> body was busy catching, cutting and drying salmon. This was when relatives from elsewhere
> might arrive, and Tlingit traders came too. It was an exciting time of feasting, dancing and
> storytelling, as well as a chance for the Yukon Indians to get European trade goods and coastal
> delicacies like dried clams or seaweed in exchange of their furs and other products.

Writing in 1888, Aurel Krause stated: 'Salt water vegetation also makes its contribution to the Tlingit household. On the seashore there are edible algae (*Alaria esculenta* Grev.) of which square black cakes are made by pressing them into a wooden box.' And later: 'Food was also an article of trade, as the oil of the candlefish which was rendered in only a few places. From the outer coast the cakes made of the leaves of *Alaria esculenta* were sent to the interior and from there came the conifer gum used for chewing.'[53] One may wonder if it was not *Porphyra* that was meant and that *Alaria* is just a translator's mistake from the German original. When I visited Yakutat in 2005, Elaine Abraham gave me vacuum-packed 'Black and Red Ribbon' seaweeds gathered by the locals.

Summarising the work of various scientists such as Jon Erlandson of the University of Oregon and Daryl Fedje of Parks Canada, the Canadian journalist Heather Pringle pub-lished an article in *New Scientist* entitled 'Follow that Kelp'. She summarises the claims that the first humans to invade north-western America came by boat and exploited the rich ecosystem of kelp forests along the ancient coast from Asia to North America.[54]

Involuntary Ingestions
During his last journey when eating and drinking Kwäday Dän Ts'ìnchí Man swallowed unintentionally various particles including pollen and spores and also microscopic algae, notably two types of snow algae which are so called because their habitat is the surface of long-lying snow beds or of snow on top of glaciers. There was also a short leafy stem of a bog moss in the faeces but it cannot be identified to the species, only to a group of species.[55] Why was it there? The remains Kwäday Dän Ts'ìnchí Man showed no signs of wounds and so a wound-dressing explanation such as advanced for Ötzi is unlikely but cannot be totally excluded because not all of the flesh was found. Bog mosses are common-est at lower altitudes, decreasing with increasing altitude, and finally peter out only a little way into the Alpine zone which begins at about 1000m. No diatoms were found in the gut (probably destroyed by the sample chemical preparation), but interestingly there were some found on the robe and they were from saltwater and likely, therefore, the robe had been on the seashore. There are silt-sized mineral particles all through the gut and they have proved important in deducing the last route. The use of environmental scanning electron microscopy with energy dispersion spectroscopy by Petra Mudie showed that during his

last journey he had drunk water from several differing altitudes and rock types. Unlike Ötzi, there is very little or no question of any alcoholic beverage having been available to Kwäday Dän Ts'ìnchí Man.

Stable Isotopes
Michael Richards was the first to investigate Kwäday Dän Ts'ìnchí Man's diet by stable isotopes.[56] He examined two bone samples and two hair samples. He stated that: '>90% of dietary protein was from marine sources.' Moreover, his studies pointed to consumption of carnivorous fish and marine mammals (such as seals and whales). These studies were extended by Michael Richards with several others and then by Linda Corr of the University of Bristol with several others.[57] Linda Corr *et al.* state: 'Thus the results of both bulk and compound specific isotope analysis provide evidence that this individual was a coastal dweller with considerable reliance on marine dietary sources.'[58] These isotopic studies are also very important part of the reasoning in the next section.

Last Journey and Death
Just as several ideas can be considered for Ötzi's social role, so there can be differing thoughts but no certainty for Kwäday Dän Ts'ìnchí Man. One of the most obvious thoughts is that he was up in the mountains hunting. As we saw for ourselves during the 2005 expedition by being pointed out to us by Bill Hanlon, a skilled hunter, there are areas in the near vicinity of the site that are favoured by Dall's sheep, which make very good eating, as do caribou, moose and other deer. Perhaps the young man had been crossing from one favoured, grassy area to another. That he was a hunter is taken for granted by Julie Cruikshank: 'In August 1999, remains of a male hunter were discovered melting from a glacier near the Tatshenshini River … he was probably travelling on one of the glacier routes between coast and interior.'[59] Another idea is that he was a messenger going from one village to another. The Tlingits are known to have had young men specially trained to be swift runners, as related to me by a reverend gentleman, a Tlingit elder during one of my visits to Haines. This matter of social role is not pursued in detail here but left to First Nations and Native Americans to consider.

Both the Tlingits and the nearby interior peoples are well known to have travelled over very extensive distances both for trading and other purposes, and frequently crossed over glaciers. Tlingit traders from Dry Bay, returning from inland, paddled downstream under glaciers.[60] Julie Cruikshank relates that two trading partners, one Athapaskan and one Tlingit, were going to the coast. The Tlingit fell into a crevasse and the Athapaskan, frightened of being blamed, nonetheless continued to the coast. When a group went back to retrieve the body they rescued their kinsman alive. She continues that 'The story underscores the perils of glacier travel but also the responsibility of Athapaskan men to their Tlingit trading partners and the uncertain ethnic boundaries differentiating them'.

In 1868 a Chilkat Tlingit chief called Kohklux, with help from his two wives, drew two maps which show routes from the coast far into the interior.[61] The Tlingit who lived at the head or north end of the Lynn Canal were widely hailed in the travel literature for their packing and long distance overland travelling ability. The story of an expedition in 1866 sponsored by the *New York Times* included the comment that a Tlingit man did 'good duty for us as packer, all art in which all T'lingit Indians are proficient'.[62] In the late nine-teenth century explorer H.W. Seton-Kerr was advised by a group of travelling Tlingits in the Chilkat area that he would need seven days to journey from their meeting point over-land via the interior Tatshenshini route. He praised the sturdiness of the Tlingits in that they could 'carry heavier packs than a white man. They can travel farther on foot and endure greater hardships. They do not require so much in the shape of clothes and bedding.' The Athapaskan peoples also made very long-distance journeys.[63]

As discussed in earlier chapters, when looking at a topographic map showing where Ötzi was found, it is an obvious thought that his last journey was from the north or the south. So, looking at such a map for Kwäday Dän Ts'ìnchí Man the thought that immediately arises is was his last journey from the coast to the interior, or to the coast from the interior, or possibly even from one part of the coast to another. The plant remains, minerals from the intestines and stable isotopes go a long way to resolving that matter.

Plant Geography: Mosses

As in so many other instances, unique in all archaeology, we know that Ötzi had deliberately carried mosses, especially flat neckera, for some purpose or other and a further 80 or so spe-cies of mosses and liverworts are important in understanding his lifestyle and environment. In contrast stands Kwäday Dän Ts'ìnchí Man, who may not have carried any mosses know-ingly but there are two mosses, each of a mere one fragment, that were in his beaver-skin bag. They are hoary fringe moss and dimorphous tamarisk moss and both species are also in the long list of mosses found with Ötzi. I have recognised no less than 12 different mosses as very small fragments on microscope slides prepared from Kwäday Dän Ts'ìnchí Man's ingesta while I found only six in Ötzi's ingesta.

Locally abundant, hoary fringe moss is one of the most common mosses in the relevant area. It is found on a variety of substrates, as at Yakutat where it grows at sea level on the ground, on rock, on wood, on rope and even on the aluminium fuselage and wings of a long-abandoned trainer aircraft. It grows at over 1600m on the scree slope immediately adjacent to the Kwäday Dän Ts'ìnchí Man site, as seen in Plate 26. Clearly it is not a very informative species regarding the aims of investigating the questions raised by Kwäday Dän Ts'ìnchí Man. Dimorphous tamarisk moss is much less common and indeed, as it happens, I have not seen it in the field in North America. For British Columbia as a whole, the noted Canadian moss expert, the late Wilf Schofield, has written: 'On stones and outcrops in open forest and sub-alpine sites, usually either in semi-arid climates or in well-drained sites, at lower elevations in the Fraser Canyon region, extending to higher elevations in the mountains, occasional in coastal areas.' In their guidebook to the mosses, lichens and ferns of north-west North America, the American bryologist Dale Vitt with two others wrote that dimorphous tamarisk moss is 'a high altitude species'.[64]

These two mosses do not tell us very much about Kwäday Dän Ts'ìnchí Man's last jour-ney but glittering wood moss and red-stemmed feather moss are somewhat more helpful. Both are abundant at lower altitudes in coniferous woodland. A few very small fragments were recovered from the robe and might have become attached during the last journey. So might a very few pieces of lichens but, more likely, the lichens came from near the site. The tiny remains of mosses extracted from the intestinal samples are somewhat more helpful.

There is a leaf fragment of water moss from the small bowel sample. This normally sub-merged moss is not a high-altitude species, indeed it only grows below the treeline. There is also the leafy shoot of a bog moss from the rectum.

Lichens

Unlike Ötzi, Kwäday Dän Ts'ìnchí Man carried no fungi as far as we know but he did carry lichens. Lichens are very seldom recovered from archaeological contexts or from peats or lake muds. I have seen some fragments extracted from the coarse sediments beside Ötzi's body. In decades of examining organic remains from ice age sediments I had never found remains of any lichen for myself until then. Then when I looked at the contents of Kwäday Dän Ts'ìnchí Man's beaver-skin bag there was a lichen which might be a horsehair lichen and also washings from his robe included another two which might be a reindeer lichen and a snow lichen.[65] With no firm identification as yet these lichens are not very informative.

So the mosses and lichens are not very helpful but there are other plants which are cru-cially important in this context. They are beach asparagus which grows only on seashores, as mentioned above, and mountain sweet cicely and mountain hemlock which both grow in abundance in the coastal zone and do not penetrate far inland; neither grows in the Yukon or if they do it is only very sparsely at the south-western fringes of the territory. There is pollen and macros of beach asparagus in Kwäday Dän Ts'ìnchí Man's gut and macros of mountain sweet cicely and mountain hemlock were removed from the outside of Kwäday Dän Ts'ìnchí Man's robe.

Beach Asparagus

This succulent, low, shrubby, green plant belongs to the genus *Salicornia* and to the family called Chenopodiaceae and, as already explained in Chapter 4, means goose foot. The chenopods include many cultivated edible plants such as beetroot and spinach, weeds of agricultural ground such as fathen and orache, as well as salt-lovers, botanically known as halophytes, growing on sea beaches and on salty or otherwise alkaline inland areas, which can be far inland, as in Xinkiang, north-westernmost China. Plants belonging to the genus *Salicornia* typify this sea coast plus interior ecology of the family. In the interior near Whitehorse there are some saline soils where the low-growing red glasswort (another *Salicornia*) grows in such abundance that its redness, standing out strongly against the white-ness of the salty encrustations, is conspicuous from a long way off (see Plates 29 and 30). On upper seashores there is beach asparagus, locally abundant, but being green, among other green halophytes, is hardly conspicuous from a distance. So we have two *Salicornia* species one only on the coast and the other only inland. There was *Salicornia* pollen in Kwäday Dän Ts'ìnchí Man's stomach and lower gut but which species had it come from — beach aspara-gus or red glasswort? Identifying the pollen of chenopods is a tricky matter. Petra Mudie set about the problem using scanning electron microscopy. The pollen is spherical with numer-ous pores and the detailed structure of the pores separates *Salicornia* from other members of the family, and the overall smaller size of the grains but with more numerous pores separates beach asparagus from red glasswort.

Where exactly does beach asparagus grow and what are its northern limits? In 2003, I have searched for beach asparagus on the seashores at Yakutat and on the adjacent islands and as far south as the mouth of the Lost River without success (see Plates 25 and 27). It is well worth stating also that Frederica de Laguna wrote a natural history section in her famous volumes on the Yakutat Tlingits without mentioning the plant even once anywhere. With Petra Mudie in 2005, I looked again negatively in that area and Petra Mudie, using a salinometer, found that the seawater at Khantaak Island was salty enough for the plant and that the beaches were suitably sheltered and gently sloping, but no beach asparagus was present. That year also, Petra Mudie and I had the chance to go to the east Alsek part of Dry Bay and we found no beach asparagus. No beach asparagus has ever been reported from Lituya Bay and Wayne Howell of the Glacier Bay National Park, well familiar with the plant, has looked twice without success there. In 2004, when we were taken to Taylor Bay by Wayne there was the plant though not in especially plentiful amounts. At the opposite extremity of Icy Strait at Point Couverden, it grows in abundance, just as it does at Gustavus. The conclusion is that the south end of the park seems to be about the northern climatic limit of beach asparagus.

Mountain Hemlock

This is a large, coniferous tree and no relation whatever of the famously Socratic, tall-growing, poisonous herb of Europe. Capable of living over 500 years and reaching to about 40m in height at the most, mountain hemlock grows under 'hypermaritime to submaritime sub-alpine boreal climates'.[66] That is just a fancy way of saying that it thrives in the very wet, mild coastal strip of the Pacific Northwest and avoids the interior, east of the mountain chains, with the much harder winters and less precipitation. Found at sea level, as at Yakutat, it goes higher up the mountains than the closely related western hemlock and there it can be very ragged in appearance with its tops and branches wind-blasted or broken off by the too great weight of frozen lumps of snow.

Fig. 7.12 Drawing of Mountain Hemlock. (*Lee Menell*)

Mountain Sweet Cicely

This is a perennial herb, related to the sweet cicely of Europe, both being members of the carrot/parsley family. Its habitats are more or less shady woodland margins on richer soils. I have seen it in just such places at Skagway and Haines, as well as at Glacier Bay in and around the National Park offices and Glacier Bay Lodge, and also on the nearby, well-named Pleasant Island where there is forest which has seen so little logging as to be essentially virgin. At Yakutat, it grows at the woodland edge by the road through the borough. It is a species with a great spread down the west side of Canada and indeed the west side of the South America. There are some other species close to this one and they can be separated on a variety of characters, including

Fig. 7.13 Drawing of *Osmorhiza* by Lee Menell.

especially the length of the fruits, which is crucial because the remains from the robe consisted of one half of a fruit which splits lengthwise. Of the relevant species the only one with fruits over 20mm long is mountain sweet cicely which does not grow in the Yukon. Fig. 7.12 shows a plant of the genus called *Ozmorhiza* to which mountain sweet cicely belongs and, bottom right, a fruit splitting in half (greater than natural size). The bristles make the fruits or half fruits stick to fur or clothing. However, I know from personal experience by getting my trousers liberally covered that the fruits mostly fall off or brush off against vegetation quite quickly.

Considering the distribution patterns of these three plants, the thought is an obvious one that Kwäday Dän Ts'ìnchí Man was on the coast and began his last journey from there – 'there' meaning somewhere between Taylor Bay eastwards to Point Couverden and the immediately adjacent Lynn Canal.

Stable Isotopes and Mineralogy

The first published paper (2004) dealing with stable isotopes led to the conclusion that 'The isotopic evidence of a mainly marine-based diet for Kwäday Dän Ts'ìnchí is very significant, as it indicates that he must have lived near the coast most of his life and moved inland less than one year before he perished and was preserved in the glacier.'[67] The second stable isotope paper (2007) confirmed that with the qualification that 'he had changed his diet in the year before his death, with input of significant amounts of terrestrial foods, although his diet was still predominantly marine-based.'[68] The third paper (2008) states: 'the Kwäday Dän Ts'ìnchí individual consumed a primarily marine-based diet in the last year of his life, which was only partially replaced by terrestrial foods in the last few weeks of life.' The fourth paper (2009) states that: 'However, the lack of a terrestrial signal in bone collagen amino acids supports the hypothesis that this was a single or very occasional journey of the Kwäday Dän Ts'ìnchí, a coastal dweller into the British Columbian interior.'

It is an omission that the kind of studies of stable isotopes in rocks, soils and waters so convincingly carried out by Wolfgang Müller to reveal Ötzi's two domiciles have not been pursued for Kwäday Dän Ts'ìnchí Man. However, there is the mineralogical study carried out by Petra Mudie.[69] The use of environmental electron microscopy with energy dispersive spectroscopy gave precise identifications of the silt particles in the gut samples. These, with the shapes of the particles (angular or rounded), were compared with silt in the water samples from the region. Combined, the results point to the last route having been up the Chilkat valley and crossing calciferous rocks into the mountains and not inland via the Tatshenshini basin and up the O'Connor valley into the mountains.

Tentatively, an account of the last hours of Kwäday Dän Ts'ìnchí Man can be proposed as follows. The coastal plants mountain hemlock and mountain sweet cicely had adhered to the robe. The faeces in the rectum are the remains of the first meal eaten probably at low altitude, perhaps even sea level, 24 hours or more before his untimely death. Carrying beach asparagus and sockeye salmon, he set off and went up the Chilkat valley. This is deduced from marine microscopic organisms as well as 'crab', beach asparagus, bog moss, charcoal and framboidal pyrites typical of marine/estuarine sediments.

Remains of the very last meal were in the stomach and were removed from the cut open but incomplete organ. It was eaten at high altitude, perhaps as much as a few hours before death. This is deduced from snow algae, 'crab', beach asparagus, fat, angular feldspar and quartz minerals.Season and Cause of Death

The important point is that there was pollen of beach asparagus in Kwäday Dän Ts'ìnchí Man's innards and on his robe. In the relevant area this plant flowers in last week of July until late August and so the death was in late summer, probably August. Nothing else was found with Kwäday Dän Ts'ìnchí Man, either internally or externally, that is inconsistent which such a conclusion. Furthermore, if indeed his only clothing was the hat and the robe that can only have been summertime attire.

The examinations of the two large parts of the body at the autopsies revealed neither evidence of foul play nor any breakages of bones that might have resulted from a fall or a deliberate blow. Similarly, the pieces of the skull and the other body parts found in 2003 gave no indications of drastic trauma. However, that cannot completely rule out either foul play or a serious accident because there could have been bad wounding of those soft tissues which were not found or a stunning fall that did not fracture the skull.

That there was ingesta all through the gut from stomach to rectum indicates clearly that Kwäday Dän Ts'ìnchí Man is unlikely to have died of failing strength or complete exhaustion brought on by lack of food with hypothermia then following as the *coup de grâce*. Of course, freezing to death could well have been the final cause. But what precisely had happened prior to that? Even though it was still summer, was he caught in a blizzard so dense as to have had very restricted vision, then becoming disoriented and, in lying or sitting down to sit out the storm, falling asleep and freezing to death? Several years ago such a scenario was posited by Julie Cruikshank thinking that he 'probably lost his way and his life in an unexpected storm'.[70] Inevitably, this paragraph is mostly speculative and, very probably, it shall never be known exactly what occurred.

Notes

1   Kuzyk, G.W. *et al.* 1999. 'In Pursuit of Prehistoric Caribou on Thandlat, Southern Yukon'. *Arctic*, pp. 214–9. Dold, K. 2004. 'Prehistory Defrosted'. *American Archaeology* 8, pp. 20–30. Hare, P.G. *et al.* 2004. 'Ethnographic and Archaeological Investigations of Alpine Ice Patches in Southwest Yukon, Canada'. *Arctic* 57, pp. 260–72. Farnell, R. *et al.* 2004. 'Multidisciplinary Investigations of Alpine Ice Patches in Southwest Yukon, Canada'. *Arctic* 57, pp. 247–59. Anonymous. 2005. *Ice Patch* 2, p. 1012. Dixon, J.E., Manley, W.F. and Lee, C.M. 2005. 'The Emerging Archaeology of Glaciers and Ice Patches from Alaska's Wrangell-St.Elias National Park and Preserve'. *American Antiquity* 70, pp. 129–43. Dove, C.J., Hare, P.G. and Heacker, M. 2005. 'Identification of Ancient Feather Fragments Found in Melting Alpine Ice Patches in Southern Yukon'. *Arctic* 58, pp. 38–43. Keddie, G. and Nelson, E. 2005. 'An arrow from the Tsitsutl Glacier, British Columbia'. *Canadian Journal of Archaeology* 29, pp. 113–23. Lee, C.M., Benedict, B. and Lee, J.B. 2006. 'Ice Patches and Remnant Glaciers: Paleontological Discoveries and Archaeological Possibilities in the Colorado Highy Country'. *Journal of Colorado Archaeology* 72, pp. 26–43. Benedict, J.B., Benedict, R.J., Lee, C.M. and Staley, D.M. 2008. 'Spruce trees from a melting ice patch: evidence for Holocene climatic change in the Colorado Rocky Mountains, USA'. *The Holocene* 18, pp. 1067–76. Helwig, K. Monahan, K. and Poulin, J. 2008. 'The identification of hafting

adhesive on a slotted point from a Southwest Yukon ice patch'. *American Antiquity* 73, pp. 279–88. Andrews, T.A., Mackay, G. and Andrew, L. 2009. *Hunters of the Alpine Ice. The NWT Ice Patch Study*. Prince of Wales Northern Heritage Centre, Yellowknife, N.W.T. Lee, C.M. 2010. 'Global warming reveals wooden artifact frozen over 10 000 years ago in the Rocky Mountains'. *Antiquity* 84, September. Hare, G. 2011. *The Frozen Past. The Yukon Ice Patches*. The Yukon Government.

2   Kwäday Dän Ts'ìnchí is the place name in the southern Tutchone (Athapaskan) tongue for the discovery site. It translates as 'Long Ago Person Found'. The author was invited to participate in the investigations of Kwäday Dän Ts'ìnchí Man by the management committee in 2000. The account in this book is first and foremost an attempt at assessing the scientific discoveries published until 2009 concerning Kwäday Dän Ts'ìnchí Man. With financial backing from Britain, Canada and the United States, the author has been very heavily involved in these investigations. No attempt has been made in this chapter to evaluate in any comprehensive way whatsoever the cultural importance for the local First Nations in British Columbia and the Yukon and also for Native Americans, especially the Tlingits of south-east Alaska. For all these peoples the importance of Kwäday Dän Ts'ìnchí Man is great. Readers should realise that in 2008 there was a symposium held in Victoria dealing with all aspects of the study of Kwäday Dän Ts'ìnchí Man, not just the strictly scientific. At the time of completion of the writing of this book, the publication of the proceedings of the symposium by the Royal British Columbian Museum still has not taken place. With principal co-authors Petra Mudie, Richard Hebda and several minor ones, the author has three contributions to these proceedings as follows: Dickson, J.H. and six others. 'Vascular plants, bryophytes, lichens and algae from the Kwäday Dän Ts'ìnchí Discovery Site in North-western British Columbia'. Hebda, R.J., Dickson, J.H., Mudie, P.J. 'Forensic Botany of the Kwäday Dän Ts'ìnchí Ground Squirrel Robe'. Mudie, P.J., Dickson, J.H. and Hebda, R.J. and Thomas, F.C. 'Environmental Scanning Electron Microscopy – a modern tool for unlocking ancient secrets about the last journey of the Kwäday Dän Ts'ìnchí Man'.

3   Loreille, O.M. *et al.* 'Integrated DNA and Fingerprint Analyses in the Identification of 60-year-old Mummified Human Remains Discovered in an Alaskan Glacier'. *Journal of Forensic Science* 55, pp. 813–8.

4   *Canadian Archaeological Association Newsletter* 19, pp. 14–8. Beattie, O. *et al.*, 2000. 'The Kwäday Dän Ts'ìnchí Discovery from a Glacier in British Columbia'. *Canadian Journal of Archaeology* 24, pp. 129–47. There was also a paper in 2001 about the chemical analysis of the hair: Martin, R.R., Biesinginger, M.C. and Skinner, W. 'Advanced Analysis of Hair from Kwaday Dan Ts'inchi'. *Canadian Journal of Analytical Sciences and Spectroscopy*. In 2002 the first of M.V. Monsalve's papers on DNA was published. Then came Dickson, J.H. *et al.* 2004. 'Kwäday Dän Ts'ìnchí, the first ancient body of a man from a North American glacier: reconstructing his last days by intestinal and biomolecular analyses'. *The Holocene* 14, pp. 481–6.

5   Ibid.

6   Ibid.

7   The six dates of wooden implements ranged from AD 1400–1955. Bone collagen of moose antlers found on the glacier downslope from the site came from the 1960s. Richards, M.P. *et al.* 2007. 'Radiocarbon dating and dietary stable isotope analysis of Kwäday Dän Ts'ìnchí'. *American Antiquity* 72, pp. 719–33. Repair patch on robe, p. 722: 'the new date … calibrates to 1730-1810 cal AD …'

8   Ibid.

9   Ibid.

10 Monsalve, M.V. *et al.* 2002. 'Brief Communication: Molecular Analysis of the Kwäday Dän Ts'ìnchí Ancient Remains Found in a Glacier in Canada'. *American Journal of Physical Anthropology* 119, pp. 288–91. Monsalve, M.V. *et al.* 2003. 'mtDNA Lineage Analysis: genetic Affinities of the Kwäday Dän Ts'ìnchí Remains with Other Native Americans'. Monsalve, M.V. and Stone, A.C. 2005. 'mtDNA Lineage Analysis: genetic Affinities of the Kwäday Dän Ts'ìnchí Remains with Other Native Americans'. In Reed, D.M. *Biomolecular Archaeology*. Carbondale, Southern Illinois University, pp. 9–21. Monsalve, M.V. *et al.* 2008. 'Brief Communication: State of Preservation of Tissues from Ancient Human Remains found in a Glacier in Canada'. *American Journal of Physical Anthropology* 137, pp. 348–55.

11 *Canadian Archaeological Association Newsletter* 19, pp. 14–8. Beattie, O. *et al.*, 2000. 'The Kwäday Dän Ts'ìnchí Discovery from a Glacier in British Columbia'. *Canadian Journal of Archaeology* 24, pp. 129–47.

There was also a paper in 2001 about the chemical analysis of the hair: Martin, R.R., Biesinginger, M.C. and Skinner, W. 'Advanced Analysis of Hair from Kwaday Dan Ts'inchi'. *Canadian Journal of Analytical Sciences and Spectroscopy*. In 2002 the first of M.V. Monsalve's papers on DNA was published. Then came Dickson, J.H. *et al*. 2004. 'Kwäday Dän Ts'ìnchí, the first ancient body of a man from a North American glacier: reconstructing his last days by intestinal and biomolecular analyses'. *The Holocene* 14, pp. 481–6.

12 Von Bonssdorf, B. 1977. *Diphyllobothriasis in Man*. London, Academic Press. Anonymous. 1981. 'Fish Tapeworm (Diphyllobothrium latum) Infections from Uncooked Alaskan Salmon'. *State of Alaska Epidemiology Bulletin* 22, pp. 1–2. Curtis, M.A. and Bylund, G. 1991. 'Diphyllobothriasis: fish tapeworm disease in the circumpolar north'. *Medical Research* 50, pp. 18–24. Reinhard, K. and Urban, O. 2003. 'Diagnosing ancient diphyllobothriasis from Chinchorro mummies'. *Mem Inst Oswaldo Cruz* 98, pp. 191–3. Martinson, E., *et al*. 2003. 'Pathology of Chiribaya Parasitism'. *Memórias Instituto do Oswaldo Cruz* 98, pp. 195–2003.

13 Ibid.

14 McCafferty, M.K. 1993. *To the Chukchi Peninsula and the Tlingit Indians 1881–1882: Journals and Letters by Aurel and Arthur Krause 1881/1882*. Fairbanks, University of Alaska Press.

15 Greer, S., Strand, S. and Mackie, A. 2005. 'The Kwäday Dän Ts'ìnchí (Long Ago Person Found) discovery: An update'. *Program and Abstracts, 38th Annual meeting, Canadian Archaeological association, Nanaimo, May 15, 2005*. Anonymous. 2002. *Yukon Wild Natural Regions of the Yukon*. Canadian Parks and Wilderness Society (Yukon Chapter), p. 119.

16 Ibid.

17 Hill, B. 2003. *The Remarkable World of Frances Barkley*. Victoria, TouchWood Editions.

18 Caldwell, F.E. 1986. *Land of Ocean Mists The Wild Ocean Coast West of Glacier Bay*. Annapolis, Lighthouse Press. Caamaño, J. 1975 (1792). 'Extracto del diario de las navegaciones, exploraciones y descumbrimentos hechos en la América septentrional por D. Año de 1792'. *Coleción de Diarios y Relaciones para Historia de los Viajes y Desubrimientos*. Madrid VII, pp. 173–135.

19 Ibid.

20 Ibid.

21 Streveler, G. 1996. *The Natural History of Gustavus*. Juneau, Greg Streveler. Anonymous. 1983. *Glacier Bay*. Washington National Parks Service.

22 http://www.empr.gov.bc.ca/Mining/Geoscience/BedrockMapping/GeologicalMaps. Douglas, G.W. 1974. 'Montane Zone vegetation of the Alsek River region'. *Canadian Journal of Botany* 52, pp. 2505–32. Pojar, J. and Stewart, A.C. 1991. 'Chapter 17: Spruce – Willow – Birch Zone'. In Medinger, D. and Pojar, J. (eds) *Ecosystems of British Columbia*. Victoria: BC Ministry of Forests, pp. 251–62. Pojar, J. and Stewart, A.C. 1991. 'Chapter 18: Alpine Tundra Zone'. In Medinger, D. and Pojar, J. (eds) *Ecosystems of British Columbia*. Victoria: BC Ministry of Forests, pp. 263–74. Shepherd, M.E. 1995. *Plant Community Ecology and Classification of the Yakutat Foreland, Alaska*. Report for USDA Forest Service, Sitka Alaska. Klinka, K., Krajina, V.J. and Scagel, A.M. 1989. *Indicator Plants of Coastal British Columbia*. Vancouver, UBC Press. Geiser, L. *et al*. *Lichens of Southeastern Alaska An Inventory*. USDA-Forest Service, Petersburg. Goward, T., McCune, B. and Meidinger, D. 1994. *The Lichens of British Columbia*. Ministry of Forests Reacher Program, Victoria. McCellan, C. 1987.

23 Cruikshank, J. 2001. 'Glaciers and Climate Change: Perspectives from Oral Tradition'. *Arctic* 54, pp. 377–93. Anonymous. 1995. *The Kohklux Map*. Yukon Historical & Museums Association.

24 http://www.empr.gov.bc.ca/Mining/Geoscience/PublicationsCatalogue/Maps/Documents/GM2009-1-2M.pdf. Douglas, G.W. 1974. 'Montane Zone vegetation of the Alsek River region'. *Canadian Journal of Botany* 52, pp. 2505–32. Pojar, J. and Stewart, A.C. 1991. 'Chapter 17: Spruce – Willow – Birch Zone'. In Medinger, D. and Pojar, J. (eds) *Ecosystems of British Columbia*. Victoria: BC Ministry of Forests, pp. 251–62. Pojar, J. and Stewart, A.C. 1991. 'Chapter 18: Alpine Tundra Zone'. In Medinger, D. and Pojar, J. (eds) *Ecosystems of British Columbia*. Victoria: BC Ministry of Forests, pp. 263–74. Shepherd, M.E. 1995. *Plant Community Ecology and Classification of the Yakutat Foreland, Alaska*. Report for USDA Forest Service, Sitka Alaska. Klinka, K., Krajina, V.J. and Scagel, A.M. 1989. *Indicator Plants of Coastal British Columbia*. Vancouver, UBC Press. Geiser, L. *et al*. *Lichens of Southeastern Alaska An Inventory*. USDA-Forest Service, Petersburg. Goward, T., McCune, B. and Meidinger, D. 1994. *The Lichens of British Columbia*. Ministry of Forests Reacher Program, Victoria. McCellan, C. 1987.

25 Ibid.

26 Banfield, A.W.F. 1974. *The Mammals of Canada*. University of Toronto Press. Nagorsen, D. 2005. *Rodents & Lagomorphs of British Columbia*. Royal BC Museum Handbook. Victoria, Royal British Columbia Museum. Eder, T. and Pattie, D. 2001. *Mammals of British Columbia*. Vancouver, Lone Pine. Nagorsen, D.W. 2005. *Rodents & Lagomorphs of British Columbia* Victoria. Royal British Columbia Museum. Lamb, A. and Edgell, P. 1986. *Coastal Fishes of the Pacific Northwest*. Madeira Park, Harbour Publishing. Anonymous. 2002. *Alaska's Wild Salmon*. Alaska Department of Fish and Game. Bolanz, M. and Williams, G.C. 2003. *Tlingit Art*. Blaine. Hancock House. Hart, J.F.L. 1982. *Crabs and their Relatives of British Columbia*. Royal British Columbia Museum, Victoria.

27 Ibid.

28 Busby, S. 2003. *Spruce Root Basketry of the Haida and Tlingit*. Seattle, Washington University Press. Mudie, P.J. *et al.* 2005. 'Forensic palynology and ethnobotany of *Salicornia* species (Chenopodiaceae) in northwest Canada and Alaska'. *Canadian Journal of Botany* 83, pp. 111–23. Worl, R. 2008. *Celebration Tlingit, Haida, Tsimshian Dancing on the Land*. Juneau, Sealaska Heritage Institute. Schlick, M.D. 1994. *Columbia River Basketry Gift of the Ancestors, Gift of the Earth*. Seattle, University of Washington Press.

29 Ibid.

30 Ibid.

31 Ibid.

32 Farjon, A. 1990. *Pinaceae*. Königstein, Koeltz Scientific Books.

33 McCafferty, M.K. 1993. *To the Chukchi Peninsula and the Tlingit Indians 1881–1882: Journals and Letters by Aurel and Arthur Krause 1881/1882*. Fairbanks, University of Alaska Press.

34 Mackie, K. 2005. 'Long Ago Person Found – An Ancient Robe Tells a New Story'. In 'Recovering the Past: The Conservation of Archaeological and Ethnographic Textiles'. 5th North American Textile Conservation Conference, pp. 35–45.

35 Hartson, T. 1999. *Squirrels of the West*. Vancouver, Lone Pine.

36 Milet-Mureau, L.A. 1799. *A Voyage round the World, performed in the years 1785, 1786, 1787 and 1788 by the Boussole and Astrolabe under the command of J.F.G. de La Pérouse*. London, G.G. and J. Robinson. Dixon, G. 1789. *A Voyage Round the World: But More Particularly to the North West Coast of America*. London, George Goulding. Cutter, D.C. 1991. *Malaspina & Galiano Spanish Voyages to the Northwest Coast*. Seattle, University of Washington Press. Joan M. Antonson. 1990. 'Chapter 13: Sitka'. In Smith, B.S. and Barnett, R.J. *Russian America: The Forgotten Frontier*, pp. 165–73. Mourelle, J.M. 1971. Anonymous. 1986. *To the Totem Shore The Spanish Presence on the Northwest Coast*. Madrid.

37 Ibid.

38 Ibid.

39 Ibid.

40 Ibid.

41 Krause, A. 1885. *The Tlingit Indians Results of a Trip to the Northwest Coast of America and the Bering Straits*. Translated by Erna Gunther, 1956. University of Washington Press.

42 Milet-Mureau, L.A. 1799. *A Voyage round the World, performed in the years 1785, 1786, 1787 and 1788 by the Boussole and Astrolabe under the command of J.F.G. de La Pérouse*. London, G.G. and J. Robinson. Dixon, G. 1789. *A Voyage Round the World: But More Particularly to the North West Coast of America*. London, George Goulding. Cutter, D.C. 1991. *Malaspina & Galiano Spanish Voyages to the Northwest Coast*. Seattle, University of Washington Press. Joan M. Antonson. 1990. 'Chapter 13: Sitka'. In Smith, B.S. and Barnett, R.J. *Russian America: The Forgotten Frontier*, pp. 165–73. Mourelle, J.M. 1971. Anonymous. 1986. *To the Totem Shore The Spanish Presence on the Northwest Coast*. Madrid.

43 Osborne, C. 1964. 'The Yakutat Blanket'. *Smithsonian Institiution Bureau of American Ethnology Bulletin* 192, pp. 187–99.

44 Krause, A. 1885. *The Tlingit Indians Results of a Trip to the Northwest Coast of America and the Bering Straits*. Translated by Erna Gunther, 1956. University of Washington Press.

45 Hebda, R. and Frederick, S.G. 1990. 'History of Marine Resources of the Northwest Pacific since the Last Glaciation'. *Transactions of the Royal Society of Canada* 1, pp. 319–42.

46 Gende, S.M. and Quinn, T.P. 2006. 'The Fish and the Forest'. *Scientific American* 295, pp. 66–71. USDA Forest Service. No date. *Fish & Forest*. Pacific Northwest Research Station. Blanchet, J.-C. and Cleyet-Merle, J.-J. 2005. *Les Eyzies-de-Tayac and the Vézère Valley*. Monum Paris.

47 Ibid.

48 Ibid.

49 *Canadian Archaeological Association Newsletter* 19, pp. 14–8. Beattie, O. *et al.*, 2000. 'The Kwäday Dän Ts'ìnchi Discovery from a Glacier in British Columbia'. *Canadian Journal of Archaeology* 24, pp. 129–47. There was also a paper in 2001 about the chemical analysis of the hair: Martin, R.R., Biesinginger, M.C. and Skinner, W. 'Advanced Analysis of Hair from Kwaday Dan Ts'inchi'. *Canadian Journal of Analytical Sciences and Spectroscopy*. In 2002 the first of M.V. Monsalve's papers on DNA was published. Then came Dickson, J.H. *et al.* 2004. 'Kwäday Dän Ts'ìnchí, the first ancient body of a man from a North American glacier: reconstructing his last days by intestinal and biomolecular analyses'. *The Holocene* 14, pp. 481–6.

50 Dmytryshin, B. and Crowhart-Vaughan, E.A.P. 1976. *Colonial Russian America Kyrill T. Khlebnikov's Reports 1817-1832*. Portman: Oregon Historical Society.

51 Dickson, J.H. and Mudie, P.J. 2008. 'The Life and Death of Kwäday Dän Ts'ìnchí, an Ancient Frozen Body from British Columbia: Clues from Remains of Plants and Animals'. *The Northern Review* 28, pp. 27–50.

52 Turner, N.J. 2003. 'The ethnobotany of edible seaweed (*Porphyra abbottae* and related species; Rhodophyta: Bangiales) and its use by First Nations on the Pacific Coast of Canada'. *Canadian Journal of Botany* 81, pp. 283–93. Pringle, H. 2007. 'Follow that kelp'. *New Scientist*, 11 August, pp. 40–3. 'Seaweeds', p. 28. Kuhlein and Turner. 1991. 'Bull Kelp. To 40m long!' *Common Seaweeds of the Pacific Coast*. Waaland, J.R.R. 1977. Vancouver. Douglas, J.J. 'Edible Kelp'. McCellan, C. 1987. *A History of the Yukon Indians Part of the land Part of the Water*. Vancouver, Douglas & MacIntyre.

53 Krause, A. 1885. *The Tlingit Indians Results of a Trip to the Northwest Coast of America and the Bering Straits*. Translated by Erna Gunther, 1956. University of Washington Press, pp. 58, 128.

54 Turner, N.J. 2003. 'The ethnobotany of edible seaweed (*Porphyra abbottae* and related species; Rhodophyta: Bagiales) and its use by First Nations on the Pacific Coast of Canada'. *Canadian Journal of Botany* 81, pp. 283–93. Pringle, H. 2007. 'Follow that kelp'. *New Scientist*, 11 August, pp. 40–3. 'Seaweeds', p. 28. Kuhlein and Turner. 1991. 'Bull Kelp. To 40m long!' *Common Seaweeds of the Pacific Coast*. Waaland, J.R.R. 1977. Vancouver. Douglas, J.J. 'Edible Kelp'. McCellan, C. 1987. *A History of the Yukon Indians Part of the land Part of the Water*. Vancouver, Douglas & MacIntyre.

55 Dickson, J.H. and Mudie, P.J. 2008. 'The Life and Death of Kwäday Dän Ts'ìnchí, an Ancient Frozen Body from British Columbia: Clues from Remains of Plants and Animals'. *The Northern Review* 28, pp. 27–50.

56 *Canadian Archaeological Association Newsletter* 19, pp. 14–8. Beattie, O. *et al.*, 2000. 'The Kwäday Dän Ts'ìnchi Discovery from a Glacier in British Columbia'. *Canadian Journal of Archaeology* 24, pp. 129–47. There was also a paper in 2001 about the chemical analysis of the hair: Martin, R.R., Biesinginger, M.C. and Skinner, W. 'Advanced Analysis of Hair from Kwaday Dan Ts'inchi'. *Canadian Journal of Analytical Sciences and Spectroscopy*. In 2002 the first of M.V. Monsalve's papers on DNA was published. Then came Dickson, J.H. *et al.* 2004. 'Kwäday Dän Ts'ìnchí, the first ancient body of a man from a North American glacier: reconstructing his last days by intestinal and biomolecular analyses'. *The Holocene* 14, pp. 481–657.

57 Corr, L.T. *et al.* 2008. 'Probing dietary change of the Kwäday Dän Ts'ìnchí individual, an ancient glacier body from British Columbia: I. Complementary use of marine lipid biomarker and carbon isotope signatures as novel indicators of a marine diet'. *Journal of Archaeological Science* 35, pp. 2102–10. Corr, L.T. *et al.* 2009. 'Probing dietary change of the Kwäday Dän Ts'ìnchí individual, an ancient glacier body from British Columbia: II. Deconvoluting whole skin and bone collagen delta 13 C values via carbon isotope analysis of individual anmino acids'. *Journal of Archaeological Science* 36, pp. 12–18.

58 Ibid.

59 Cruikshank, J. 2001. 'Glaciers and Climate Change: Perspectives from Oral Tradition'. *Arctic* 54, pp. 377–93. Anonymous. 1995. *The Kohklux Map*. Yukon Historical & Museums Association.

60 Ibid.

61 Ibid.

62 Ibid.

63 Carcross-Tagish First Nation and Greer, S. 1995. 'Skookum stories on the Chilkoot/Dyea trail'. Carcross-Tagish First Nation, Whitehorse, Y.T. Schwatka, F. 1891. 'The expedition of the "New York

Times" (1866)'. *Century Magazine* 19, pp. 865–72. Seton-Kerr, H.W. 1891. 'Exploration in Alaska and north-west British Columbia'. *Proceedings of the Royal Geographical Society* II, pp. 865–72. McClellan, C. 1975. 'My old people say. An ethnographic survey of southern Yukon Territory'. Part 1. *Publications in Ethnology* 6. National Museum of Canada. Anonymous. 1988. *From Trail to Highway. A highway guide to the places and the people of the Southwest Yukon and Alaska Panhandle.* Victoria, Champagne-Aishihik Indian Band.

64 Schofield, W.B. 1976. 'Bryophytes of British Columbia III: habitat and distributional information for selected mosses'. *Syesis* 9, pp. 317–54. Vitt, D. H., Marsh, J.E. and Bovey, R.B. 1988. *Mosses Lichens & Ferns of Northwest North America.* Edmonton; Lone Pine Publishing, p. 83. Brodo, I.M., Sharnoff, S.D. and Sharnoff, S. 2001. *Lichens of North America.* Yale University Press. With many colour photographs, this is one of the best-illustrated volumes in all of botanical natural history. Geiser, L.H., Dillman, K.L., Derr, C.C. and Stensvold, M. 1994. *Lichens of Southeastern Alaska An Inventory.* Petersburg, USDA-Forest Service. Goward, T., McCune, B. and Meidinger, D. 1994. *The Lichens of British Columbia Illustrated Keys Part 1 Foliose and Squamulose Species.* Victoria, Ministry of Forests Research Program.

65 Ibid.

66 http://www.empr.gov.bc.ca/Mining/Geoscience/PublicationsCatalogue/Maps/Documents/ GM2009-1-2M.pdf. Douglas, G.W. 1974. 'Montane Zone vegetation of the Alsek River region'. *Canadian Journal of Botany* 52, pp. 2505–32. Pojar, J. and Stewart, A.C. 1991. 'Chapter 17: Spruce – Willow – Birch Zone'. In Medinger, D. and Pojar, J. (eds) *Ecosystems of British Columbia.* Victoria: BC Ministry of Forests, pp. 251–62. Pojar, J. and Stewart, A.C. 1991. 'Chapter 18: Alpine Tundra Zone'. In Medinger, D. and Pojar, J. (eds) *Ecosystems of British Columbia.* Victoria: BC Ministry of Forests, pp. 263–74. Shepherd, M.E. 1995. *Plant Community Ecology and Classification of the Yakutat Foreland, Alaska.* Report for USDA Forest Service, Sitka Alaska. Klinka, K., Krajina, V.J. and Scagel, A.M. 1989. *Indicator Plants of Coastal British Columbia.* Vancouver, UBC Press. Geiser, L. *et al. Lichens of Southeastern Alaska An Inventory.* USDA-Forest Service, Petersburg. Goward, T., McCune, B. and Meidinger, D. 1994. *The Lichens of British Columbia.* Ministry of Forests Reacher Program, Victoria. McCellan, C. 1987.

67 *Canadian Archaeological Association Newsletter* 19, pp. 14–8. Beattie, O. *et al.*, 2000. 'The Kwäday Dän Ts'inchi Discovery from a Glacier in British Columbia'. *Canadian Journal of Archaeology* 24, pp. 129–47. There was also a paper in 2001 about the chemical analysis of the hair: Martin, R.R., Biesinginger, M.C. and Skinner, W. 'Advanced Analysis of Hair from Kwaday Dan Ts'inchi'. *Canadian Journal of Analytical Sciences and Spectroscopy.* In 2002 the first of M.V. Monsalve's papers on DNA was published. Then came Dickson, J.H. *et al.* 2004. 'Kwäday Dän Ts'inchí, the first ancient body of a man from a North American glacier: reconstructing his last days by intestinal and biomolecular analyses'. *The Holocene* 14, pp. 481–6.

68 Richards, M.P. *et al.* 2007. 'Radiocarbon dating and dietary stable isotope analysis of Kwäday Dän Ts'inchi'. *American Antiquity* 72, pp. 719–33.

69 Corr, L.T. *et al.* 2008. 'Probing dietary change of the Kwäday Dän Ts'ìnchi individual, an ancient glacier body from British Columbia: I. Complementary use of marine lipid biomarker and carbon isotope signatures as novel indicators of a marine diet'. *Journal of Archaeological Science* 35, pp. 2102–10. Corr, L.T. *et al.* 2009. 'Probing dietary change of the Kwäday Dän Ts'ìnchí individual, an ancient glacier body from British Columbia: II. Deconvoluting whole skin and bone collagen delta 13 C values via carbon isotope analysis of individual anmino acids'. *Journal of Archaeological Science* 36, pp. 12–8. Dickson, J.H. and Mudie, P.J. 2008. 'The Life and Death of Kwäday Dän Ts'ìnchí, an Ancient Frozen Body from British Columbia: Clues from Remains of Plants and Animals'. *The Northern Review* 28, pp. 27–50.

70 Cruikshank, J. 2001. 'Glaciers and Climate Change: Perspectives from Oral Tradition'. *Arctic* 54, pp. 377–93.

8

The Importance of
Ancient Glacier Mummies

This account of ancient human mummies melted from glaciers began with Ötzi, the Tyrolean iceman, for the substantial reason that 20 years ago the late Neolithic (or Chalcolithic or Copper Age) man quickly and rightly became world famous. His body, both inside and out, and his set of clothes and numerous items of equipment have been minutely examined. The circumstances of his life and death have been deduced therefrom. The number of scholarly studies runs into many hundreds, if not thousands, and that number will grow and should do so. The publications are in English, German, Italian and French. No doubt there are accounts in other tongues too but I have not tried to cope with them, or even to find them.

By contrast, there are only few investigations of the Porchabella Shepherdess, the Theodulpass Mercenary and poacher Norbert Mattersberger, all three found in Central Europe, and of Kwäday Dän Ts'ìnchí Man, alone in North America. Even combined the investigations of these four frozen human remains are nowhere nearly as numerous as those about Ötzi. Nor are the results as immediately and globally newsworthy, if only because the remains are much more recent than those of Ötzi. Nonetheless, all have marked interest in one way or another with Kwäday Dän Ts'ìnchí Man being second only to Ötzi in what we have deduced about some of the events of his last days.

Freezing, in the permafrost or in glacier ice, can produce splendidly preserved corpses. Because of instantaneous preservation by freezing, human bodies melted from glaciers are outstanding sources of information about humankind from periods long ago. Depending how good the preservation has been after hundreds or thousands of years, they tell us much about the precise moments of death in ways that other archaeological remains cannot, certainly not in such comprehensive ways. In falling into a crevasse or however they came to die, they can reveal how the person had looked, dressed, been equipped, how healthy, what they had just eaten and where they had travelled during their last few days.

The intestinal contents of ancient glacier mummies are encoded diaries and maps. The trick is learning how to crack the codes. At the most the diaries are likely to be only a few days, perhaps only one day or less than 48 hours. The faeces in the rectum and colon are older than the contents of the stomach if only perhaps by several hours. The analyses by microscopy of Ötzi's intestinal contents unexpectedly revealed complex journeying during his last hours. At the age of about 47 and with a variety of ailments, he began his last few days at high altitude and then he had travelled down Schnalstal and finally back up again to meet his end on the col between that valley and Niedertal, the very uppermost part of Ötztal. The precise period between May and September remains disputed by some; late spring is the likely season.

Similarly, Kwäday Dän Ts'ìnchí Man had a long journey, if perhaps a less complex one, as far as we can tell as yet. So, on the basis of the present distribution pattern of beach asparagus, mountain hemlock and mountain sweet cicely combined with the stable isotope studies, as well as the study of the minerals in the samples from the gut, the following can be argued. When he was perhaps less than 20 years of age Kwäday Dän Ts'ìnchí Man set out in late summer on what became his last journey. Carrying seafood, he had left from somewhere between the west end of Icy Straight and Klukwan and he then took the Chilkat valley to go up into the mountains where on the glacier he met his sad, untimely end.

In one way if not more, the investigation of Kwäday Dän Ts'ìnchí Man is more satisfying so far than that of Ötzi. His stomach was partially full and so we already have a good idea of his very last meal. Due to the recent radiological work of Patrizia Pertner now we know that Ötzi's stomach was full. So we can find out what he had eaten just before his death. Likely it will be similar to his immediately previous meals. However, samples for microscopy and DNA will confirm that thought. On 12 January 2011 Patrizia Pertner sent me an email stating: 'On 6 November 2010 the whole stomach content was emptied in order to carry out several examinations on the mummy.' So we may soon know exactly what his very last meal was, with any unintentional ingestions. Let there be meat, cereals, other plants – sloes perhaps? The omnivorous iceman! Let there be flat neckera and bog moss too!

The elucidation of the last hours of these two ancient men by microscopy as well as by stable isotopes and mineral particles is unique in archaeological science and is likely to remain so unless more well-preserved glacier mummies with full or partly full innards come to light high in the mountains. Where? Alaska, the Andes, the Himalayas? At least for the scientist, how very satisfying it is that we can carry out such reconstructions, all the more so in the case of Ötzi who lived so very long ago.

As the great antiquity of the body was not realised soon enough, unfortunately Ötzi was ripped from the ice. How much better it would have been if the frozen corpse had been carefully excavated. But the initial discovery was both accidental and not remotely antici-pated, as indeed were all the four other frozen bodies discussed in detail in this book. Glacier mummies really are very special and so differ from all other ice mummies. That is not to say that the other ice mummies are not of much interest – far from it. Enough has been said in Chapter 1, I hope, about the Greenlandic bodies, the Siberian tombs and sacrificed Andean children, for instance, to make that abundantly clear.

My first direct involvement as an environmental archaeologist took place when I was 23 in 1960, though at the time I did not know I was such a person. I thought I was a botanist helping archaeologists. The term environmental archaeology first came into use several years later. As the collector of samples for pollen analysis and radiocarbon dating at the behest Professor Harry Godwin, I assisted Professor Grahame Clark. This was Professor Clark's last of the very few excavations he ever did and it concerned the Neolithic and Bronze Age layers stratified into the peat of the fenlands of East Anglia, where Sir Grahame and Sir Harry, as they became, had first investigated in the 1930s during their long Cambridge

University careers.[1] The resulting dates helped to push the onset of the British Neolithic back many hundreds of years. The point of relating this is not to name drop – though they are good names to drop – but that I learned very young and from direct personal practical experience that the more we delve into humankind's distant history the earlier and earlier important developments seem to become. That Ötzi had lived 5200 years ago came as a surprise to some, even archaeologists. I do not think it should.

Ötzi's set of archery equipment is not just tantalising in its obvious uselessness but it is the oldest bow with a quiver full of arrows yet to have come down to us. This discovery is a delight to toxophilists worldwide. It has been known for years that hunting with the bow was taking place in Europe 5000 years or more before Ötzi lived. Just exactly when bows were invented is unclear but it had happened by 12000 years ago. This is established by the discovery of pine-wood arrow shafts with flint heads and notched proximal ends well preserved in peat at Stellmoor near Hamburg, Germany. Possibly there were bows and arrows as much as 19,000 years ago because what appear to be flint arrowheads, beautifully crafted, have been found in Iberian sites of Solutrean times, such as Parpalló in Valencia, Spain. Archaeologists are cautious, such as F. Bernaldo De Quiros and V. Cabrera Valdès. If they were not for arrows, then what was their purpose? It is a puzzle. There is a claim, backed up by a variety of studies, by Marlize Lombard and Laurel Phillipson in the journal *Antiquity* (2010) that bows and stone-tipped arrows were in use no less than 64,000 years ago in South Africa. Really? I would like to think so.

Seemingly only two retouching tools have survived from antiquity; there is that belonging to Ötzi and that from the grave at Fontaine-le-Puits in France, and both are late Neolithic. Perhaps there are others lurking unrecognised. Such were very useful tools for making very small flints and tiny flints are known from the Mesolithic. Can the discovery of Mesolithic retouching tools be predicted? I think so.

Ötzi's clothes show beautifully neat stitching. He was no ragamuffin, though his leggings were very well worn with numerous patches and his jacket had clear make-do-and-mend characteristics. Indeed, some think him to have been smartly dressed, at least in his jacket, if that is what it was. No Mesolithic or Palaeolithic clothing has survived. If and when such clothing is found (fingers crossed!) it is likely, I predict, that it will be found to be surprisingly neat. The famous statuette, the Venus of Willendorf, of some 25,000 years ago, may not have a stitch on her generous, better perhaps to say obese, body, as you can see in the wonderful natural history museum in Vienna. However, she sports either a neat hairdo or a very tight-fitting, elaborately made hat.[2] Our remote prehistoric ancestors cared about their appearance and no surprise there really. Cartoonists please do not stop producing funny images like the ones reproduced in this book but do take note and desist from showing Ötzi as a crudely dressed caveman!

Especially in the cases of Ötzi and Kwäday Dän Ts'ìnchí Man, the study of such corpses tells us dramatically how extremely well our distant ancestors knew their environment: the useful properties of plants, fungi, animals and rocks. They had, of course, to know such properties to some basic extent just to survive – to feed, clothe and shelter themselves. However, their knowledge was very sophisticated, more so than many may realise. From Ötzi we now know that two different fungi could be carried, one being a clear case of use for fire-making, the other very likely to have been medicine. What we do not yet know from scientific studies of Ötzi or any other Neolithic or even earlier persons is when mycophagy (fungus-eating) for nutrition or tastiness first took place. There is also the bog moss from Ötzi's gut which is, I contend, plausibly interpreted as an unintentionally ingested fragment of a wound dressing. How very much I would like to know if this is correct. Archaeologists please find me more evidence, before the Curse of Ötzi gets me at long last.

The Cambridge University archaeologist John Robb has complained about the way Ötzi has been treated. There are statements that 'Facial reconstruction, whether necessary or accurate, is often carried out principally for its ability to suggest a living person; a face is much more a person than a skull' and 'the study of Ötzi has been a predictable exercise in the transformation of a physical body into a social person'.[3] What's so wrong with that? There is little or nothing in my view. I have been happily engrossed to be part of that process which produces results of outstanding interest to a great many people.

In a short commentary called 'Time to leave Otzi [sic] alone?' in 2002 in the noted medical journal *The Lancet* 360, p.1530, David Sharp stated: 'I cannot help wondering if there will soon be a limit to what the Tyrolean iceman can usefully tell us.' Such a thought is deplorable in my opinion and I cannot accept it at all. If one considers all the techniques that have been invented in the last hundred years and have produced such fascinating information about Ötzi, think what might become known to us by 2100 or 2200, when there will have been techniques applied that are undreamt of now. There will be a great deal, I venture, and the decision of the south Tyrolean authorities should be applauded unreservedly for providing Ötzi with a suitable, frigid resting place for all time in theory (and hopefully in practice if not for all time then for a very long time indeed).

All humankind has an innate curiosity about the past, not just the recent but the distant past too. The studies of ancient glacier bodies revealing such intimate details of lives lived long ago, in my firm view, lead us to respect our remote ancestors greatly, to appreciate more and more their skills, to realise more fully than ever their humanity. This strengthens the bonds between us.

Given that ancient glacier mummies are so very important and subject to rapid deterioration when exposed, would it not be good sense to try to anticipate where and when such remains might be found? Here is a cautionary tale. In June 2004, along with no less than 12 co-authors, mostly Canadians, I published the paper entitled 'Kwäday Dän Ts'ìnchí, the First Ancient Body of a Man from a North American Glacier: Reconstructing his Last Days by Intestinal and Biomolecular Analyses'. At the very time of that paper going to press a few months earlier, I gave a public lecture in Scotland mainly about Ötzi but I mentioned Kwäday Dän Ts'ìnchí Man, without giving any of the then unpublished results. In the audience was Mrs Rosamund Stenhouse-Stewart who told me an unexpected story and soon after, at my request, sent me a letter. In the 1890s her father Thomas Livingstone Haig (b.1866) had been a magistrate in south-eastern British Columbia. While based at Revelstoke, he did not merely hear of but 'was shown by an Indian fur trapper the body of a completely preserved Indian trapped within the ice'. The letter continues: 'I do not know where but he mentioned its preservation and complete condition. I believe that he understood that the gathering thickness of the ice had begun to make the body gradually less visible'.

Of course, I realised instantly that this discovery might take precedence as the first ancient glacier mummy from North America, if we could find out more about it and, even better, obtain radiocarbon dates if any part of the body and associated organic artefacts had been kept anywhere. By email, I informed Alexander Mackie, the British Columbia government archaeologist very prominent in the studies of Kwäday Dän Ts'ìnchí Man, and Al immediately took steps to start enquiries but, disappointingly, nothing positive has ever transpired, except that before and after the 1890s there had been reports from the Revelstoke area of a body in a glacier. Newspapers mention a French Canadian prospector or fur trader or a Salish Indian or an advance scout for the Canadian Pacific Railway. It is said that the unfortunate man had fallen into a crevasse in the glacier on Mount Begbie. Dominating the region, this striking mountain is about 12km south-west of Revelstoke and reaches 2732m (8963ft) and the glacier is on its north-east slope. The first known ascent was not until June 1907.

We might well never know just when the person came to be frozen in the ice and so we do not know if he was an ancient or modern glacier mummy. In any case, there have been, of course, no scientific investigations and, indeed, there could not have been the kinds of studies discussed in this book because many of the techniques had not been invented at that time and others were much less advanced than now.

Then, in July 2007, with Geneviève Lécrivain, I visited Revelstoke and had very helpful discussions with Cathy English, the curator of the Revelstoke Museum and Archives, whose research into the matter began to convince me that there never was a Mount Begbie Iceman. It is just a good story kept alive by raconteurs, journalists and credulous people. In the *Revelstoke Review* of 30 June 1940 there is very long article by Arvid Lundell about this Iceman. Cathy English was told by the journalist's daughter that her father had simply made the article up. In the 1890s Thomas Haig was a very prominent citizen in Revelstoke, then a small town that had quickly grown up because of the construction of the Canadian Pacific Railway. Had he really seen a frozen body on Mount Begbie he would, presumably, have written an official report and the matter would have been in a local newspaper, such as *The Herald*; searches of official documents and of the appropriate newspapers by Cathy English and her assistant Kirsten Gonzales revealed nothing. Immediately after I broadcast on local Revelstoke radio about the story, I was contacted by Mr Scott Gallicano who told me that his grandfather Tangres Gallicano related the story of the remains of an Indian but this time on Mount Macpherson, a few kilometres north-west of Mount Begbie, and where, it can be added, no glacier exists.

After studying topographic maps, Jenny and I flew by helicopter around Mount Begbie twice and looked down on the glacier, which is shrinking, like almost all other glaciers. It makes little sense that there could ever have been a frozen body there. In the cases of the Porchabella Shepherdess and the Theodulpass Mercenary, discussed in Chapter 6, and also of Ötzi, the bodies had been found in or near passes; they had been going from A to B or B to A. The same is likely true of Kwäday Dän Ts'ìnchí Man. To ascend Mount Begbie is to go nowhere but up the mountain. Of course, the person could have been a hunter going from A and intending to go back to A, like Norbert Mattersberger, or a prospector, but why would it have been necessary to make a potentially dangerous crossing of the glacier at 2500m or more? In her 1998 *Revelstoke History and Heritage*, written with much assistance from Cathy English, R.M. Nobbs did not see fit to mention the Mount Begbie iceman. This iceman equals the Yeti, the Loch Ness Monster, Ogopogo, Big Foot and UFOs – just an engaging tale, nothing more. A plausible origin of the story is that, seen from certain positions near Revelstoke, the skyline of the Mount Tilley range, just a few kilometres west of Mount Begbie, looks like a supine, sleeping Indian with his hands across his chest.

So how can we ensure the swift and best possible retrieval if more discoveries of real ancient frozen bodies are made, as is very likely? This will be very difficult. Melting ice patches, already known to be productive, can be searched easily enough each year by dedicated enthusiasts on foot in the very reasonable expectation that finds of arrows or darts or other artefacts lost by hunters may be made as more ice melts. But how can human bodies melting from glaciers be predicted with certainty? The answer is that they cannot. However, it would be a help to study maps to find cols very close to glaciers, which in the past were liable to have been used as passes, like Schnidejoch in Switzerland or Hauslabjoch in Ötziland. My near namesake, the American James E. Dixon, with two others, has pursued this matter in detail. They say, with an emphasis on Alaska: 'Monitoring melting ice is necessary to identify these unique, rare and ephemeral archaeological remains.' It is made all the more urgent by global warming. With publication in 2005, they devised a geographic information system MAPIS, 'Modelling Archaeological Potential of Ice and Snow', to assist aerial reconnaissance and pedestrian survey. It is to be hoped that this proves to be a productive step forward.[4]

How wonderful it would be if the well-preserved frozen body of a Neanderthal came to light. But where, if anywhere in the European mountains or elsewhere, is there ice more than 30,000 years old that might have held such a corpse until now? Nowhere is the disappointing answer. We shall need to make do with frozen modern humankind and that is marvellous enough.

Notes

1   Clark, G. and Godwin, H. 1962. 'The Neolithic in the Cambridgeshire Fens'. *The Antiquaries Journal* 36, pp. 1–33. Fagan, B. 2001. *Grahame Clark. An Intellectual Life of an Archaeologist.* Oxford, Westview Press. Godwin, H. 1978. *Fenland: Its Ancient Past and Uncertain Future.* Cambridge University Press.

2   Lammerhuber, L., Kern, A. and Antl-Weiser, W. 2008. *Venus.* Baden, Edition Lammerhuber.

3   Robb, J. 2009. 'Towards a Critical Ötziography: Inventing Prehistoric Bodies', pp. 100–28.

4   Dixon, J.E., Manley, W.F. and Lee, C.M. 2005. 'The emerging archaeology of glaciers and ice patches: Examples from Alaska's Wrangell St Elias National Park and Preserve'. *American Antiquity* 70, pp. 129-43. Lee, C.M. 2010. 'Ice on the Edge: Methods and Recommendations for Conducting Ice Patch Surveys in Rocky Mountain National Park'. Unpublished report for the National Park Service.

Epilogue

At an early stage of my career I had dealings with the media because of my participation as a botanist on the Royal Society expedition of 1962 to study the effects of the volcanic eruption on Tristan da Cunha. At 24 I had never been outside Europe until I went to that very remote island in the South Atlantic Ocean. Much later there was the Glasgow Garden Festival in 1988 for which I led a five-man plant-collecting expedition to Papua New Guinea. Soon after that there was the publication of my book on the *Wild Plants of Glasgow*. These events too interested the press, radio and television. However, it was my involvement with the investigations of Ötzi from 1994 onwards that really embroiled me with the media.

First mention is necessary of the silly Curse of Ötzi story, espoused enthusiastically by the media, just as the equally silly, if more famous, Curse of Tutankhamun had been several decades earlier. On page 3 of the edition of 13 November 2003 *The Sunday Mail*, a red-top Scottish newspaper of no great distinction, there appeared the headline 'CURSE OF THE MUMMY SCOT NEXT ON THE LIST'. That person is me. I had been interviewed on the phone by a young lady reporter who, clearly firmly believing the curse to be feared, was taken aback by my expostulations of dismissal. The story had come about by the deaths of various people such as Konrad Spindler, who died at the age of 63 in 2005, Tom Loy also at 63 in 2005 and the co-discoverer of Ötzi, Helmut Simon, at 67 in 2004. There is even a book *Le Malediction d'Ötzi 7 morts mystérieuses autour d'une momie de 5300 ans* written by two French journalists. Where the mysteries are escapes me. To pad the book out the authors added a synthesis of the science, including my work. It is not too bad an attempt as far as it goes but, as could be expected, they did not know the half of it.

As this book is published I am 74 and I have investigated Ötzi for many years, including pouring over the contents of his innards. He does not seem to be too offended at this unseemly intrusion, as yet anyway, though I can hardly hope for ever. While sitting in the lounge of Geneviève Lécrivain's home overlooking the pleasant, heavily wooded countryside of Franche-Comté, I was interviewed live by BBC Radio Scotland news and the interviewer was surprised when I said Ötzi is my benefactor and not my malefactor. After all, he was the reason why Jenny and I met in the first place. *Vive Hibernatus*! (as the French have charmingly called Ötzi.)

I was interviewed by the science editor of *The Observer*, the well-known broadsheet newspaper, about the mosses carried by Ötzi and I mentioned that toilet paper was a possible use. The larger, softer mosses are entirely suitable for that purpose, as attested by the Viking cesspits excavated in Dublin and many other archaeological layers. Mosses have my seal of approval in that and other respects. To the exclusion of all other and perhaps more likely explanations that particular one was spread across the bottom of the front page of the newspaper the next Sunday. The *Daily Express* followed with 'Soft, strong and very old' and the *Vancouver Sun* had 'Iceman mystery wiped away'. I cringed repeatedly, if perhaps with hindsight somewhat pompously, and gave worldwide radio interviews to try to bring back some semblance of balance. Listeners to the ABC and CBC, for instance, heard my complaints. A later headline, however, that pleased me was 'Inspector Moss' produced by my local rag. Well done *The Milngavie and Bearsden Herald*!

Now there are much more serious media matters to relate. There have been numerous television programmes about Ötzi. I cannot recall one that has really satisfied me and I have been badly annoyed by some, even to the extent of hurling a half brick at the television set (just kidding, but that is how I have felt). For instance, after consultation with me and being sent my publications, BBC2's flagship science series *Horizon* broadcast to the world that the Innsbruck botanists had identified the suite of mosses indicating a southern provenance for Ötzi. But that was my work carried out in Glasgow University. I complained three times by letter and first to the producer, then the controller of BBC2 and finally the director general of the BBC. All three wrote back with the apologies becoming more fulsome up the hierarchy. However, they all ended: 'Our working practices make such mistakes inevitable.'

Later, I spent in all some eight hours helping a researcher who assured me that this new *Horizon* program would be based on good science and he listened to my warnings, some very strong, about this and that, not least Tom Loy's lack of publication of the basic data concerning his remarkable claims such as the death in battle theory. When I saw the result I realised none of my advice had been taken and furthermore neither I nor my university was even listed in the credits. Working practices again perhaps?

When my participation in the investigations of Kwäday Dän Ts'ìnchí Man became widely known I was approached by a British television company wanting to make a film. Over lunch I spent some two hours or more explaining the science to a young researcher. I recounted how we had worked out his coastal rather than interior connection, his marine diet, details of his last journey, season of death and so on. Fascinating stuff, I feel it not too unreasonable to claim. All this with the stunning background of beautiful landscapes and seascapes with great mountain chains, enormous glaciers, some reaching the sea, with dangerous animals often encountered, moose and both grizzly and black bears. I cautioned that the local tribespeople would not allow photographs of the badly fragmented body to be used and furthermore there was no evidence that foul play had been involved in the death. It was simply, as far as we could tell, an accident on the glacier. A couple of weeks later I got a letter from the boss of the company stating they were no longer interested because of the ban on photographs of the body and the lack of a gory death (very words). Is this the kind of attitude we want concerning science TV programmes? Sensationalism or nothing – deplorable!

However, a television news broadcast that made me smile was the sight of a group of white-coated, po-faced Austrian medical professors gathered round the supine Ötzi in his bare scuddy. One of them was using a spatula to hold up the tiny, shrivelled genitals (the condition is not too surprising, perhaps, after over 5000 years at sub-zero temperatures). This event was to show the world that Ötzi had not been castrated, as claimed ludicrously by some German newspapers. It is not just British newspapers that can be repellent.

Thirdly, there are politics and personalities, an even more serious matter. There have been no scientific publications about Ötzi in the British world-renowned scientific journal *Nature* other than criticism, the most important being by Paul Bahn and the late Katherine Everett in 1993. And rather damning it is. They wrote an article 'Iceman in the cold light of day', published not so long after the discovery but long enough for appropriate action to have been taken by the Austrian and Italian authorities. Though some of the more minor aspects of their criticisms were dealt with in due course (or were not well founded in the first place), their main charge remains valid to this day in my view: no international team of appropriate top world authorities has ever been set up not just to deliberately guide but to actively drive the research forward. That should have been done immediately once the great age of the corpse was established.

From the outset, there have been academic, national and international political difficulties and very strong personality clashes; the latter, however, is hardly an unusual occurrence in science, as in other walks of life. Nonetheless, in my opinion, progress has been retarded for a large part of the last 20 years. There are various studies of Ötzi crying out to be done. An obvious one, in my view, is an assessment, carried out by appropriately qualified medical men, of his state of health just before his death. Just how ill was he, seriously or not? Well muscled and sturdy he may have been, but was he in a physically fit state to have made a swift ascent, descent and ascent again over not just rough but in places very steep ground and finally to have reached the great altitude of well over 3000m? Another intriguing matter is the finding of raised values of both copper and arsenic in Ötzi's hair. Was he involved with copper smelting or not? After approaching 20 years since the first publication on this particular topic science has moved on and improved techniques could be brought to bear on this intriguing question in the not unrealistic hope of sorting the matter out. Another one concerns the identifications of the animals used to make Ötzi's clothes and gear. From an early stage goat, deer, cattle, chamois and brown bear have all been listed. Nobody claimed sheep until 2008. Four hair samples had been provided by Konrad Spindler to Klaus Hollemeyer of Saarland University with three others. They state that sheep had been the animal used to make the upper-body clothing (jacket/coat) and leggings, and cattle had been used for the upper part of his shoes. So the whole matter needs reinvestigating. Yet another matter is the state of Ötzi's teeth and that also should be examined again.

In early February 2011 I asked Albert Zink, Director of the EURAC Institute for Mummies and the Iceman in Bozen, what projects on Ötzi were approved. Here is the list:

Investigation of blood traces on the clothing and tools of the Iceman

Development of a system with a modified atmosphere dedicated to the preservation of the Iceman

Histological and nanotechnological investigations of different wounds on the hand and back of the Iceman

Photoscan of the whole body of the Iceman mummy

Database for Mummies and the Iceman

Life in the Iceman: a search for psychrophil [cold-loving] microbial flora

Molecular investigation of the nuclear DNA of the Iceman

Investigation of the stomach contents of the Iceman

These are all worthwhile projects but many others could be set up both to satisfy scientific curiosity and be of interest to the public. Apart from the several just mentioned above, here are two more suggestions that occur to me.

Why was the database not set up and running years ago? It would be very useful to know who had published what where and when about Ötzi. Then nobody, not the media, nor students nor academics nor the interested public, would have any excuse for being badly informed.

Gilberto Artioli has written:

It is evident that a thorough physico-chemical investigation of the axe is needed at the present stage. Such research would provide a valuable characterization of the object, and novel information on metallurgical technology in the fourth millennium BC. That, nearly 20 years after the discovery, proper usewear analysis has yet to be performed is unfortunate; it might reveal what the axe had been used to do.

The preface of this book complained about the media for poor and over sensational reporting of Ötzi and the science applied to him. At the end of the book here is yet another complaint – a very recent one at that. This time it is about the world-famous, high-impact journal *Nature*. In the edition of 3 March 2011 there is an account by a journalist of the new exhibition in the Iceman Museum, particularly concerning the reconstruction of Ötzi. It is riddled with errors and misleading statements:

'Ötzi did not freeze to death'. He was killed quickly by an arrow to his back. This has been known worldwide for years. That he was pursued by attackers (*plural*) is not established scientific fact. That he was being pursued at all is speculation. Only two people were certainly involved in Ötzi's death – Ötzi himself and the person who shot the fatal arrow.

The artists, the Kennis brothers, 'previously put a face to Neanderthal man'. So what? It is not the first time for Neanderthals. Years ago, the late Gyula Skultéty reconstructed the face of the man from La Ferrasie, Dordogne, to give just one example.

The defrosting of the mummy on 20 November 2010 was not the first time since the discovery of Ötzi.

The removal of the stomach contents that day was not just to study bacteria. Various other studies are being carried out. (This author hopes to study the mosses therein, if there are any found by Klaus Oeggl!)

That Ötzi looked fragile is most definitely disputable. The best paper on his physique claims he was sturdy, like a modern Olympic wrestler. (Can such a person look fragile unless in poor health?)

If all that is what we get of science news reporting from the illustrious *Nature* what hope is there that newspapers will improve?

Three weeks after this book went to the publishers the following headline, with explanatory text, appeared online on 23 June 2011 in *National Geographic Daily News*. It is based on a presentation at the 7th World Congress on Mummy Studies in San Diego:

'Iceman's Stomach Sampled – Filled with Goat Meat
Missing until 2009, mummy's stomach found to contain lumps of meat'

If readers find convincing some or all of the arguments I put forward in this book then they will find various statements in this new *National Geographic* article questionable or misleading. The stomach was not missing but unrecognised. We do not know that Ötzi was a hunter (we do not know with certainty what he was), there is no scientific evidence that he encountered murderers (one killer, of course, but killers no). The headline 'Goat' is misleading. Readers who do not persist to the end of the article may think it refers to a domestic goat. But it is alpine ibex which is a totally different species.

Finally, the article contains the direction to open 'Wounded Iceman Made Epic Final Journey, Moss Shows'. Readers will be surprised by that. 'Moss' shows nothing of the sort. Mosses are very clearly an important, revealing part of the archaeobotanical science of the iceman, particularly flat neckera and the bog moss. The former relates to his southern provenance and the latter to the intriguing possibility of his use of it as a wound dressing for the badly cut right palm.

Citations, Basic Sources and Notes

Each chapter has its own bibliography in which the citations are listed numerically and referenced throughout. Where appropriate I have added explanatory notes, some of which are lengthy. Where there are more than three authors, I have given the citation as Other, A.N. *et al.*, followed by the usual details. The exceptions are the basic sources on Ötzi. There are four volumes of archaeological and scientific papers which are connected with the University of Innsbruck. In the text these books are referred to as *Innsbruck* 1, 2, 3 and 4, followed by the page number where needed:

Innsbruck 1 is mostly in German but with English, French, German and Italian summaries, as do
    all the four volumes. Höpfel, F., Platzer, W. and Spindler, K. 1992. *Der Mann im Eis. Band 1.*
    Eigenverlag der Universität Innsbruck.
Innsbruck 2 is mostly in German. Spindler, K. *et al.* (eds) 1995. *Neue Funde und Ergebnisse. Der
    Mann im Eis Volume 2.* Wien, Springer Verlag.
Innsbruck 3 is in English. Spindler, K. *et al.* (eds) 1996. *Human Mummies. The Man in the Ice Volume
    3.* Wien, Springer Verlag.
Innsbruck 4 is in English. Bortenschlager, S. and Oeggl, K. (eds) 2000. *The Iceman and His Natural
    Environment. The Man in the Ice Volume 4.* Wien, Springer Verlag.

There is a considerable variety of other books and scientific papers aimed at the general public as well as at scholars. These are presented here in chronological, rather than alphabetical, order.

Barfield, L., Koller, E. and Lippert, A. 1992. *Der Zeuge aus dem Gletscher.* Vienna, Uberreuter.
    This was the first serious book on Ötzi. It was never translated into English. Konrad Spindler
    never referred to this book in any of his publications.
Egg, M. *et al.* 1993. 'Die Gletschermummie vom Ende der Steinzeit aus den Ötztaler Alpen'.
    Jahrbuch des Römisch-Germanischen Museums 39, pp. 1–128. This is mostly in German.
Spindler, K. 1993. *Der Mann im Eis Die Ötztaler Mumie verrät die Geheimnisse der Steinzeit.*
    München. In C. Bertelsmann. 1994. *The Man in the Ice.* London, Weidenfield and Nicholson.
    Referred to in the text as *Spindler* 1, this is the best-known book on Ötzi which was written very soon after the discovery. It was first published in German, then in English. Issued
    as a paperback in 1995 in both German and English, it was revised and updated with some
    important additions and reissued until at least 2001. Referred to in the text as *Spindler* 2, it is
    now very out of date. Apart from German and English the book was translated into Spanish,
    Portuguese, Swedish, Estonian, Czech, Korean and Japanese. A bestseller, this book was subjected to severe scholarly criticism by archaeologist Paul Bahn.
Barfield, L. 1994. 'The Iceman Reviewed'. *Antiquity* 68, pp. 10–26. This long, descriptive review
    written by an archaeologist with much experience of northern Italy includes not just text
    but maps and drawings of the equipment, clothes and shoes.

De Marinis, R.C. and Brilliante, G. 1998. *La Mummia del Similaun L'Uomo Venuto dal Ghiaccio.* Venezia, Marsilio. Second edition 2004. In Italian. These authors report extensively without qualification on Tom Loy's work on traces of blood, collagen, starch and other remnants on the dagger, the axe head, arrow shafts and bow.

Fleckinger, A. and Steiner, H. 1999. *The Fascination of the Neolithic Age. The Iceman.* Bozen, Folio Verlag. This large book is in German, Italian and English; it has numerous colour photographs of the clothes and gear. A year earlier they had published a small book: *The Iceman.* Bozen, Folia Verlag.

Spindler, K. 1999. 'Forschungen an dem Beifunden des Mannes aus dem Eis zwischen 1991 und 1997'. *Schriften des Südtiroler Archäologiemuseums* 1, pp. 61–8.

Fowler, B. 2001. *Iceman.* London, Macmillan. Second edition. Written by a journalist, this book is much concerned with personalities of the scientists involved. The epilogue written because of the work of J.H.D. *et al.* (2000) puts J.H.D. in the University of Scotland, an institution that never was.

Sulzenbacher, G. 2002. *The Glacier Mummy Discovering the Neolithic Age with the Iceman.* Vienna, Folio. This slim book is informative and attractive with every page full of colour photographs but beware of botanical clangers. The leaves from the birch bark container being called beech (*Fagus sylvatica*) instead of Norway maple (*Acer platanoides*) is an example and another is that reed sweetgrass (*Glyceria maxima*) was not that grass used to make the grass cape.

Fleckinger, A. 2003. *Ötzi, the Iceman, the Full Facts at a Glance.* Folio, Vienna. Fitting easily into a pocket, this is a 100-page booklet, again full of colour photographs and informative but with mistakes; for instance, 'Lucy' being twice referred to as 300 million years old instead of 3 million. A botanical blunder is that the very important pollen from Ötzi's gut is not hops (*Humulus lupulus*), a climber, but hop hornbeam (*Ostrya carpinifolia*), a small tree. The so-called second edition (2005) differs in no significant way from the 2003 publication.

Dickson, J.H., Oeggl, K. and Handley, L.L. 2005. 'The Iceman Reconsidered'. *Special Archaeological Edition Scientific American* 15, pp. 4–13. This was first published in 2003 and then brought up to date two years later. In 2003 we were sceptical about the arrowhead but in 2005 accepted it as properly established.

Dal Ri, L. 2006. 'The Archaeology of the Iceman'. *Schriften des Südtiroler Archäologiemuseums* 3, pp. 17–44. This survey is in volume 3 devoted to Ötzi in the new journal of the South Tyrolean museums. Volume 1, 1999, and volume 4, 2006, also concern Ötzi.

Rastbichler Zissernig, E. 2006. *Der Mann im Eis Die Fundgeseschichte.* Innsbruck University Press. This is in German, with no English translation. It contains a highly detailed account of the numerous visits to Ötzi's corpse before it was removed from the ice.

Egg, M. and Spindler, K. 2009. *Kleidung und Ausrüstung der Kupferzeitlichen Gletschermumie aus den Ötzaler Alpen.* Römisch-Germanishes Zentralmuseum, Mainz. Entirely in German, this tome has superb drawings and photographs of the equipment and clothing. It is an update of the 1993 book.

Samadelli, M. 2009. *Iceman photoscan.* Pfeil, München. In English, Italian and German, this has beautiful close-up photographs of the mummy, including 3D shots. It 'provides a full and detailed photographic documentation of the mummy's entire body, and which can be easily accessed by anyone via the internet'.

Flackinger, A. (ed.) 2011. *Ötzi 2.0. Eine Mumie zwischen Wissenschft, Kult und Mythos.* Vienna, Folio. This large format, colourful book celebrates the opening of the new display in the Iceman Museum to commemorate the 20th anniversary of the discovery. As of spring 2011 it is only in German or Italian. There are 14 contributors dealing with different aspects of Ötzi.

Index

Entries in **bold** refer to the plate numbers.